PRAISE FOR JEN LANCASTER

Jeneration X

"Fans of the witty memoirist are delighted to see her back."

—*The Philadelphia Inquirer*

"Hands down, Jen Lancaster's funniest memoir yet. . . . It's the comedic tales she shares that suck you in for a wild ride as you hungrily devour chapter after chapter of Lancaster's witty moments."

—SheKnows Book Lounge

"Hey, growing up is a process, and Jen's is especially hilarious."

—Persephone Magazine

"Chatty. . . . Lancaster provides some laugh-out-loud moments."

—*Kirkus Reviews*

If You Were Here
A Novel

"Witty and hilarious." —*People*

"A perfect summer read." —*USA Today*

"Jen Lancaster leaps into the fiction arena with her rapier-sharp wit in one hand and a fistful of Home Depot gift cards in the other."

—Joshilyn Jackson, *New York Times* bestselling
author of *Backseat Saints*

"Hilarious and irreverent."

—Carrie Ryan, *New York Times* bestselling author of
the Forest of Hands and Teeth series

"Proves once again that Jen Lancaster is in a master class when it comes to infusing books with wit and charm."

—Sarah Pekkanen, Author of *Skipping a Beat*

My Fair Lazy

"[Jen] is one of the best and most entertaining real-life-chick-lit writers out there and her latest offering proves it all over again. . . . Her transformation (complete with footnotes, which are hilarious) makes her even more relatable and funny. . . . *My Fair Lazy* does not 'suck it.' It rocks it."

—Examiner. com

continued . . .

"[*My Fair Lazy* is] light and fun and full of pop culture musings."
—*Chicago Sun-Times*

"One of the things I love most about her work is that she writes like I think she talks over blueberry mojitos next to the pool with her best friend. . . . The book will make you laugh out loud, which is something all of 'the real' self-help books recommend." —Associated Content

"[A] pithy, clever collection of essays." —*Redbook*

Pretty in Plaid
"A hilarious tribute to her early fashion obsessions." —*People*

"Scathingly witty." —*Boston Herald*

"Laugh and cry at this hilarious collection of essays that chronicle Jen's fearless fashion faux pas through the ages, her eleven (yup) years of undergrad, and her not so glamorous entry-level jobs. You'll revel in the lessons she gleans from her travails: primary among them, that the ability to laugh at your mistakes is the best skill you'll ever learn." —*Redbook*

"She pegs her memories to outfits—a green dotted Swiss dress, some stylin' Jordache jeans, crocodile skin pumps—in a way that will win the hearts of all of us who still remember the dusty green of our 1980s-variety Girl Scout uniform (with its fetching beret and knee socks!)."
—*San Antonio Express-News*

Such a Pretty Fat
"She's like that friend who always says what you're thinking—just 1,000 times funnier." —*People*

"Believe it or not, losing weight can actually be a laugh riot. . . . [Jen Lancaster] mercifully infuses much-needed humor into the life-altering process." —*Chicago Sun-Times*

"[Details] what it's like to be large, in charge, and totally hilarious."
—*Metro*

"A surprisingly charming weight-loss odyssey . . . with the winning honesty and humor [Lancaster's] fans have come to expect."
—*Publishers Weekly*

Bright Lights, Big Ass

"A bittersweet treat for anyone who's ever survived the big city (and it's so funny, I can almost forgive Jen Lancaster for being a Republican)."
—Jennifer Weiner, #1 *New York Times* bestselling author of *Fly Away Home*

"Refreshing, hysterical, illuminating! From the title on, *Bright Lights, Big Ass* is an anti-haute hoot. In a voice that's charming and snarky, hilarious and human, Jen Lancaster tells the ultraglamorous truth about real big-city living. And it's better than anything on TV."
—Lori Jakiela, author of *Miss New York Has Everything*

"Wickedly funny, refreshingly honest, and totally unapologetic."
—Caprice Crane, author of *Family Affair*

"Jen Lancaster may be one of the few authors around capable of writing her own sitcom; she's smart, wry, and never afraid to point out her own short-comings while letting us into her uniquely funny world."
—Melanie Lynne Hauser, author of *Jumble Pie*

Bitter Is the New Black

"The woman is nothing if not spunky, and she does have her funny moments, particularly when sticking it to The Man."
—*The Washington Post*

"Carrie Bradshaw meets Barbara Ehrenreich in this memoir about white-collar unemployment after the dot-com bubble burst."
—*Kirkus Reviews*

"Jen Lancaster's confessions should be mandatory reading for the absurdly salaried young smart-arses around town . . . an honest, insightful, and ultimately feel-good handbook for what to do when ruin beckons."
—Deborah Hope of *The Australian*

"A classic story of comeuppance written from real-life experience by the funniest new author from the blogosphere. A strong debut and a must read for any American princess."
—Jessica Cutler, author of *The Washingtonienne*

"She's bitchy and sometimes plain old mean, but she's absolutely hilarious."
—*Chicago Sun-Times*

Other Titles by *New York Times*
Bestselling Author Jen Lancaster

Bitter Is the New Black

Bright Lights, Big Ass

Such a Pretty Fat

Pretty in Plaid

My Fair Lazy

If You Were Here

Here I Go Again

Jeneration X

One Reluctant Adult's Attempt to Unarrest
Her Arrested Development,
or
Why It's Never Too Late for Her Dumb Ass to
Learn Why Froot Loops Are Not for Dinner

Jen Lancaster

NAL New American Library

NEW AMERICAN LIBRARY
Published by the Penguin Group
Penguin Group (USA) Inc., 375 Hudson Street,
New York, New York 10014, USA

USA / Canada / UK / Ireland / Australia / New Zealand / India / South Africa / China

Penguin Books Ltd., Registered Offices: 80 Strand, London WC2R 0RL, England
For more information about the Penguin Group visit penguin.com.

Published by New American Library, a division of Penguin Group (USA) Inc.
Previously published in a New American Library hardcover edition.

First New American Library Trade Paperback Printing, May 2013

REGISTERED TRADEMARK—MARCA REGISTRADA

New American Library Trade Paperback ISBN: 978-0-451-41716-9

THE LIBRARY OF CONGRESS HAS CATALOGED THE HARDCOVER EDITION OF THIS TITLE AS FOLLOWS:

Lancaster, Jen, 1967–
Jeneration X: one reluctant adult's attempt to unarrest her arrested development, or why it's
never tool late to learn why froot loops are not for dinner/Jen Lancaster.
p. cm.
ISBN 978-0-451-23317-2
1. Lancaster, Jen, 1967– 2. Authors, American—21st century—Biography. 3. Maturation
(Psychology)—Humor. 4. Conduct of life—Human. 5. United States—Social life and
customs—Humor. I. Title.
PS3612.A54748z46 2014
8144'6—dc23 2011048451 [B]

Printed in the United States of America
10 9 8 7 6 5 4 3 2 1

PUBLISHER'S NOTE
Penguin is committed to publishing works of quality and integrity. In that spirit, we are proud
to offer this book to our readers; however the story, the experiences and the words are the
author's alone.

The recipes contained in this book are to be followed exactly as written. The publisher is
not responsible for your specific health or allergy needs that may require medical supervision.
The publisher is not responsible for any adverse reactions to the recipes contained in this book.

The publisher does not have any control over and does not assume any responsibility for
author or third-party Web sites or their content.

For former slackers everywhere and
for Karyn, who gives good title

C·O·N·T·E·N·T·S

Contents

We were stuck between meanings. Or we were the last dribbles of something. The fall of the Soviet Union, this was, the death of analog. The beginning of aggressively marketed nachos.

—Milo Burke, Sam Lipsyte's *The Ask*

Generation Xers were brought up on television, Atari 2600s, and personal computers. They are the generation that was raised in the 1970s and 1980s, and saw this country undergo a selfish phase that they do not want to repeat.

—Jennifer Jochim, *Outpost*

We're the middle children of history . . . no purpose or place. We have no Great War, no Great Depression. Our great war is a spiritual war. Our great depression is our lives.

—Tyler Durden, Chuck Palahniuk's *Fight Club*

Jeneration X

P·R·O·L·O·G·U·E

January 2010

"Thanks for completely ignoring me."

I'm standing here in my cashmere coat, shaking. Whether it's from cold or from fury, I've yet to determine.

"Huh?"

"I said *thank you for completely ignoring me*. I sat out there with my hazards on for the past twenty minutes."

The valet blinks heavy-lidded eyes that don't quite function in unison. "Guess I didn't see you."

"Didn't see me?"

I am incredulous. How did he *not* see me? I was in an SUV the size of a school bus and let's just say I was liberal with my use of the horn. I was impossible not to see. Helen Keller could see me. Andrea Bocelli could see me. Stevie Wonder would be all "*Do I Do* see you!"

I'm trying hard not to punch this guy smack in his red windbreaker, so I'd wager it's the anger that's making me shake.

"Didn't see you," he confirms, not meeting my glance. Instead he scans the street looking for other vehicles he might park.

This is *exasperating*. Not only did I wait twenty minutes for his attention, but once I realized he was never getting to me, I had to park myself. Normally this wouldn't be a big deal, but a) because I'm very, very lazy I specifically get my hair cut here since they have a valet, b) he'd already made me late for my appointment and c) the nearest garage was blocks away.

I had to drive down three stories into the belly of this semi-abandoned building to find a cavernous parking area where the only light came from a handful of fifteen-watt incandescent bulbs hanging from the ceiling thirty feet above. I never met a parking garage that didn't feel all *CSI* and like a sexual assault could happen any minute, but this? *This* was the rapiest rape garage that ever raped.

Then after I took the elevator upstairs I found myself in the atrium of an eight-story, vacant shopping mall. The only reason I could even see where I was going was because a few stores up front were still open and casting light, but ninety percent of the rest of the stores were dark and empty and foreboding. George A. Romero wouldn't have to make a single change if he wanted to film another *Dawn of the Dead* movie here. That no one tried to eat my brain is nothing short of a miracle.

Which is why I can't let this go.

I level my gaze. "Listen, I was in a six-thousand-pound SUV fifteen feet away from you right next to the sign that says VALET PARKING. I beeped, I waved, I sent up little smoke signals from the tepee in the backseat. Then, when I got out of the car to talk to you, you jumped into the car behind mine. When you came back, you ran over to the car next to me, yet you walked so close to my car that you set off my parking sensor. So, with all of these factors in mind, *how do you claim to have not seen me?*"

He shrugs. "I don't know." When he exhales, I smell Snoop

Dogg's tour bus. Ah, that would account for the slow blinking and vision obstruction and serves to piss me off more. Seriously, in an economy with people begging for jobs, this asshole thinks it's kosher to get baked at work and then drive my car?[1] Unacceptable.

I fight the urge to ask if he knows who I am.

Because I suspect that if I don't walk away, who I am is the lady who gets her car shat in the next time she valets.

---

[1] In theory, I mean.

A·U·T·H·O·R'S N·O·T·E

When Douglas Coupland wrote *Generation X*, he was writing about me.

I mean figuratively, not literally.

I read *Generation X* in my second[2] senior year of college, in the time in which I briefly traded my loafers for Birkenstocks, khakis for flannel, and Wham! for Nirvana. As a poster child for all things considered "slacker,"[3] I clearly recall nodding my head and saying, "Yeah, man. You *get* it."

Until I stumbled across *Bridget Jones's Diary* six years later, I'd never identified more with a novel. Coupland gave voice to the ennui that every twentysomething felt at the time, back in the day when we were long on promise and short on opportunity. He understood us because he was one of us—trapped between the perpetual, collective optimism of those he labeled "Global Teens"[4] and their Baby Boomer parents, our generation defined ourselves by . . . nothing.

Technically, that's not true. Our generation defined ourselves

....

[2] Of six total.
[3] Including cynicism, apathy, and un-cute plaid shirts.
[4] Later characterized as Generation Y or the Millennials.

by our perpetual fear of a Soviet invasion, playing Cold War mix-tapes on our Walkmen. *Oh, Sting,* we'd lament, *we also hope the Russians love their children, too.* If iPods were around back then, we'd have had entire thermonuclear war playlists, filled with songs like "99 Luftballons," "Wind of Change," and "Toy Soldier."

Before John Hughes made them household names, we had Matthew Broderick and Ally Sheedy in *War Games* trying to per-suade a Soviet supercomputer via dial-up modem that the only way to win a nuclear war is not to play.

We had *Red Dawn* and a pre–*Dirty Dancing* Jennifer Grey carrying not a watermelon, but an AK-47.

We had "Wolverines!"

Then, just like that, the Cold War ended and we lost the one thing that made our generation unique.

Those of us born between 1965 and 1980 had none of the benefits of the generations that came before or after us. We know nothing of the kinder, simpler America from the Camelot days, nor were we born with an innate understanding of how to operate Mi-crosoft Windows.

Today, we're a beeper generation in a smartphone world.

Complicating matters is that neither the generation that came before us nor the one that's come after has demonstrated any real desire to act like adults themselves. Financial planning advertise-ments show Baby Boomers running away from corporate life to pursue dreams that, in this economy, are downright ridiculous. This is *not*, in fact, the time to quit your job with your 401K and health insurance to go build custom boats. I know Dennis Hopper told everyone it was okay, but he's dead now.[5]

....

[5] And he had the kind of cash and cachet only Hollywood could create.

On top of that, we've got folks in their late twenties to early thirties so wrapped up in quasi-political Facebook friend requests and Spotify and Farmville that Soviet troops could *actually* roll down Main Street and they'd never even notice. Or care.

Of course this doesn't pertain to every member of Generation Y,[6] but it's not that far-fetched either. Um, hey, Counselor, can you stop streaming *Gilmore Girls* on Netflix long enough to present your case to the jury? KTHXBAI.

Watching this generation operate makes me very glad that people my age understand that tools like technology and social media are a means to an end and not the end itself.

My generation didn't play soccer so we know that when the game is over, not everyone gets a trophy. Yet here we are, trapped in middle management between two massive cases of generational arrested development.

And what we've determined from watching everyone else is that deciding to grow up has been our ultimate act of rebellion.

So that's what those of us in Generation X have done to define ourselves. We've become the only adults in a world full of children.

I mean, if I could finally grow up? Anyone can.

Maybe I've moved to the dark side, but it's clean and nice and we never run out of toilet paper. And honestly, getting here wasn't that hard. All I had to do was make the conscious decision to grow up.

Whether you're a Boomer, a Millennial, or a still-reluctant Xer who's not yet read the memo because you don't understand how to

------

6 Or Baby Boomer, for that matter. Or you, no matter what your generation, as you've shown remarkably good sense in having picked this book.

download attachments on your phone, *Jeneration X* is your invitation to join me because it's never too late.

I know it sounds hard, but fear not: I've done the legwork for you! Each chapter in this book illustrates a painful lesson I learned about becoming more of an adult, so I hope you'll find this guide useful.

Although this book will help you navigate the treacherous waters of many aspects of reluctant adulthood, if I leave you with no piece of wisdom but this, please understand that at a certain age your body can no longer efficiently process all the artificial colors in a dinner-sized serving of Froot Loops, regardless of how delicious they may be.[7]

And you won't realize this until it's already too late.

Far, far too late.

Unless you have a particular affinity for crying on the toilet, you may just want to trust me on this one.

Best,
Jen Lancaster

---

[7] Particularly with a dash of half-and-half.

Involuntarily Voluntary

I'll often yell at homeless people. "Hey, how's that homelessness working out for you? Try not being homeless for once!"

Okay, fine.

I've never actually said this. Coach Sue Sylvester on *Glee* did. But considering the first line in my memoir *Bitter Is the New Black* reads, "Camille said you stole a bag from a homeless guy," imagining my saying this isn't such a stretch.

Having come within five days of losing my apartment and moving back with my parents not so long ago, you'd think I'd be a little less glib about other people's circumstances.

You'd be wrong.

The thing is, my life is good right now . . . I suspect a little too good.

I fear that I'm starting to forget what it felt like to struggle. My memories of the bad old days when the bank took our car and ComEd disconnected our electricity are fading and sepia-toned. So when Coach Sylvester offered her suggestion, I found myself nodding in agreement. Why *don't* they try not being homeless for once? You know, get a job and such. How hard could it be, right?[8]

Success has paved the way for me to revisit some old, bad habits. I'm concerned that my confidence is quietly morphing back into arrogance and my hard-won humility is turning to hubris. More often than not, snotty has once again become the new black. My tolerance is nil and last week while shouting at the valet I'd deemed incompetent, I realized how dangerously close I was to asking him if he knew who I was.

This is not good.

Instead of asking someone if they know who I am, I *should* be asking myself who it is I want to be.

The last time I behaved in such a childish, petulant manner, Karma knocked me out of my penthouse and onto my ass. Although I learned to appreciate those lessons in retrospect, at the time, life *sucked*. And I'd like to never live through anything like that again.

Thankfully I finally have the ability to take one giant step back from myself and right my terrible attitude before my life tumbles like so many houses of cards again.

I need to give back the good I've been so selfishly taking in.

I need to repay the karmic debt I've incurred.

I need to actually grow up instead of just saying it.

And now my job is to figure out how.

....

[8] Plus, there's probably some cake somewhere. Let them eat that.

You know who volunteers?

Grown-ups.

Also, people sentenced with community service after a DUI.

But mostly grown-ups.

Doing charitable work seems like it would be soup and sandwich to my desire to give back as well as my need to mature, so I'm looking into it. The only volunteer work I've done previously was with shelter dogs and I really enjoyed it, but it turns out I'm a "take work home with me" kind of gal. As my husband, Fletch, and I live with a pit bull, a German shepherd, and five cats, we are at capacity in the stray pet department. Until we lose some members to attrition, I should stick to groups of creatures I don't want to bring home. Like children and the homeless.

I sign up on a couple of Chicago volunteer databases, so I figure finding projects should be a snap. I mean, I'm smart,[9] I have skills to offer,[10] I'm willing and able,[11] so surely there's some stuff out there at which I'd excel. Or, barring that, at least wouldn't hate. I log in to the first calendar and begin to peruse volunteer listings. I'm free all week, so let's see what's available.

Okay, here's something for Girls on the Run . . . well, now *that* sounds vaguely fun in a frenetic kind of way. Zippy and upbeat and useful. I wonder what they do? Maybe this is a charity that helps women balance their busy schedules? Or it provides gals on the go

....

[9] Relatively.
[10] Limited.
[11] In theory.

with some kind of relaxing downtime? If that's the case, I bet my friend Angie could benefit. In the summer her minivan turns into a Mobile Command Unit and she stuffs it full of uniforms and pads and equipment before she shuttles four stinky boys to various sporting practices, camps, and workshops, all day, every day.

Angie's always throwing out her back because she's perpetually perching on steel risers cheering on her fourth track meet of the week, or hauling coolers full of enough gluten-free, dairy-free, sugar-free, tree nut–free snacks for the whole team.[12] On away game and tournament days, she's on the road from six a.m. until ten p.m., fueled by nothing but a bucket of coffee and a handful of back pills. How cool would it be if Girls on the Run could come out and, like, bring her some sangria or give her a quick shoulder massage? I'd definitely work to support those efforts.

I click over to the charity's Web site and see that this is *"A nonprofit prevention program that encourages preteen girls to develop self-respect and healthy lifestyles through running."*

No sangria, then?

This charity isn't what I thought, but I like the idea of a nonprofit prevention program that encourages preteen girls to develop self-respect and healthy lifestyles. Empowering young women is never a bad idea.[13] I'm all for Girls on the Run . . . except for the part that might include *me* running.

As my proficiency is less "running" and more "chugging along on the treadmill, sweating and swearing, at speeds no faster than 4.0 and for lengths no longer than a quarter of a mile," I imagine

---

[12] Did you know that peanut butter's now considered a hate crime? Because it totally is.

[13] It's not as good an idea as a mobile soccer-mom sangria-delivery service, but still.

I'm not the role model these tweens seek. What am *I* going to teach them? That it's fine to take a cab for three blocks, particularly if cute shoes are involved? How to pick up the remote control with one's feet in order to avoid bending? The key to mixing the perfect dirty martini?[14]

Next!

On Saturday I can work at the Tour de Fat, which is "a celebration of bicycles and creative community." The project entails pouring beer for three hours and then cleaning up after people who've been drinking said beer. The last time I had anything to do with serving cocktails was when I worked at a dive bar in college. The money was nice, but the downside of the job was the cleaning-up-after-people-who'd-been-drinking bit. Due to the abundance of biohazards, I had to poke head and arm holes in the contractor garbage bags I wore over my *Dirty Dancing* jean shorts and sorority T-shirt to avoid the backsplash that came from hosing down the bar.[15]

I'm going to say Strike One on the potential for being gross.

"The Tour de Fat festival celebrates Chicago's growing biking community."

That may be a problem because I *loathe* most of Chicago's growing biking community. I'm infuriated at how bikers interpret traffic laws at will, plowing through stoplights, zipping in and out between cars, and riding on the sidewalk. Last week I almost nailed some mutton-chopped, forage-capped hipster who was completely oblivious to traffic due to his preoccupation not only with chatting on the phone but also smoking, thus leaving him with zero

....

[14] Double the olive juice.
[15] Fact: every drunk person barfs up pineapple chunks.

hands on the handlebars. When I honked he was all, "Bicycle rights, you fascist!" to which I replied, "Hey, Johnny Rebel—this car weighs six thousand pounds. Your ten-speed weighs twenty-five. If we crash I guarantee I'll win."

Strike two.

I check out the rest of the event description. The festival helps support environmental charities and having recently seen an incredibly guilt-inducing Discovery Channel special about polar bears, I'm on board. That is, until I stumble across a sentence that stops me dead in my tracks.

"Volunteers are encouraged to come 'in costume.'"

That's a problem because I have an irrational fear of adults wearing costumes.

By "fear" I mean "deeply seated hatred."

I'm of the mind-set that if you're too old to solicit candy from your neighbors, you're too old to dress as a Ninja Turtle. I still have flashbacks from when I had a professional job and coworkers would show up for the day done up as superheroes and Raggedy Ann. They'd be all, "Hey, won't this be fun when we see clients today?"

Um, you're not coming to *my* meetings, Batman.

In case you're wondering, I despised costumes even before I gained enough weight to limit my masquerade options to Saucy Pirate Wench or Viking-Horned Opera Singer. Thank you, no. And by the way? If you've ever gone to a Halloween party done up as a Sexy Nurse or Sexy Policewoman, please know that you appear to be one pizza delivery/cable repair away from starring in a porno.

Strike three, Tour de Fat, thanks for trying.

Let's see . . . would I like to build houses in Munster, Indiana, for eight hours?

Not with a fresh manicure, I wouldn't.

Do I want to staff the gates at one of Chicago's ubiquitous summer fests? Yeah, I'm over forty, flighty, and fluffy—I'd say I'm not ideal bouncer material.

Shall I call BINGO numbers at a local church? Pfft, if those BINGO participants are as vicious as I've seen portrayed on television, I'd be better off trying to talk local gang members into voluntarily disarming.

What else . . . oh, looks like I could teach homeless men to use the Internet through an urban ministry charity. The notion of this intrigues me, but I can't quite get past my cynicism that the second I teach these guys to do a Google search they're not heading for ICanHasCheezburger.com. This is probably the root of all those Nigerian prince e-mail scams, too. Teach a man to fish and he might just take the opportunity to steal all your lobster pots.

Hey, here's one about "keeping current." I quickly scan the description and I see that participants would be tasked with having engaging conversations about current events. Hey, I like current events! I like conversations! I'm engaging! I bet if I did this one, I could practice some of the higher-culture skills I learned for *My Fair Lazy*.

I jot down the contact information in order to sign up. I wonder, would I be working with kids or seniors? If it's seniors, I'd be fascinated by their take on how the world differs today than when they were young. I bet I'd hear a lot of sentences start with, "In my day . . ."[16] That would be totally enriching; I'm sure I'd get more out of the conversation than they would.

....

[16] I'd award bonus points for any sentence that ended, "And stay off my lawn!"

If it's kids, then I'd have the chance to be the elder statesman and I could talk about what life was like when calculators were the size of bricks and we got only three TV stations (unless you counted public TV) (which I didn't) and if you wanted to send your friend a message, you needed a pen, a spiral notebook, and the ability to do an origami fold.

I'm about to send the project coordinator an e-mail requesting to join in when I notice a few words I'd previously skimmed over. Turns out I wouldn't be having these scintillating conversations with youth or the elderly. Apparently I'd be chatting up gentlemen just released from *prison*. And this takes place in a halfway house, so their participation is likely involuntary. Suddenly this doesn't sound like such a great idea.

To be fair, maybe these conversations are totally beneficial to the ex-cons and perhaps they can't fully mainstream back into society without being able to connect with regular people. I bet having the civilian perspective helps them right the thought processes that led them down the wrong path in the first place. Yet I know myself well enough to say I'd be far too uncomfortable around these men and that the interchange wouldn't benefit any of us. Plus, I'd probably try to cross-examine them about their past crimes in order to better judge them, because even though I've made the conscious decision to become an adult, that doesn't preclude me from being an asshole.

Moving on.

Now, hey, this one's right up my alley. *"Come be surprised by how much joy an animal can bring into someone else's day. The XY Senior Center is a facility for seniors and other residents who need skilled nursing care. Pairs of volunteers make the rounds with a friendly cat or dog to socialize with residents in individual rooms. Volunteers without pets can pair up with pet owners."*

Yes! Score! Ding ding ding! I've finally found a use for my menagerie! Perfect! I love the idea of having old folks connect with animals. Pets are so therapeutic, at least when they're not vomiting in one's shoes[17] or climbing the curtains[18] or whizzing on the leg of the pool table because it vaguely resembles a tree trunk.[19] I mean, when I'm stressed or sad, nothing in the world makes me feel better than spooning Maisy, feeling her scratchy paintbrush fur against my cheek and inhaling her eau de corn chip scent.

Years ago when I worked for an HMO, I had a few peripheral dealings with nursing homes. All the best ones included pet therapy programs. Lots of places even had big, docile dogs and sweet-natured cats who lived in the facilities; they made such a difference in the residents' lives.

I absolutely adore the idea of bringing the elderly and pets together. But given the nature of my pets, I wonder if I shouldn't try to pair up with someone? Maybe I should ask.

I copy down the contact information and shoot the organizer a quick e-mail.

Hi, Kim,
I'm interested in volunteering for the XY Senior Center project. I'm wondering, though, if I need to be paired with someone who has a pet. I have two dogs who are seriously friendly but one of them is a 75-lb pit bull and the other is

---

[17] Tucker.
[18] Gus.
[19] Loki.

a 105-lb shepherd mix. They're both sweet as can be, although they tend to jump and head butt and I'd worry about them in a roomful of folks with limited balance and fragile hips.

Otherwise, I've got three kittens who couldn't be more charming, although they're still kind of feral. They're great around our house but I wonder if they might not slingshot around a room looking for a place to hide should they encounter strangers.

My elderly cats are pretty calm, but one doesn't groom himself and he looks like a bath mat. (He's also missing all his teeth but that doesn't stop him from woofing down dry dog food!) The other one is about a thousand years old and somehow I imagine petting the feline manifestation of Mr. Burns from The Simpsons wouldn't be nearly as nice as touching something fat and furry. But maybe it would work because she's spry and feisty?

Anyway, if you feel like my pets might be appropriate, let me know. And if you'd rather just pair me up with another owner, that'd be great, too. I'd love to be a part of this.

Best,
Jen Lancaster

I send my e-mail and await confirmation.
Which never comes.
Damn.

As always, my friend Stacey is a willing partner in crime, which is why I'm able to rope her into an Indianapolis road trip. We're going to an event with the GlamourGals Foundation, a nonprofit whose mission is to inspire and organize teens to provide complimentary makeovers to elderly women living in senior homes. Julia Porter, the Director of Programs, has been incredibly helpful in guiding me to various volunteer opportunities, so when I have the chance to repay the favor, I'm all over it.

We spend our day giving manicures and makeovers to the elderly residents and within five minutes, I can tell what a valuable program this is. When you're holding someone else's hand or touching her face, it creates an instant bond and an intimacy that you won't find in a garden-variety conversation.

The thing about the elderly is they don't dick around with a lot of social niceties. No time for that. So I can't help but appreciate when one of the ladies grills Stacey on her marital status.

"Are you married?" Stacey's elderly manicure client asks.

"No, but I'm dating someone exclusively," Stacey replies.

"Are you shacking up?" I have to stop rouging my gal's cheeks because I have to clap my hand over my mouth to keep from snorting.

Stacey smiles patiently. "We don't live together."

"Why not? Time's a-wasting."

And then I die laughing until she turns to me and asks why I don't have kids.

However, these ladies' ability to be blunt and articulate exactly what they want and need is why I believe this is such an amazing program. I feel like kids today have trouble expressing themselves, particularly when they can't hide behind tweets and text messages, and knowing there's a cadre of outspoken old ladies in hot pink lipstick forcing them outside their comfort zone makes me weep a little less for the future.[20]

Unfortunately, with the *My Fair Lazy* book tour coming up and the out-of-town locale, I'm not able to get to other events, so I search for opportunities closer to home.

Stacey and her family volunteer every year at the Glass Slipper Project, a nonprofit organization that gives away free prom dresses and accessories to high school juniors and seniors in the Chicago area. This is another one that makes my heart smile. If *Pretty in Pink* taught us anything, it's that no girl should ever miss her prom, Blaine. Except Molly Ringwald's dress was tragic so I'm particularly on board with the idea of needy young ladies receiving a new or gently used dress so they don't have to bust out their sewing machines.

A few days before the event Stacey calls me.

"What size do you wear?" she asks.

I already dislike where this is going. "Why?"

"Because I need to know what size T-shirt to get you for the Glass Slipper Project."

I feel a quick whoosh of relief. "Oh, no, thanks. I don't want a shirt." In my brief tenure as a professional volunteer thus far, I've learned that the shirts are kind of a status symbol. Everyone shows up to volunteer in T-shirts advertising other charities where they've worked, kind of like concert tees, only for do-gooding. It's like ev-

---

[20] Please go to GlamourGals.org if you'd like to help this amazing organization.

eryone's trying to one-up another; *I see your 5K Fun Run for MS tee and I'll raise you one Half Marathon for Habitat for Humanity!* Personally, I choose to break the cycle of one-upmanship by forgoing the swag.

I'm excited about the day because it sounds like fun and Stacey says everyone's always so happy. Last year she was a personal shopper, meaning she helped various girls find their dresses, accessories, makeup, etc. However, she says the best job is doing checkout because you get to see what everyone has picked, which may work for me because I'm more nosy than helpful. Mind you, I remember her story from a while back when one of her girls didn't think to wear any undergarments—any, *at all*—and Stacey spent her day functioning as a human shield. So when she mentioned the checkout area was the only place with chairs and I wouldn't have to see anyone naked, I was sold.

"Actually, you do. Everyone wears matching T-shirts to indicate who's staffing the event. Kind of like they do at Target."

Nooooooo! Wearing matching T-shirts is the first step towards donning a costume. I panic a little. "What if I don't want to wear a stupid shirt?"

Stacey's all matter-of-fact. "You have to wear the shirt in order to volunteer."

But I'm having none of this. "You know who made people wear matching shirts?" I ask. "Nazis, that's who."

"Is this really an issue for you?"

I begin to break into panic sweat. "Absolutely! One day it's matching T-shirts and the next it's me and a bunch of other assholes dressed as Stormtroopers and Ewoks and Yodas and shit going to Comic-Con. Matching T-shirts are the gateway drug to all things Dungeons and Dragons. So, no. No shirt. No, sir. No, thank you. I'm going to sit this one out." Immaturity trumps altruism every time.

Every week Stacey and I meet our best girlfriends, Gina and Tracey, for lunch. To say that none of us suffers fools gladly would be an understatement, but no one quite takes this to the extent that Gina does. There's a certain phrase that Gina reserves for the most obstinate, the most ridiculous, and the most frustrating among us. She reserves it for dire situations, like when dealing with a third-world call center. She'll take whatever bullshit they spew and simply restates it so that whoever said it first can hear exactly how stupid they sound. Trouble's afoot when you hear Gina begin a sentence with, "So what you're telling me is . . ."

Stacey pauses a moment to collect her thoughts before she says, "So what you're telling me is that you don't want to help needy girls with their prom dresses because you're afraid it will one day cause you to dress like C-3PO."

I mull this over.

"I'll take whatever size shirt you get."

"All righty. See you on Saturday!"

Reluctant Adult Lesson Learned:

Taking feels good but giving feels great, even if you have to do it in a stupid shirt.

The Evolution of a Bad Idea

10:15 P.M.—Hmm, getting late. I should get ready for bed.

10:30 P.M.—Hmm, getting even later. I should get ready for bed.

10:45 P.M.—Someone on the Internet is mistaken and I must express my displeasure with many uppercase letters and exclamation points.

11:00 P.M.—It's really not getting any earlier, is it?

11:10 P.M.—Nightly skin inspection in bathroom mirror. Not perfect, but not bad for my age/lifestyle/aversion to sunscreen.

11:11 P.M.—Hey, what would happen if I used a magnifying mirror during my inspection?

11:12 P.M.—SWEET JESUS, MAKE IT STOP!

11:13 P.M.—Reinspect by light of bedside lamp. Ah, all better.

11:14 P.M.—But what if I put in a brighter bulb?

11:15 P.M.—IS FURRY BEAST! KILL IT! KIIIIIIIIL IT!

11:16 P.M.—"What do you think I'm doing? I'm looking at my skin in this mirror. And I've either got to wax this mustache or start giving rides on it, ha ha!"

11:16 P.M.—"What do you mean, '*I don't think that expression means what you think it means*'?"

11:17 P.M.—Oh. Then that man at Target with the FREE MUSTACHE RIDES logo was wearing a very dirty shirt.

11:18 P.M.—"I would like to amend my previous statement. I need to wax this mustache or learn to twirl it, ha ha!"

11:19 P.M.—I should tweeze this thing.

11:20 P.M.—I should find my tweezers.

11:21 P.M.—Ow. Ow. Ow. Ow. Ow.

11:22 P.M.—Screw this. I need a professional waxing. Must make an appointment.

11:25 P.M.—Can't. Stop. Fondling. Mustache.

11:30 P.M.—Fine, I'll do the goddamned thing myself.

11:40 P.M.—Can't find new tub of wax I purchased for just this very occasion, so locate old container. Is very old. Is possibly the exact same tub that Moses' wife used to remove her unwanted facial hair. (Desert light is unforgiving.)

11:41 P.M.—But it's wax. It's not like it could go bad, right?

11:42 P.M.—"I'm not *'banging around and keeping you awake.'* I'm doing something important."

11:43 P.M.—Microwaving.

11:44 P.M.—Microwaving.

11:45 P.M.—Microwaving.

11:46 P.M.—Microwaving.

11:47 P.M.—I think my microwave may be broken.

11:48 P.M.—Ah, there we go.

11:49 P.M.—I don't have a stick, so I'll just use my finger to stir this hot, molten lava.

11:50 P.M.—"Well, what do you expect? I just seared off my own fingerprint!"

11:51 P.M.—Blow and cool. Use damaged digit to spread wax liberally on my Tom Selleck.

11:52 P.M.—Wait for wax to harden so can pull off unsightly hairs in one (briefly painful) fell swoop.

11:53 P.M.—Is not hardening.

11:54 P.M.—Is not hardening.

11:55 P.M.—Is not hardening. Is sitting on upper lip in a big, sticky blob.

11:56 P.M.—Begin to tentatively peel off wax millimeter by millimeter. (Hate metric system.)

11:57 P.M.—Is like removing chewing gum from underneath cafeteria table, only ouchy.

11:57 P.M.—Hurty.

11:58 P.M.—Hurty.

11:59 P.M.—So very hurty.

12:00 A.M.—Use sticky bits of already-peeled wax to slowly pry off other gummy bits.

12:01 A.M.—Oh, yeah, this is WAY better than waiting nine hours and paying a professional ten dollars to handle this in five seconds.

12:02 A.M.—The good news is the hair is coming off.

12:03 A.M.—The bad news is, so is my skin.

12:04 A.M.—How mad will he be if I wake him up to help me?

12:05 A.M.—On second thought, he'd be mad for a second, but the mocking would last a lifetime. Must cowboy-up and finish job myself.

12:06 A.M.— . . . And it's finally off!

12:07 A.M.—Except for those small, tacky bits with the Kleenex stuck to them.

12:08 A.M.—I know, I'll use baby oil. That gets rid of sticky stuff.

12:09 A.M.—Hmm, I don't have baby oil. Instead opt for canola oil. (Is heart-healthy.)

12:10 A.M.—Wax is off, now to remove oil. Need toner.

12:11 A.M.—But tossed out toner after that whole "who thought it was a good idea to make this stuff the exact same shade of blue as the nail polish remover?" incident.

12:12 A.M.—Will use Fletch's toner. Quietly.

12:13 A.M.—!!!

12:14 A.M.—"WELL MAYBE THEY SHOULD HAVE WRITTEN 'GLYCOLIC ACID' IN BIGGER PRINT ON THE BOTTLE!"

12:15 A.M.—Probably should plan to make an "I'm sorry I got shouty after midnight" mousse tomorrow.

12:16 A.M.—Inspect skin in magnifying mirror by light of new bulb. Hair is gone, but lip is swollen in manner of Simpsons character.

12:17 A.M.—So this is what I'd look like if I had the ability to grow a big, red Fu Manchu mustache. Noted.

12:18 A.M.—In retrospect, perhaps "learn to twirl it" wasn't such a bad idea.

12:19 A.M.—Is really late. Must get ready for bed.

12:20 A.M.—I wonder if anyone else on the Internet is wrong?

Reluctant Adult Lesson Learned:

Philosophy makes a moisturizer that states on the label that you won't find so many imperfections if you don't go looking for them.

The manufacturers of Philosophy products are a bunch of baby-booming hippies.

My philosophy is you won't find so many imperfections if you simply have that shit lasered.

C·H·A·P·T·E·R T·H·R·E·E

Flipping the Script

"What are you guys doing for Thanksgiving?"

"Ignoring it."

"Ha. Right."

When I don't respond, Stacey cuts her eyes away from the road to glance over at me. "No, seriously, what are your plans?"[21]

I reply, "I'm being serious. We plan on pretending that Thanksgiving isn't happening."

Stacey and I are on our weekly pilgrimage to the Kingsbury Street Whole Foods Market. Stacey was out of the country when the place opened this May, so it was me who took her here for the first time when she returned in June. And now? It's our special

---

[21] A shorter "fictionalized" version of this story is available in Stacey's fabulous book *Off the Menu*, in stores July 2012. Even though *Jeneration X* comes out first, Stacey wrote hers before I did. I felt that should be noted.

place; it's kind of like our church, if churches specialized in locally sourced, grass-fed beef.

I've always loved going to the grocery store, long before I learned to cook. There's something about the cool, crisp, refrigerated air, the pyramids of glossy, precisely stacked fruits and vegetables, and aisle after aisle of neatly faced cans and boxes that deeply appeals to my inner need for order.[22] My favorite time to shop is early afternoon, before the after-work rush, because that's when everything is at its calmest and tidiest. (Before you ask, *of course* I'm the shopper who rearranges the jars of tomato sauce after I select one to keep the shelf pristine and symmetrical.)

So if grocery shopping in an orderly, well-stocked store is good, then imagine doing so in the third-largest WFM in the world. Situated on the river, the Kingsbury store boasts an entire promenade where shoppers can stroll and dine and watch boats pass. In fact, the best view of the Chicago skyline can be seen from the top of the three-story parking garage. And that's just the outside!

The inside of the store is nothing short of monolithic. The fresh produce area alone is the size of a football field and it's bordered by a coffee bar. The fact that they're all about being "organic" and I can't get a damn Splenda for my latte is an annoyingly first-world problem for sure, but that's why I always carry extras in my purse.[23]

Did I mention the coffee bar serves beer and wine, too, and always has sports on the flat screen? For me, this isn't as much of a selling point as you'd think because certain members of the WFM

....

[22] Or my inner need to "control things" as per Fletch.

[23] You never know when you'll have to sweeten on the go.

customer base are cluelessly aggravating enough without adding public intoxication to the mix.[24]

Beyond the produce section is the fresh seafood area where the mongers wear those big rubber boots-pants you see on the fish-tossers at Pike's Market in Seattle. Even though I'm pretty sure the staff members just got off the El and not a Bering Sea crabbing vessel, I appreciate the nod to authenticity.

There are places to sit and have a cocktail or meal throughout the store. Between the dairy and wine sections is a big wine-and-cheese bar, and past that you'll find an upscale food court area, with everything from barbecue and hand-tossed woodfire pizza to fresh sushi.

And the bars—don't start me on the bars. There's a make-your-own trail mix bar, a choose-your-own seafood bar, a decant-your-own honey bar, a mix-and-match cookie bar, and a hot food bar with enough variety to satisfy everyone from the most humorless vegan to the world's biggest carnivore.[25] One day I stopped by early after a dentist appointment and I stumbled across the breakfast bar, complete with biscuits and gravy. So magnificent was the sight that I wept a little.

When other grocery stores dream of an afterlife, this is what they picture, with twenty kinds of fresh gelato and sorbet made daily and cheese sellers who say, "Hmm, I haven't tasted that particular *tomme de chèvre*, either—let's open it up and sample it together!"

Through the confluence of unbelievably fresh product, a little

....

[24] Although to the person who always parks his Range Rover in the ALTERNATIVE FUELS ONLY parking spot? I like your style.

[25] Which is the Southern Elephant Seal. (I looked it up.)

training, and finally owning some decent equipment, I've come to love cooking. Turns out I'm fearless in the kitchen and Fletch is constantly delighted by the dishes I make. Yeah, there's an occasional misstep—candy apple pork chops, I'm looking at you—but I've found real Zen at the bottom of my enamel cast-iron pot.

In fact, last year Fletch and I tackled our first fully blown, fancy-set-table, official Thanksgiving dinner as our attempt to create a new holiday tradition. In the past we'd gotten together with family, but as our relationship became increasingly strained,[26] we thought we'd be a lot happier on our own and this was our first go of it.

Our menu was outstanding and I'm not sure what the best part was. The prosciutto-wrapped asparagus was the perfect blend of crisp and salty and the creamed pearl onions made me want to bury my face in the chafing dish and go at them feeding-trough-style.

But as Fletch and I sat there at our grown-up table in our first real dining room—with a chandelier and everything!—eating a wonderful meal and drinking out of proper wineglasses, the venture into new traditions felt like a waste of time. I spent two days in the kitchen and we finished stuffing ourselves in about twenty minutes. The end result, although delicious, wasn't worth the effort and felt like a huge letdown.

Our other Thanksgiving option, going out to dinner alone, feels equally depressing, so we decided that our *new* new tradition is full-on denial.

I tell Stacey, "We're just going to be all, *'Thanksgiving? Sorry, I think you dialed the wrong number.'*"

....

[26] Read: certain members became bat-shittier.

Stacey keeps stealing confused glances at me while she drives. "Let me get this straight—you plan to ignore Thanksgiving?"

"Exactly."

"Honey, denial is not a strategy."

"Pfft. Denial is *absolutely* a strategy, particularly for the kind of holidays that depress you. For example, how did you celebrate Valentine's Day last year?"

Stacey's lips get all scrunchy, and her voice is clipped. "I don't remember."

"See? Denial. Works like a charm.[27] Can you blame me for not wanting to recognize the day because it bums me out? All holidays do. Always have. I've hated the time period between my birthday in November and January second since I was a kid because, without fail, every single holiday devolved into big-time family chaos."

"How so?" Stacey gets distressed when I bring up familial insanity, likely because she comes from a functional family where everyone not only loves each other, but actually likes one another, too. No one tells anyone else they're fat and no one gets into a screaming match over using too much hot water, nor does anyone continue to hold a grudge about shit that happened in 1976.

It's so weird.

"Give me a specific," she prompts.

"Let's see . . . well, every year like clockwork my mother would try to punish my father because he liked being home for the holiday instead of driving seventeen hours in the snow each way over a

....

[27] Please don't worry about Stacey. When this happened, she was about four days away from meeting the man of her dreams. They got married in May 2011, and he gives her the best Valentine's Days anyone could possibly imagine. I'm talking diamonds, champagne, and poetry. He treats her like the (bossy) goddess she is.

weekend so she could be with her extended family, none of whom he liked, so that was fun."

"That's it?"

I roll my eyes. "Oh, please. We'd spend the week leading up to the holiday dealing with her sulking and pouting and I'd be all, *'What are you, fifty?'* Then the actual day of Christmas or Thanksgiving or Easter would roll around and she'd freak out because she spent so much time pouting and sulking that she'd be entirely off schedule in creating the meal. And despite having help from me, my dad, and later my sister-in-law, dinner wouldn't be ready until ten p.m. and she'd be mad at us for complaining that we were hungry. Of course, she'd sabotage a situation already made super-tense due to starvation by unilaterally deciding madness like, *'I'm going to make this a fat-free Thanksgiving!'"*

Stacey blanches. "That is a crime against humanity."

"Right? Plus, she believed that we should be all Norman Rockwell–y and, like, sit around in candlelight and listen to carols, and you know what? That's a lovely thought and we should pencil that in. But when everyone's gathered in the family room and we're all quietly enjoying each other's company for once by hanging out and watching the James Bond marathon on TBS, *that* is not the time to yank the television cord out of the wall and demand we share our feeeeelings. Because we feeeeel? Like watching *Goldfinger*."

Stacey laughs and says, "That can't possibly be true," while I nod emphatically. We arrive at WFM and find a cherry parking spot on the second floor next to the door. We exit the car and enter the store, taking the long escalator that dumps out right by the bar. "Need to cocktail up before you finish the story?"

"Yes, but I won't. Oh, and this *totally* happened, most recently from Thanksgiving 1992 through 1994 until my brother's family entirely stopped coming for that holiday, and Christmases 1999 through 2006."

"Oy." We grab matching carts and begin to peruse the most perfect stack of Honeycrisps. Each one is the size of a softball and they easily weigh one and a half pounds. We both murmur in admiration while we stuff them in plastic produce bags.

"Yep. Hey, speaking of—sometimes my mother would take the thing my father dreamed about all year, her one home-run swing, the apple pie—and she'd substitute zucchini instead. Just because. Ask me how well that went over. I mean, I appreciate her looking out for my father's health, but it's one freaking dinner over the course of three hundred and sixty-five days. Hey, how about we *don't* make it a fat-free Thanksgiving? I'm not saying she was all Joan Crawford because that's certainly not the case, but believe me when I say I never looked forward to any holiday."

Stacey pats me on the arm as we wend our way past the fancy lettuce display. "Then? Every meal ended in recriminations when we'd make my mother angry by accusing her of hiding the butter and emptying all the saltshakers and filling them with No Salt. Which, of course, she did. By the way? When you put Smart Balance HeartRight Light Spread on mashed potatoes? I totally *can* believe it's not butter. Passive aggression; it's what's for dinner."

Stacey stops in front of the fresh-cut fruit fridge. "Oh, peanut, I'm sorry."

"It is what it is." I shrug. "I mean, I'm not all scarred and I don't need therapy or anything. It's just that the idea of going over the river and through the woods? Holds no appeal."

"What about Fletch?"

"Ironically, our traditions were a step up for him. At least *we* had James Bond. Poor Fletch used to get stuck in the mountains of Virginia with no television and his grandmother would boil a chicken for Thanksgiving dinner. She'd serve the big, flaccid, gray mass of meat and say, 'Let's eat and get it over with already.' So when we're all *A Christmas Story* and order Chinese this year, don't feel sorry for us because we're going to have the best non-Thanksgiving Thanksgiving ever."

Stacey furrows her brow while debating pineapple chunks or rings. Then, after a few seconds she says, "No."

"No pineapple?"

Stacey bangs on her shopping cart. "No. No, no. You need to celebrate Thanksgiving."

"What part of my *I hate the holidays* diatribe did you not understand?"

"You don't *hate* Thanksgiving. You hate conflict. You hate bad food. You hate chaos. Thanksgiving is inherently happy. No one hates Thanksgiving." She stops herself. "Well, Native Americans maybe. Point is *you* can't not be happy on a day where pie figures in so prominently. What you need to do is *reclaim* Thanksgiving. You need to flip the script."

"We tried that last year and it was lame."

"Because it was just the two of you. This year, you invite guests."

I protest, "Who's going to come? Everyone always has Thanksgiving plans."

"Yeah, miserable plans. *I can, in fact, believe it's not butter* plans. Plans they're dreading because they never had your awesome Thanksgiving Day dinner as an option before. Start asking around. You'll be surprised at how many people would rather go to your house. I'm telling you, flip the script."

"But—"

"Flip it."

"I can't—"

"Flip. It."

We're still debating when we run into our dear friend Gina. She spots us from her table on the second floor where she's having lunch when she hears the familiar sound of us squabbling.

"Gina, settle an argument for me," I say. "No one would come to my house on Thanksgiving, right?"

Gina cocks her head. "Why not?"

"Because they have plans. Like you. Where will you be on Thanksgiving?"

"Probably in my house, drinking wine, ignoring the day so I don't have to be with my annoying relatives," she replies.

"Aha!" Stacey crows. "*This* is what I'm talking about. If Jen had a Thanksgiving Day dinner, would you come?"

Without hesitation, Gina replies, "Absolutely! I'd much rather drink wine at your house."

Stacey turns to me. "Told you so."

I admit it, I like the idea of flipping the script, but the actuality of it may be too much for me to handle. "I panic when I have to cook for more than three people. Remember my dinner party this summer where half the guests never even got fed before they had to leave and I accidentally got hammered?"

Gina helpfully adds, "If I recall, the problem was more that you got hammered and forgot to start dinner. Those cocktails were delicious, though." I mixed equal parts of passion fruit juice, elderflower liqueur, Prosecco, and Stoli Razberi and all the girls slammed them like Gatorade on a hot day.[28] Eventually Fletch had to step in to work the grill because he thought we were all so soaked in alcohol that we'd ignite if we got too close.

You see, I've become a bit of a mixologist—or, according to Fletch, I'm the Queen of the Girl Drunk Drinks. When we started dating, I drank Johnnie Walker Black and soda. Now when we go out, I'm all, "What do you have with lychee nuts in it?" To me? This is not a bad thing. I mean, I don't do shots anymore because I hate how they make me feel in the morning. Coincidentally, this is also why I no longer eat Lucky Charms for dinner. Much as I enjoyed both acts, I haven't the liver or the stomach of a college kid anymore.

Stacey waves away my protests. "When we get home, I'll send you my Thanksgiving time and action plan. My plan contains everything you need to do from start to finish, so the whole thing is foolproof. No worries."

"Does this mean we're having Thanksgiving at your house, Jen?" Gina asks.

"Um . . ." I stammer.

"Yes," Stacey replies. "This year Jen learns to flip the script. Now, I think we have some shopping to do."

Within a few hours, my Thanksgiving Day goes from nonexistent to hosting a dinner for twelve.

Holy crap.

....
[28] Primarily because I forgot to tell everyone I included a bottle of vodka.

Later in the evening, I receive Stacey's time and action plan. I sit here at my desk blinking at it, overwhelmed by its precision. Not only does this multiple-paged tome contain an entire menu complete with recipes, but there's a whole shopping list divided by department and the time action plan breaks out my week in fifteen-minute increments, beginning on Monday.

This is a masterpiece of planning and precision.

To the extent that it's freaking me out.

I e-mail Stacey the following: *"Somewhere in Connecticut, a chill just raced down Martha Stewart's back."*

She responds: *"Poor Martha. Sadly, she is not chilled at all. 1) No Jew could ever out-Thanksgiving a WASP like her and 2) I don't forge my own silverware or weave my own tablecloth, which just makes me lazy. Go over with Fletch, and make your own menu. You can then delete items off the shopping list for the stuff you aren't making, and add anything new that you need. (Check your herbs and spices, since I have a good stock of those and they aren't on my shopping list.) Once you have the menu set, we can make an equipment list."*

Equipment list?

I am so over my head right now.

Things begin to go off the rails before I can even get to step one on Monday. Between finishing edits for *My Fair Lazy* and driving downtown for an interview for a syndicated columnist position with Tribune Media Services, I lose the whole day. I'm officially in panic mode despite having three whole days before the dinner.

"Thanksgiving is ruined!" I wail.

"Nothing is ruined. The world's not going to end because you couldn't get to the cranberry sauce or pickled carrots today. Just relax, you can do this," Stacey assures me. Well, of course she's calm—she's not even making dinner. Her extended family switches off holidays, so this year, all she's got to do is cook soup.

Stacey talks me off the ledge and even promises to spend the day with me on Wednesday helping to prep.

She doesn't know it yet, but her reward for helping will be watching *Twilight* with me on DVD.[29]

I lose another entire goddamned day to edits, despite my trying to rush. So if you run across errors in *My Fair Lazy*—and you will—please cut me some slack because Stacey's time and action plan says nothing about budgeting a day for rewrites.

Fletch is delighted with the idea of a houseful of guests. He's way more excited than I am, actually, likely because he doesn't grasp the enormity of the work in front of us. He's making himself useful and he's even added his own steps to the time action plan, including:

Steam clean the rug

Finish wiring project

Polish floor

Pick up turkey

Iron linens

---

[29] No good deed goes unpunished, eh?

Secure weapons[30]

Because of other priorities, we don't get to WFM until Tuesday afternoon. The minute I see cops directing traffic in and out of the garage, I know we're in trouble.

"I was going to the worst place in the world and I didn't even know it yet," Fletch quotes from *Apocalypse Now* as he tries to navigate past a hybrid that seems to be entirely held together by bumper sticks mocking my every belief. And yet this parking lot chaos is nothing compared to what we find inside.

Ever seen those photos of the two hundred thousand Chinese people at the beach in Qingdao during a heat wave? And there's not a single grain of sand that isn't covered by a Chinese dude in a Speedo and a Chairman Mao haircut? And you can't tell where the ocean of people stop and the ocean proper begins because it's such a mass of humanity? And you could literally stick out your elbows and be carried into the sea by fellow sunbathers?

That's exactly what the produce department is like here tonight. For a minute I think we're going to have to skip the mashed potatoes when the crowd sweeps me over to the onions, but I manage to swim my way back upstream to the tubers.

"This may have been a mistake," Fletch notes, after we're wedged into a corner by the Manchego display when hipsters flood the wine bar. I see my favorite cheese monger struggling to keep his head above water as shoppers swarm ten-deep around the counter. I catch his eye as he mouths, "Help."

"You think so?" I respond.

And that's when the after-work crowd arrives.

....
[30] It's probably a good thing we didn't have access to any kind of weapons (other than salmonella) during old family holidays.

Two hours and a river of blood, sweat, and tears later, we're done shopping. Those who've never lived through the repugnance of war can't possibly comprehend what we went through, so let me sum it up—we were in the shit. We had only two ways home: death, or victory. Francis Ford Coppola would win another Academy Award were he to make a movie about our experience.

On the way back to the house, we pledge to never speak about the experience again in an effort to keep the post-traumatic stress at bay. If we don't, someday you'll see us at the entrance to the expressway holding signs saying Kingsbury Whole Foods Thanksgiving Vet.

We discover our next problem once we arrive home.

"What is all this?" Fletch asks, staring at the boxes currently filling the entire fridge.

"Tracey can't cook so she sent over some pies as her contribution," I reply. "FedEx delivered them earlier today."

"How many pies are there?" He leans deeper in the fridge and begins to count. "Seven? We have seven pies! For nine adults and three children. Does that seem right to you?"

"Why, is that not enough? I'm also making a cake."

The expression he's wearing tells me everything I need to know about my ability to do dessert math. We pack all the boxes back into the dry ice they arrived in, then place them in coolers on the back deck, with zip ties adding an extra measure of security against rats. In holidays past, my mother used to store all our leftovers on the hood of the car in the garage, so my dad's vehicle always had little dings on it from the Pyrex bowls of unwanted fat-free stuffing. Fletch threatens me with an untimely death if I try to do the same to his car, so deck it is.

I still make a cake, though, because you just never know.

Stacey's been here next to me, working through lunch and now dinner. We've been ass-deep in pans and pies and potato peels and plungers.[31]

"It's so hard. Why is it so hard?" I cry as I use a floury hand to wipe my sweaty brow.

Stacey, covered in bread crumbs and homemade cream of mushroom soup splatters, is almost too shell-shocked to answer. She rocks a little when she finally replies. "Time and action plan meant for many days, not one day. Not one day. Never one day."

"Maybe we should have some pie to help us along?" I suggest.

"No pie. Just finish. Just finish. See vampires. Just finish."

I hug her briefly before continuing to peel my butternut squash over the open garbage can. Peels are falling all over the previously clean floor and at this point, I don't care.

I just want to be done.

I just want to sit down.

I just want to share the magic of *Twilight* with Stacey.

I just want us to watch Bella make out with her creepy, stalker boyfriend who, really, should be arrested on statch charges because she's seventeen and he's what, at least a hundred years old?

I just want her to roll her eyes with me over the wooden performances and stilted dialogue, despite still secretly wanting to hug myself afterward because I love all of it so much.

....

[31] Here's a fun fact—don't put potato peels in the garbage disposal unless you like having mung water back into every sink on the first floor after they've already been cleaned in anticipation of the big day. Also, invest in a wet-dry vac. Trust me on this one.

And as soon as the butternut soup is set to simmer, we can do this. Fletch has the DVD cued up and everything.

We still have to get through peeling and de-seeding the mountain of squash before we can sauté the chunks with onion and butter. After everything softens up, we have to use an immersion blender to break the squash into small bits and mix it with the pumpkin, and then we'll make it extra creamy and smooth via chinois strainer before we can add the cream and nutmeg.

I steal little bites of everything during the cooking process and am confident that this dish is going to kick off the dinner in the most delicious fashion possible.

We need to let the soup cool before we put it away, and now the plan is to grab something to drink and finally get off our feet.

"Stace, you want some wine? I have an open bottle of some decent Chardonnay."

"If I have one glass, I'll pass out and die. How about some water?"

I go over to the cabinet next to the stove to retrieve a glass. Because we've been extremely conscientious about not having to work around dirty dishes, we've been vigilant about unloading the dishwasher and thus, our undersized glass cabinet is stacked a bit too tightly.

It's stacked so tightly, in fact, that when I open it, one of my favorite juice glasses falls out and breaks on the countertop.

Right next to the uncovered pot of soup.

And when I say "break," I don't mean a couple of big chunks that could be reassembled. I mean, smashed, pulverized, exploded, stomped on like a Jewish wedding and tempering joy by flinging tiny bits of juice glass to the four corners of the kitchen.

"Do you think the soup's okay?" I ask. "Like, if we strained it?"

She mournfully shakes her head. "Oh, honey, no. That juice glass didn't just break; it detonated. That soup was a shopkeeper's window and the glass was an SA storm trooper. That was Kristall-nacht. Serve the soup to your guests and you're going to kill them and their families will sue and then you'll *really* hate this holiday."

All of which means if I want to serve soup tomorrow, I've got to go back to Whole Foods for more butternut squash. Tonight. The evening before Thanksgiving.

The horror . . . the horror . . .

We don't have enough room at the big table for everyone, so I have to annex the table in the kitchen for the kids. Growing up, I was always stuck at the kids' table and it sucked so I wanted to make sure this wasn't the case for our young guests. I decorate the table with tons of candies and little games and flowers. I've made it so appealing that I kind of want to sit there.

We ironed all the linens earlier in the week, and I started to set the table days ahead of time until I found cats sitting in the soup bowls. I chased them away thinking, *I wonder if Martha Stewart has to put up with this shit?* I had to unset and wash everything and we don't redo it until this afternoon once we put the cats away.

It's five o'clock and the guests should begin to arrive any minute.

After what feels like forty-eight hours of hard labor, I'm ready for this.

Okay, fine, I have mashed potatoes in my hair, the sink is

stacked to the ceiling with dishes, and Maisy just barfed up shrimp tails on the living room rug, but the liquor's chilled and I'm happy.

The next six hours are a blur of good food, great wine, and loosened belts. There's football and Bond flicks playing on televisions throughout the house and although there's a little shouting, it's only so everyone can hear each other over all the laughter.

There's enough pie left over to send every family home with one, and, due to Stacey's meticulous planning, we stocked up on GladWare so we could make sure everyone has leftovers on the day after Thanksgiving. Even though it takes us two days to finally get every dish washed and stored, the effort has been worth it.

This Thanksgiving has been the best holiday ever and the beginning of a new set of traditions.

The script has been flipped.

Reluctant Adult Lesson Learned:

Forgive the cliché, but friends are truly the family you choose.

Lucky Nineteen

*E*ighteen places.

Since I graduated from high school and moved out of my family's house, I've lived eighteen different places. That means I've moved eighteen times in twenty-five years. Gypsies don't move that much, nor do carnies, nomads, or Deadheads. I'm exhausted just thinking about it.

That's eighteen bedrooms.

Eighteen bathrooms.

Eighteen rounds of scouring stoves and wiping cabinets so I can get back my security deposit. No wonder I've had such a hard time trying to grow up. How the hell am I supposed to establish roots and mature when I move on to the next joint every 1.38 years? That's barely enough time to have my magazine subscriptions forwarded!

However, that's all about to change because Fletch and I are planning to buy a home!

For the past year and a half, our intention has been to buy the place we've been renting in the city because it's nicely sized, it boasts lovely finishes, and is Stacey-adjacent. Also? We're already here and the notion of boxing up all my shit one more time makes me weak in the knees.

Of course, now that we've finally saved up enough for a down payment, we wonder if we really want to do business with our landlord. Our country's stringent libel laws prevent me from coming right out and calling him the dirtbag I believe him to be, so I'll share a few recent incidents so you may draw your own conclusion.

For example, not long ago we found a big orange violation sticker on our front gate saying that our water was going to be shut off if we didn't cough up the five hundred dollars we owed in past-due bills immediately.

Um . . . we're renters. According to the standard City of Chicago lease, we don't *have* a water bill. That's not our responsibility. And if we did have a water bill—which we don't—how could it be five hundred dollars?! The average city water/sewage bill runs about fifteen dollars/month.[32] At five hundred dollars, that would mean the water bill hadn't been paid even once since this house was built *almost three years ago.*

After forty-five minutes spent on hold with the Chicago Department of Water Management . . . bingo. Confirmation. That's three years of unpaid bills and we've only been here half that amount of time.

....

[32] Not that I would advise it, but this is when it's fortuitous to have AC-CIDENTALLY opened someone else's mail so you know this kind of shit.

I quickly take care of what's past due and deduct the amount off our rent because if I leave it for the landlord—for simplicity's sake, let's call him Dick—it will never get done. How do I know?

Because the same damn thing happened with our electricity.

Dick isn't your prototypical slumlord, which is why all of this is so frustrating. He's an Ivy League grad with an assload of higher education degrees and he really should know better. In fact, he's a professional real estate speculator, so none of what happens next should be new to him.

When we moved in here in October of 2008, I attempted to establish electric service in my name. When I hadn't received a bill in December, I started calling ComEd because I worried when we did finally receive one, it would be so huge I couldn't pay it. As I'm fully versed in what it's like to live without power, I'm anxious to make sure nothing like this ever happens again, so I call around for answers.

Turns out our place had never passed the final electrical inspection after being built because some junction box was placed in the wrong area. Until the house passed city inspection, a meter couldn't be installed and thus an account couldn't be established. The house had essentially been siphoning energy for free since it was built.

Yes. Let that sink in for a moment.

Stealing from the electrical grid.

Is that not some Dr. Evil/supervillain shit or what?

According to ComEd, they'd sent many, many letters to Dick trying to right this egregious wrong to no avail. We called him and he promised to take care of everything.

"Taking care of everything" resulted in Dick doing, well, *dick* for three months, as well as the first of the big orange cutoff stickers slapped on our front gate. Do you know how frustrating it is to finally have yourself together enough to keep the lights on only to almost lose them because of the guy whose mortgage we pay? ARGH.

From start to finish, the process of establishing an electric bill in my name took eight months. Oh, and when Dick's moronic subcontractors finally moved the box to pass inspection, they cut the line to our alarm system. So, unbeknownst to us, from April until November our expensive radio-controlled system that we installed and paid for *didn't work*. We found this out only when a battery needed to be changed and our landlord claimed he "couldn't remember" the name of the alarm contractor who originally wired the house. Fortunately, we still had his card.

What's interesting to note is the alarm contractor was *very* familiar with Dick's name, due to over ten thousand dollars' worth of unpaid invoices. And that's when we decide that buying this house might result in too many more unpleasant surprises. At some point, someone's going to *send some guys* (if you know what I mean) and I'd like to not be here when it happens.

A few years ago our plan was to buy a house in the North Shore suburbs but we never quite got there. We couldn't decide which town we might like best and then, once we made a decision, a mold infestation forced us out of our old rental house and completely changed our buying timeline. Now that it looks like we don't want this house, we revisit the decision to move to Lake County, largely because of Maisy.

My beautiful pit bull Maisy is pretty much the light of my life. She's a huge reason I tried so hard to establish a writing career; I couldn't bear the idea of having to leave her every day to work an office job. Whenever I'd go out without her, she'd mournfully gaze at me with these soulful brown eyes, made almond shaped because of her kohl eyeliner–type markings, and I'd be overcome with guilt because I hated having her miss me. Whenever I'd leave the house, she'd be perched on the back of the couch, right by the door, waiting for me. The second she'd spot me on the sidewalk, her whole body would wag, like my coming back was the greatest thing to ever happen in her life. So now when people ask me why I became a writer, I tell them it's because my dog was a nudge.

Anyway, every few weeks, she and I travel thirty miles up the expressway to the Veterinary Specialty Clinic in Buffalo Grove so she can undergo chemotherapy for mast cell tumors. Fortunately, we caught it early enough for treatment. She's been in remission for a while and the majority of time she does very well, but when she gets sick, it's very serious and very scary. If she didn't have cancer, I'd be comfortable taking her to local emergency vets, but because she does, we go directly to her clinic. Over the past year, she and I have taken many snowy, white-knuckled, midnight rides.

Fletch and I find a map and draw a big circle around a ten-mile radius of the clinic and decide we're living somewhere within those boundaries. We're torn between two communities I know to be green and lovely, but what clinches our decision is Highland Park's stance on pit bulls. In short, they don't want them. In 2009 the mayor proposed bans on this breed, so even though it would be legal to have my dog there,[33] she wouldn't be welcome. You don't want my dog? Then you don't get my tax dollar.

....

[33] At least for now.

Ultimately we choose to search for homes in Lake Forest because I like lakes and I like forests and that place has both in abundance.

Of course, before anything can happen, we need a mortgage approval. With the way the lending market has been collapsing in on itself like a dying star, we're not quite sure how this is going to work.

We had our own financial meltdown in the not so distant past, so we're not ideal mortgage candidates, at least not on paper. For a bank to agree to lend us money, we've got to make a case for why we're not the deadbeats our slow-to-improve FICO scores claim.[34] Our friend introduces us to a broker and we meet him for lunch at a sushi place to discuss our situation.

Here's the thing: I like sushi. I like it a lot and not just boring stuff like California rolls. Maybe I'm not at the Jeremy-Piven-human-thermometer-level of sushi lover, but I dig it. Raw halibut, flounder, trout, salmon, and tuna . . . if you roll it up in *tobiko* and dip it in eel sauce, I'm game. But anyone who's ever been to a sushi joint knows that there's one small, scary portion of the menu consisting of the superweird stuff that blurs the line between "fish," "insect," and "sci-fi movie mutant." Yet when the mortgage broker suggests we order from the dark side, I'm all for it and I eat every bizarre bite that's set in front of me, until we receive a big wad of raw quail egg–topped sea urchin.

"You might not like it," cautions Ryan, our potential mortgage broker.

....

[34] I'm not one to advocate anarchy, but sometimes I think Tyler Durden had it right.

When the platter of what appears to be small tongues wrapped in seaweed and topped in ectoplasm arrived at the table a minute ago, I kind of gathered that I wouldn't.

Yet if eating sea urchin is what determines whether or not I spend another year paying Dick rent, then sea urchin is suddenly my favorite dish. (Of course, Fletch is a culinary coward and sits out this round.)

I pick up the small, vaguely orange, tongue-shaped[35] sea slug in front of me and I steel myself for what's about to happen next. I approach the piece with an open mind, knowing that some of my favorite foods—foie gras, escargot, and caviar—gave me nightmares until I actually tasted them.

I stuff the sea urchin in my mouth and I have trouble chewing it because I'm unsure where my tongue ends and the sea urchin begins, not unlike when I've eaten dinner before all the Novocain wears off after a trip to the dentist. As the sea urchin lolls around my mouth, I feel like I'm being French-kissed by a Japanese fishing boat.

And the slimy raw quail egg? The texture does this bite no favors, either.

I do not love sea urchin.

I do not like sea urchin.

I do not want to put sea urchin anywhere near any of my orifices ever again.

Yet in downing it, I prove to myself that I can handle any food challenge were I ever to make it onto *Survivor*.

Also? I get us a mortgage.

....

[35] With what appear to be taste buds and everything!

Our friend is a Realtor here in the city and we ping her to help us find our new home. We want to buy a place so we can move before I leave for my book tour.

Not happening.[36]

Since February, we've made three offers and each has imploded due to poor inspections[37] or issues with the seller doing a short sale. Our buying process has morphed into a high-stakes game of Card Sharks wherein all parties involved shout "Higher!" and "Lower!" willy-nilly and the potential sale inches along until someone draws a seven card, the action freezes, and we have to write Dick yet another rent check.

We table our hunt until I finish my book tour in May. In the interim, our friend has to deal with some family business, so she helps us select a local Realtor named Nancy.

Nancy asks what kind of house we'd like and I send her a seven-page manifesto on what my ideal home might be. Attached to that are dozens and dozens of houses from the MLS with notes on what I like and dislike about each of them. (Two enthusiastic thumbs up on pools, fenced yards, and brick, and two down for Dryvit, lack of basements, and anything mauve.)

I anticipate that our search will be endless because when we were looking in late winter/early spring, we saw so many places

....

[36] If you enjoy stories about idiots buying their first home and all the things that can go wrong, I humbly suggest you check out my first novel, *If You Were Here.*

[37] Chris Rock is wrong; I do not want a nice, moist house.

and the few that were right didn't work out. I figure the process will take a few months and that we're going to have to make tons of trips so we can see everything on the market. And that's totally cool because I love seeing how other people live. For someone as snoopy as I, the notion of opening refrigerators and peeking in closets with impunity as part of a decision-making process is a dream come true. What kind of soap do they use? How many shoes do they have? This is the kind of stuff I need to know.

The thing is, Nancy is not only the spitting image of Jane Lynch's character in *Best in Show*,[38] she has the same no-nonsense personality, too. Out of the forty places I'm dying to see, she immediately dismisses almost all of them for a variety of reasons (e.g., you don't want to deal with a foreclosure, the place is overpriced and underwater, the seller isn't serious, etc.) and my dream of learning the *Secret Lives of North Shore Wives* dies immediately.

Nancy takes us to exactly four houses.

But I'll be damned if each of them isn't exactly what we want.

She is the Real Estate Whisperer.[39]

We narrow our choices down to two homes—a neighborhood-y Tudor style where the interior is move-in ready without a fence or pool, and a tree-surrounded Colonial that needs a face-lift in the decorating department but the yard boasts lots of rosebushes and an in-ground pool.

I bring Stacey to see both of them and despite its being filled with window treatments she refers to as "Satan's Golf Pantaloons"

....

[38] Less butch, though. She wore pretty shoes, lipstick, and had a shell pink mani/pedi.
[39] Or a consummate professional who knows a dawdler when she sees one.

she believes we'll be happier in the Colonial. She says you can't deny the place's good bones, notwithstanding the owners' deep and abiding love of monkey-covered wallpaper.[40]

The time elapsed from making an offer to moving in is a little over a month, which isn't nearly enough time to pack everything and yet affords me ample opportunity to freak the hell out.

Until this moment, the most expensive thing I've ever purchased is a handbag and here I am, saddling myself with thirty years of debt. THIRTY YEARS. And you know what? Handbags never need new roofs. Handbags don't flood or catch on fire. Handbags don't get termites. Handbags have never made me eat sea urchin. When I get bored with a handbag, which, coincidentally occurs every 1.38 years, I'm not obligated to keep carrying it. I can just get something new without involving Realtors and banks and mortgage brokers and attorneys. Yes, I've complained about living in eighteen places, but just about every time we moved, I've been ready to go.

But now, like it or not, I'm going to have some real roots in this new place. And that terrifies me.

What are we going to do in a home where we're responsible for everything? As of now, every time something breaks in our place we giggle and say, "That sounds expensive!" and then we call Dick. Generally he does nothing until we withhold our rent, but at least it gets done eventually and not on our dime.

During a particularly panicky moment, Fletch sits down next to me on the deck and says, "If you want to grow up, this is your chance. Being an adult isn't just paying taxes and investing in a Roth IRA; it's about making decisions that scare you and following

....

[40] As it turns out, the monkey wallpaper is *bank*. And it stays.

through with them anyway. However, if for any reason you feel we're not ready, we can stay here."

I'm generally not one who believes in signs, but when I hear a gunshot in the distance after he says this, I pay attention. We close on our house two weeks later.

The best day of my life isn't when we're handed the keys to our new place. Rather it's today, the day after we close. Fletch left early this morning to run some items up to our new place. I head north, too, only I have to take Maisy to chemotherapy first. (Loki always comes with us because what dog doesn't enjoy a road trip?)

Maisy receives her treatment and is in excellent spirits as we spend the next twelve minutes driving from the clinic to the house. When we pull into the garage, the dogs are confused and as I let them loose in the new, empty house, they go crazy Vegas-style. They might not understand the details, but they grasp the concept that this is somehow now theirs.

Fletch is out back replacing lightbulbs but when I let everyone fly into the yard, they don't even notice him—or all the grass and trees and roses—because they're so distracted by the big, blue pool.

And that's when my sweet little girl, back leg bandaged from the blood draw and wobbly from receiving a dose of toxic chemicals, dives right in.

It is *awesome*.

Loki splashes in after her and starts swimming laps and biting at the water. As we watch them paddle around the pool, my heart bubbles over with joy and I'm overcome by the sense of having made the right decision.

This would be a lovely place to end this missive with the reluctant adult lesson that even if you're scared, you should do it anyway.

Of course, this is *us* we're talking about.

We move out of Dick's place a week later and for the first time, we don't scour the stove or wipe cabinets ourselves. Instead, we hire a crew to do so. We also have the carpets professionally cleaned and we leave the house in better shape than when we moved in. Because we've learned not to trust Dick, we have the photos to prove it, too. We even paid for a home inspection in case we ever had to go to court and needed an impartial third party's report.

Of course Dick keeps our entire security deposit, claiming he had to replace all the carpeting and repair all the imaginary holes we knocked in the walls.

Of course he does.

He even sends us receipts for alleged damage . . . from the construction company he just so happens to own. The thing is, once a Dick, always a Dick. So I send Gina and her boyfriend Lee in for a covert operation posing as potential tenants. They schedule an appointment with an apartment broker and they go over the place with a fine-tooth comb. They return with photographic evidence that he did none of the work for which he submitted receipts. Gina even has the broker send her e-mail confirmation that the landlord states the carpet is just fine and there's no need to replace it.

I not only want to go all HULK SMASH and bash in Dick's face with my good whacking shovel but I'd also like to engage in a war of social media.

Our real estate attorney advises against both courses of action.

Instead, she sends him what she calls a "liar, liar, pants on fire" letter but ultimately nothing happens because (if my Google stalking is to be trusted, and I think it is) he's in a world of financial trouble and his last priority is writing us a check. She says we could sue, but it would cost far more in terms of dollars spent and aggravation and that our best revenge is living well here in our nineteenth, permanent home.

But for me?

I think the best revenge is writing a shaming essay about the situation that will live on in the Library of Congress forever.

Reluctant Adult Lesson Learned:

Don't be a Dick . . . because you never know who might be documenting your bad behavior.

C·H·A·P·T·E·R F·I·V·E

The Queen of Kings

I'm holed up in my office when I hear their rising voices.

I don't speak Polish, but I do speak *panic*, and from the tone of what they're saying, there's trouble afoot.

As I hear the slap of flip-flops barreling down the hallway, I think to myself, *This can't be good.*

To backtrack, I spend every Friday from eleven to two hiding in my office when our cleaning ladies come. Mind you, this is the new maid service, as we fired the old team for pinching a bunch of stuff, including a video camera. I don't know if they thought we were famous because of all my framed posters from Barnes & Noble book signing appearances, but if they were looking to cash in on a celebrity sex tape, I'm afraid they were going to be sorely disappointed with all the kitten footage.[41]

....

[41] How many times do I have to say this, people? The Internet is FOREVER.

Yes, cleaning ladies are an extravagance, but Fletch and I made a deal—as long as I'm working on a project, I'm allowed to outsource our housekeeping. At the moment, my "project" is watching TiVoed episodes of *The Real Housewives of New York*, but that's on a need-to-know basis.

One of the ladies is calling, "Excuse! Excuse!" which generally means they're finished, but it's only eleven fifteen and the house is disgusting. At this point, it occurs to me that neither of the ladies has ever actually said anything to me except for "excuse," no matter how much I try to engage them in conversation. Fletch told me that once when he was here alone with them, one of the gals held a cell phone to his head and demanded he, "Ask boss," when he inquired if they could fold a couple of baskets of laundry.

I hate that I missed it because I'm crazy in love with an Eastern European accent. Some people dig the melodious tones of French or Italian, but me, I'm all about a language that comes out somewhere between spitting and barking. There's something so refreshingly direct about the Slavic way of speaking; it's all "it MUST" and "you WILL," as opposed to our very American "if it's not too much trouble" and "as long as that's okay." When no one's around, I make Maisy talk in an East German accent. *Maisy need. Maisy need NOW.*

I open my office door and find one of the ladies in what can best be described as a state. "Is something wrong? Can I help?" I ask. Whatever the problem is, I can fix it. If someone hurt herself, I can grab our first aid kit, call 911, or do an ER run. If something broke, I can glue it back together. If they simply want to express their disgust at how dirty the floors got while I was away at SxSW and Fletch was in charge of the house, I can invite them to join the club.

Seriously, WTF? Was he hosting a rodeo in here?

The cleaning lady replies to my offer of assistance by saying the one thing without a readily apparent solution.

"The shit is small."

Beg your pardon?

I repeat to her, "The *shit* is small?" I say it a couple of times while I try to work it all out in my head.

She nods emphatically and points in the direction of the master bedroom at the end of the hallway and enunciates every word. "The shit is *small*."

As we both rush down the hall, my head races with grim possibilities.

Where did the small shit come from?

Where is the small shit now?

Is the small shit on the duvet? That's no real biggie because it's machine washable.

Is the small shit on a linen chair cushion? Um, more problematic because I'm not sure how to launder it. Scrub brush? Dry cleaning?

Oh, God, please tell me there's no small shit on my prized Persian rug with the delicate swirls of celery and cerulean blue woven through the magenta wool.[42]

Wait, is this like the time one of our cats barfed in the cleaning lady's shoe, only a million times more gross?

Did Loki deposit another "I got nervous" bomb?

....

[42] Fletch ruined our old jute rug after I asked him to clean it. My assumption was that he'd use a Rug Doctor. In all the lousy places we've lived and with all the ridiculous neighbors we've ever had, nothing has ever been more white trash than when I spotted him standing in the front yard like Cousin "Shitter's Full" Eddie, squirting the rug with a garden hose.

Or did something go horribly awry in the bathroom due to my cavalier attitude about using an antique banana in Fletch's smoothie yesterday?

I get to the master bedroom expecting chaos . . . carnage . . . destruction, or, at the very least, a diminutive pile of something steaming.

Instead, I find that I've laid out the wrong bedding, accidentally setting out a Queen set instead of King and for the better part of five minutes, they've been attempting to wrestle them onto the bed.

Oh . . . I get it.

The *sheet* is small.

I start to laugh; then I apologize profusely, swapping out Queens for Kings. I head back to my office where I spend the next two hours and forty-five minutes watching TV and giggling over the shit being small.

And then it occurs to me . . . this is probably why our old cleaning ladies stole from us.

Sheet.

<hr>

Reluctant Adult Lesson Learned:

Angie's List exists for a reason. Use it.

Get Off My Lawn

There's one truth that I live by: *Hell hath no fury like a middle-aged woman in a fuzzy pink robe, hopped up on a winning combination of allergy medicine,* Alias *reruns, and anger.*

Reside in the city long enough and you learn to steel yourself against shit going down because if you don't, you're going to be a victim. The second you let your guard down and are all, *"My apartment's only two blocks from this bar—taking a cab would be silly,"* is the exact second when a gang of miscreants springs out of a darkened alley, steals your new iPhone and Coach bag, and punches you in your bourgeois mouth, ruining a significant investment in dental work.

That's what they take if you're lucky.

So you keep your guard up all the time. And you know what?

Living like this is exhausting and it's one of the million reasons we're decamping for the suburbs in three weeks.

But we just wouldn't be *us* if the city of Chicago didn't send us off with a parting gift. Thanks, Mayor Daley!

I'm in my office around midnight, finishing up an e-mail before heading to bed. Because the room's at the very front of the house on the top floor, I have a premiere vantage point for my self-appointed position as the Queen of Neighborhood Patrol. Trust me when I say I'm delighted to turn over my Constant Vigilance™ sash, crown, and scepter to anyone who wants 'em when we leave Logan Square forever.

I'm just switching off my computer when I hear a few weirdly muffled thumps and a light clattering of metal, followed by a familiar clang.

The familiar clang is that of my front gate closing.

I roll my chair over to the window a couple of feet away and notice one person standing outside my gate while another ascends my front steps. In my head I'm all, "Hey, who's come to visit?" until a split second later my city-brain takes over and I realize that no one should be there, what with this being midnight at a single-family property with a perpetually locked gate.

I don't recognize these people. My friends not only have day jobs, but also the courtesy to phone before dropping by, and I quickly deduce the two people looming around the front of my house aren't here on a social call.

Also? I'm pretty sure none of my friends take crystal meth.

Politely as I can, I open my window in order to inform them that I shan't be receiving any visitors today.

"HEY, TWEAKERS! THIS IS PRIVATE PROPERTY. GET THE HELL OUT OF HERE!"

To which the dreadlocked white guy[43] replies, "Mind your own fucking business. We're allowed to be here."

From my perch in the window, I assure them they are *not*, in fact, allowed to be here and go off on an entire tangent about the notion of private property. I explain how my concept of ownership is influenced by the capitalist school of thought and how I don't subscribe to their clearly more Marxist views of said concept, although really, Marx was more about the people owning the *means* of production and not so much about that which is considered "social wealth," such as Coach bags, iPhones, a mouthful of veneers, and any sort of high-end electronics that might be stuffed in the large, empty sacks they're carrying.

To which he responds, "Fuck you."

Seriously? A brilliant monologue like that and the snappiest of rejoinders he can muster is instructing me to sex myself up?

You, sir, are neither a gentleman nor a scholar.

I inform them of my plans to call the local constabulary and the woman, who is Stevie Nicks's younger, druggier doppelganger, again suggests I go spend some quality time with myself in an intimate manner while her partner informs me of his plans to come inside to "fuck you up."

Oh.

Really.

As I've reached the limits of my own negotiating capabilities, I'm left with no choice but to call in the big guns.

....

[43] Oh, honey, Counting Crows called. They want Adam Duritz's look back.

No, not those.[44] I mean Fletch.

He's on the other side of the second floor in the bedroom. He hears me squawking, *"Perimeter breach! Perimeter breach!"* as I thunder down the hallway. He assumes I'm on a bad Ambien trip, perhaps cut with a side of crazy, but I assure him that other than Claritin, I'm entirely sober. I brief him on the sitch and he takes off up the street after them while I call 911. His goal isn't to confront them as much as maintain visual contact and direct the police to them.

After dialing, I, too, take to the street, fancying myself a high-kicking, martial-arts-knowing, wig-flipping CIA operative like the divine Miss Jennifer Garner starring as Sydney Bristow. But she must practice more often because I'm able to jog all of fifteen feet before I get a stitch in my side.

Fortunately, Fletch can run more than half a block before collapsing in a heap of pastel terry cloth, sock monkey slippers, and a mud mask, so he manages to catch up to the perps. Because I'm still spitting distance from my house sucking air and hugging my knees, Fletch has to fill me in on what happens next.

Quick caveat? It's possible he caught up to them not because he's a paragon of physical fitness. The more likely explanation is that the miscreants are all weighed down in the kind of layered hippie clothing last seen praying for a miracle at a Grateful Dead show, so they aren't exactly truckin'.

As Fletch walks up behind them, he says, "My wife tells me you decided to pay us a visit."

....

[44] Until it's legal to shoot someone for being an asshole, my weapon of choice is a shovel.

The couple becomes visibly agitated and Stevie Nicks asks, "Um, who's your wife?"

To which he replies, "The woman I married."

That's the extent of Sergeant Fletcher's interrogation before the police arrive.[45]

I guess as soon as the police are on the scene, both the tweakers immediately begin to cry, with Stevie sobbing that she thought her friend lived there. Yet when questioned, neither one of them has any idea of what their friend's name is. The woman begs for a warning because she really needs a miracle, man.

Not to be all heartless, but let's look at this story with a critical eye. These people decide to stop in and see their Friend With No Name. And they choose to pay a visit to said nameless friend at midnight. On a Tuesday. In a darkened house. And instead of say, ringing the doorbell like every other goddamned person who walks by my house, they force their skinny arms through the extremely tight metal bars of the security gate, reaching around to unlock it before heading to the stoop to peek in the windows. And then when questioned by authorities about said trespass, they request a miracle.

Yes. Clearly this is the most logical explanation.

When I initially popped out of the window, instead of offering a genuine reaction like, "Shit, this isn't Holly's place? I'm so sorry!" (or even "Nice robe, fatty!") their first response is to swear at me, threaten me, and jog away carrying a whole bunch of empty bags. Right. Seems innocent enough to me.

....

[45] For as many complaints as I've had with the CPD's response time, I must give them kudos for arriving in a flash in this instance.

The fact that Stevie Nicks is carrying no ID and is currently on probation *after serving time for breaking and entering* doesn't lend a lot of credibility to her story.

Fletch is up the street with one set of officers while another talks to me. I fill him in on all the ways that our house has been marked lately. "We've been tagged almost daily and we keep finding odd items, like pennies glued to our mailbox and soda bottles lined up on our fence posts in distinct patterns, like crop circles or some weird paranormal shit." Plus our doorbell rings all day long and I can't imagine that all of it relates to little kids heading to the park, especially when it happens after dark.

The officer nods gravely. "Ever considered moving?"

"We're off to Lake County in three weeks."

"The economy's making it worse and worse around here." The officer begins looking at me very pointedly. "So there's no misunderstanding, you realize that wasn't a social call, ma'am. I suggest you press charges. Can you tell me if they tried to open the door?"

"I heard it and I didn't understand what it was at first, but yes, I'd say they did. However, I didn't *see* it happen."

"Are you sure? I need to know *if they tried the door*." He keeps looking at me in what I interpret as a meaningful way, but maybe he's just trying to guess how big my pores are under this mask?

I shift in my slippers. "Again, I can't say I saw it. The knob's not visible from my desk. But I heard it."

"Ma'am, this is very important. I need to ask you one more time, *did they try the door?*"

I scratch the side of my face and bits of clay crumble onto my robe. "I definitely heard what sounded like someone thumping against it. I'd bet *my* life on it, but in good conscience I can't bet anyone else's. I didn't *see* them try the door with my own eyes. So in all fairness, I can't say that they did."

The officer seems to deflate a little as he takes down this bit of information.

I have to appear in court next month now. Because I didn't *see* them try the door with my own eyes, they're charged only with simple assault and trespassing. Yet there's not a single doubt in my mind that they tried the knob. I know what I heard. I firmly believe they wanted to enter my house and fill all their empty bags with my stuff. Period.

What really chaps my ass is how much volunteering I've done lately with organizations that help women on parole. As part of my efforts, I've been teaching computer skills to women in a halfway house. At first the ladies just wanted me to help navigate Facebook so they could find old boyfriends, but after they began to trust me, they let me see their résumés. I've done some creative writing in my time, but I'm stretched to an entirely new level when tasked with explaining an eight-year gap in employment history.[46]

The thing is, I really enjoyed working with the women. I coached them on job skills and we worked on interview questions. I tried to make them feel empowered and confident, helping them recognize the positive things they've done in their lives. As we spent more time together, I wondered exactly how much of their crimes stemmed from poor choices and how many were

....

[46] Ten were it not for good behavior.

due to being in the wrong place or getting involved with the wrong man. As far as I was concerned, they paid their debt to society and helping them transition back into it felt like I was making a difference.

Yet with this one instance, I suddenly question all the times I've been at the halfway house and I wonder if some of these women weren't smiling politely while wondering how they'd look wearing my pearls or driving my car. I'm so angry that an ex-felon, likely one who's gone through the exact kind of program where I've been coaching, let herself into my locked gate and thumped my front door that I'm not sure I want to continue working with the program. Suddenly, I feel a whole lot less charitable, like my efforts have been for nothing.

Afterward, while Fletch gets ready for bed, I sit on the side of the tub and keep him company. As we conduct a postmortem of the event, we discuss how it feels like society has gone downhill since we were kids. Growing up, I couldn't even fathom the idea of a potential home invasion. The greatest crime I could name back then was that Brooke Shields didn't personally respond to my fan mail.

Okay, technically I wrote to extend the hand of friendship . . . and also hit her up for some free Calvin Klein jeans, but still, I'm sure she had plenty to spare and my letters were *charming*.[47]

While we chat, it occurs to me what the catalyst has been for our societal slide.

"You know who started this whole downward spiral?" I query.

....

[47] People were just being polite about the unibrow, honey. If you'd have responded to me, as your real friend, I'd have told you the truth.

"Um . . . Liberals fighting with conservatives?" He's just finished washing his face and I hand him a towel.

"Nope."

"The Cold War?"

"Guess again."

"The implosion of the subprime lending market?"

"Bzzt. One more guess."

"Ted Turner's introduction of the twenty-four-hour news cycle?"

"You're never going to guess because the answer is Starbucks. Our downward spiral can neatly be placed at the feet of Starbucks."

Don't get your lattes in a bunch—please understand that I have nothing but admiration for how the Starbucks Corporation runs their business. I respect their use of Fair Trade products, their concerns for the environment, and their groundbreaking efforts to provide benefits for part-time employees. That shit changes lives, you know? And I adore Starbucks' consistently high-quality products so much that at any given time my blood type is Iced Caramel Macchiato with Two Splendas.[48]

Fletch loads up his Sonicare with toothpaste. "This should be good. Continue."

"Starbucks has high operating costs because they're paying out a lot of money for health insurance. Just imagine how many of their employees need MRIs after helmetless bike accidents and how much they must shell out on antibiotics for piercings gone awry. Not cheap, right? *That's* why they're charging four dollars for a cup of coffee. Overhead, baby, overhead."

....
[48] Unless it's Gingerbread or Pumpkin Spice Latte season, of course.

Through a mouthful of foam he asks, "How does this relate to a couple of tweakers scaling our fence?"

"Ah, I'm glad you asked. See, the consumer is willing to shell out four bucks for delicious coffee because it is delicious."

He gives me an odd look in the mirror. "Did you already take your Ambien?"

"Shut up, and no, I'm doing that right now." I wash down my Ambien with a quick sip from his water glass. "I'm high on Vitamin A—adrenaline. Tell you what, those tweakers are lucky my shovel wasn't handy. ANYWAY, when people drop four dollars on a cup o' joe, they're way less likely to throw it away when they head into previously beverage-free bastions like stores, churches, classrooms, what have you."

Fletch blinks in a manner that I interpret as encouragement. I continue. "My theory is that our compulsive Starbucks consumption prompted us to stop following the 'No Food or Drinks' rule. Now here's where it gets tricky—"

He spits and rinses, blotting his mouth with a towel. "I'm all ears."

"The issue is that the no food or drinks tenet has been just as much of a societal pillar as other biggies like 'Thou Shalt Not Kill' and 'Respect the Sabbath' and 'No Shirt, No Shoes, No Service.' So my point is that being allowed to circumvent one of the very basic rules of society has opened the gateway to our growing more lax in all things moral, ethical, and legal."

"Is this the kind of thing you do after I go to bed? I always suspected you were up late looking at LOLCats or Real Housewife gossip, but clearly you've been hitting conspiracy theory Web sites."

He exits the bathroom and heads into his closet, returning with a pair of SpongeBob-print pajama bottoms. If our tweakers arrived five minutes later, I wonder if he'd have seemed quite so imposing clad in those.

I follow along behind him into the bedroom where we find Maisy and Loki fast asleep on the bed. Nice watchdogs, eh? But if a squirrel had tried to break in, we'd be telling a different story right about now.

I climb into my side of the bed. "I'm not claiming that the Java Chip Blended Beverage is responsible for two idiots attempting to gain entry to our home."

He yawns and stretches and resets our house alarm before getting into bed. "That's for a judge to decide."

I puff my pillow and pull up the covers, attempting to eke out the portion of the bed not covered in dog. "All I'm saying is that I worry that our culturally cavalier attitude towards the basic rules could lead us down the slippery slope to complete and total anarchy."

Fletch gives me a kiss and turns out his light. "That's a lot to ponder . . . especially without your good aluminum-foil thinkin' cap. But nice work tonight. You were very brave."

"Thank you."

We lie there in the dark and I can hear his breathing slow as he begins to drift off.

"Hey, Fletch?"

"Yeah?"

"Do you think I can bring coffee to the trial?"

"I guess we'll find out."

But we don't find out because I write down the wrong date and I miss my day in court.

I guess the tweakers got their miracle after all.

Reluctant Adult Lesson Learned:

If you don't want to be a victim, employ Constant Vigilance™ . . . and buy a date-book.

Generation Y Don't You Do It for Me?

*M*y professional career began when I graduated from college and landed a position at an HMO. Unlike most of my Gen X peers, I was actually able to nab a job that didn't require wearing an apron and black Reeboks, so I was thrilled.[49]

I'll always be grateful to my friend's mom who worked for the HMO. She was kind enough to give my résumé directly to the hiring manager instead of having to navigate HR. The introduction got me in the door and I'd be remiss if I didn't mention it.

In 1996, Larry Page and Sergey Brin were a couple of nerdy PhD students kicking around the Stanford campus while I was getting ready to graduate. It would be a solid two years until they got their first round of venture capital to start up the company that eventually became Google. What I'm saying is that researching a

---

[49] Kids, this recession ain't our first rodeo.

company wasn't as easy as typing a few lines into a search engine back then. I couldn't ping the Dun & Bradstreet database on my Android phone nor could I Facebook stalk the hiring manager to find our common ground, like how she was really into Bob Mould and *ER*.

Everything I knew about the HMO came from me skulking around the basement of the Purdue University libraries, scanning sheet after sheet of microfiche. Information was hard to come by back then, so the onus was on me to sell myself because I wasn't impressing anyone with my mad library skills. I spent days poring over my management textbooks and practicing sample interview questions.

Ultimately, I was successful in being hired on my own merits.

Turns out, even though I got the job, I *hated* the job. For six months, my professional life revolved around keeping the physician provider manual up-to-date and my days were endless, filled with calling office staffs to inquire if they were located on Sheridan Street or Sheridan Road. It was crazy-making and I wonder if I wouldn't have been happier as a waitress. At least I'd get a shift drink at the end of the day.

Around that time, my friend's mom landed an incredible gig at a top-tier consulting firm and it was everything everyone in my company dreamed about. I'm talking serious Golden Ticket here. As I watched her pack her desk, all I could say was, "Take me with you!"

To which she replied simply, "You're not ready. You need to serve your time here before you can move on."

As I've built my career, first as an executive, and then as an author, I've never forgotten that piece of advice.

I don't know what it's like to be searching for a job now right out of college. In a lot of ways, because of access to information, it has to be easier than trawling around a basement, squinting at microfiche. And yet, because technology's leveled the playing field, it must be challenging as well, so I respect anyone who takes a creative approach in trying to make it. When it's appropriate and when I can, I do my best to help those who ask.

What I don't respect is the portion of Generation Y—and to be clear, I believe it's only a portion and that there are plenty who shouldn't be painted with this brush—who've grown so lazy and entitled that they can't even be bothered to try.

That brings me to Ashley.

Ashley embodies everything I loathe about the Millennials. Following, you'll find the letter she blast-e-mailed to a number of successful contemporary authors[50] a couple of years ago. (My comments are in italics.)

Hi, my name is Ashley and I'm currently working on my first novel. Writing a novel has always been a dream of mine, but I'm pretty nervous and worried that I'm going to fail. I was hoping that you would answer the following questions for me, to help me get started?

1. How do you develop your characters? Are they people you know?

   I write nonfiction which seems like it would be obvious by the word "memoir" on the cover of

---

[50] Including me.

each of my books, but apparently not. Since I write about real people, the characters pretty much develop themselves.

2. How do you come up with their names?

   Really, most of the credit goes to their parents.

3. Did you have any formal training in order to become a writer? Classes? A degree?

   Yes.

4. How do you get ideas for stories?

   How do you not get ideas for stories?

5. What do you consider the most important principle of fiction?

   This is something I've never thought about considering I don't write fiction.[51]

6. How do you, when writing dialogue, make sure that each character sounds like a unique person?

   I, when writing dialogue, try to phrase things in a way that sounds completely natural. Because

---

[51] Okay, fine, I do now, but didn't at the time.

who wouldn't, when writing dialogue, try to make conversations sound conversational? Again, when writing dialogue, it's easier to make unique individuals sound like unique individuals when they are unique individuals. When writing dialogue.

7. How do you set up your books? Do you outline them first or do you have an idea and just go with it?

   From tallest to shortest, left to right, with a heavy bookend butted up against the small end.

   Oh, wait. I answered that before I read the whole question.

   I find ideas overrated. Outlines, too.

8. How do you decide how long a book should be?

   Well, I certainly wouldn't spend ten seconds Googling "how long is a novel?" to find out what the industry standard is. Instead, I'd e-mail John Grisham.

9. How do you decide on a title for your book?

   Scotch.

10. How do I go about getting an agent? Where do I look for one?

Obviously you look for one by asking me. (I keep them in my guest room.)

11. How do I know which agent is best for me?

I'm going to go out on a limb here and say this probably won't be an issue.

12. How much should I expect to pay an agent to represent my book?

You should pay them whatever they ask, because, again, a ten-second Google search on "how much do I pay a literary agent?" wouldn't reveal that an agent works for you and only gets paid once you sell your writing.

13. Will an agent expect me to sign a contract? Should I sign one?

Yes, in blood. Yes, right before you give them a blank check.

14. How & why did you become a writer?

Because I wanted to bring back the ampersand.

15. Does this process ever get easier?

No.

16. Have you ever doubted yourself while writing? If so, how do you get over it?

    Yes. Scotch.

17. What should my manuscript look like?

    Um, about 6'2", dark, neatly trimmed hair, well polished shoes, and eyes that crinkle when he smiles.

    Shit, I just described my husband.

    I guess I don't understand the question.

18. How long did it take to publish your first book?

    I certainly never mention this in any of the books I've written so it must be that I don't know the answer.

19. Do you typically do a lot of research for your books?

    Typically.

20. What is the hardest part of writing for you? The easiest?

    The hardest part is trying not to be an asshole when people send asinine e-mails. The easiest is cashing checks.

21. Do you have any favorite authors? Books?

    Pfft, writers don't read. And if they did, they certainly wouldn't detail all the stuff they loved on their Web site and in their books.

22. I'm pretty nervous about writing my book and trying to get it published. I guess I don't have much for self-confidence when it comes to this. Do you have any advice?

    Scotch.

FYI, I didn't send this to her, tempting though it was.

Instead, I exercised a heroic amount of self-restraint and demonstrated maturity by e-mailing this reply:

"Ashley, this is not how you become a writer."

The great irony here is that Ashley had the nerve to tell me that I was out of line, like *I'm* the one at fault because she lacked the willingness or intellectual curiosity to make any effort to become a writer outside of finding my e-mail address . . . like *I* should ignore my current deadlines in order to share my hard-won knowledge of the publishing world with someone who hasn't even bothered to read one of my books.

Frankly, I'm shocked to have heard back from her and not one of her helicopter parents who've clearly been good-jobbing her to the point where she feels like the world not only revolves around her, but also owes her the benefit of its collective experience.

So, Ashley, please understand there are plenty of Millennials out there who don't share your nonexistent work ethic.

They recognize that technology is only part of the equation and it's to be used in addition to, and not in lieu of, making an effort.

And they're going to eat you alive.

Reluctant Adult Lesson Learned:

You're not an asshole for demanding that Generation Y pay their dues, regardless of what Ashley thinks.

A Barbie Girl in a Barbie World

"Excuse me, ma'am?"

I'm sitting at my desk, deep in concentration, trying to make sense of what to pack and what to pitch.

These drawers are shameful. I don't know how I can be so organized in some aspects of my life and so utterly disordered in others. Every contract I've ever signed, sorted by dates and dollar amounts, lives in a tidy bundle in the bottom file drawer. They're next to folders for all bills we've paid in the last three years, chronologically ordered, time-stamped with check numbers and, if paid online, attached to confirmation receipts.

Yet one drawer up from that is an office supply graveyard, brimming with dead pens and old stamps and expired prescriptions. I'm talking business cards from people I can't recall meeting and Post-it notes covered in random sums, surrounded by expired gift cards and rusty paper clips and the world's oldest pack of gum, all shellacked into one giant mass by an oozing bottle of clear nail polish.

Pathetic.

I'm not a pack rat—really, I'm not, although sometimes in an effort to be more efficient, I trend that way. For example, my office is on the second floor and that's where I tend to spend most of the workday. Because it's located an entire flight of stairs away from the filtered water on the fridge door, I find myself going thirsty rather than taking the trek to the kitchen.

(Yes, I understand exactly how lazy this is.)

(Do I need to remind anyone of how I once considered hiding a bucket in the first floor pantry of our old town house rather than climbing twelve stairs to the bathroom?)

(Fletch wouldn't let me, by the way, which is bullshit because I have a pretty good idea of what went down in the mop sink when Fletch would drink beer in his basement man cave.)

Anyway, I came up with a rather elegant solution. I'd buy a case of water and store it upstairs. Ergo I'd never get thirsty to the point of dizziness again. Genius![52]

I bought the water, brought it upstairs, and deposited it on the guest bathroom counter where it was profoundly in the way for the next few days. Although I shower in the master bathroom down the hall, I do everything else in here. Fletch is a bona fide bathroom hog and there's nothing more annoying than having to stay up an extra half hour waiting to floss while he's busy reading *War and Peace* on the mug.[53]

....

[52] A tiny bit pathetic, but mostly genius!

[53] If anyone out there shares a bathroom with her husband, I implore you to either move to a larger space or add on to your existing space because this is the key to marital bliss.

The problem with my genius solution is that I had to work around the bulky case when I brushed my teeth, washed my face, conducted whisker patrol,[54] etc., so I needed to find a place to store it. I thought the laundry room might work, but it was so tiny that I'd have to rearrange everything in the cabinets and that smacked of the exact type of effort I hoped to avoid.

Turns out the solution to my problem was right next to me. I drew back the shower curtain in front of the unused guest tub and placed the case in there, spic, span, and out of the way. Added bonus? If one of the bottles started to leak, the water would go right down the drain. Again, genius!

When Fletch arrived home, I proudly whipped open the curtain to show him where I'd stashed the water.

He slowly looked from the case to me. After a long pause, he finally responded, "You've decided to store items in an empty tub. Congratulations. You've just taken the first step to seeing yourself on *Hoarders* in twenty years."

I moved the bottles. I'd rather be thirsty than on TV for the wrong reasons.

I'm so lost in thoughts about accidentally becoming one of those cat-flattening hoarders[55] that the woman in the doorway has to clear her throat to grab my attention.

"Oh, gosh, I'm sorry. What can I do for you?" This lady is part of the team busy packing up our house for the move. We thought we could do it all ourselves but we quickly became so bogged down in the decision-making process that we fell behind schedule and had to call in experts.

....

[54] Shut up.
[55] There's always at least one flat cat on those shows. Always.

The packer appears somewhat perplexed, which is odd. Thus far she's known how to pack everything from CD collections to a free-range assortment of Christmas ornaments. Fletch and I have been awed for the past day as she and her crew systematically disassemble every bit of our house, so I wonder what could have possibly thrown her off her game.

"Ma'am, what would you like for me to do with . . . your head?"

She holds up my blond, bodiless Barbie styling head, ordered one night years ago while on an Ambien trip. I've since learned that I can't be trusted to be near a computer while on prescription sleeping medication, so I made sure to move my computer as far away from my bed as possible. (In fact, in the new house, my office will live on an entirely different floor.)

As for the Barbies, I simply tell everyone that I'm a collector. Of course, true collectors never take their prizes out of the box to see if they can finally master the art of cutting bangs, but whatever.

"Just give it to me and I'll deal with it," I say all businesslike and officious, quickly stuffing Barbie into one of the bags we're moving ourselves. Then I try to look busy so she doesn't ask why a forty-two-year-old woman is still playing with dolls.

While I attempt to chisel apart my office supplies, it occurs to me:

I should find a more grown-up hobby.

Between moving and unpacking and settling into my first real home, I sort of forget about my deep and abiding love of all things

Barbie. I still keep my *Mad Men* Barbies on display because they're so impeccably assembled. I mean, Miss Joan is wearing a tiny bustier and seamed stockings! Betty has a wee gold compact with a mirror inside! That's just badass at any age. But the rest of my collection lives in the closet and has seen the light of day only when friends' daughters have visited.

I can't say that I fell out of love with my Barbies but there's something about writing my first mortgage check that made me go, "You know what? Not so into the toys anymore."

Plus, many of the enriching activities I learned about while writing *My Fair Lazy* actually stuck. Turns out I'd rather spend time crafting my own elaborate updo than Barbie's, particularly when it means I'm going somewhere fancy; convenient because . . . Joanna and I are opera aficionados now!

Okay, by aficionados, I mean we went once but we both seriously dug it! The thing no one tells you about the opera is how many cocktail breaks are involved. With multiple intermissions, one never needs to lose one's buzz and champagne makes everything better.

We saw *A Masked Ball* in December and were absolutely taken by the spectacle of it all. Between the music and the costumes and the set, the whole night left us breathless.[56] As much as I love to people watch, the opera is the perfect place for it because every walk of humanity is represented, at least sartorially. There were folks from kids in jeans to men in tuxedos, capes, and big top hats, and all fashions in between.

Because we really want to make tonight's showing of *Carmen*

---

[56] Oh, and we found out my friend Caprice was wrong and it actually isn't appropriate to shout, "Show us your tits!" after a particularly stirring solo.

special, we're treating ourselves to a hotel room. I want to do it up right because in the fifteen years I lived in town, I never once stayed anywhere except my own apartments. So I figure if I'm going whole hog, I'll book us at the Peninsula.

Joanna and I debated whether or not we wanted to share a room, but we realized we spent our entire freshman year in an eight-by-ten cinder-block dorm room, and that's without the benefit of room service or seven hundred fifty thread-count sheets, so we'd probably manage being together for sixteen hours.

Before the show, we have dinner at the Purple Pig, a restaurant known for charcuterie. We sit at a community table and make friends with the conventioning Minneapolis-area anesthesiologists sitting around us—sharing a couple of bottles of wine and bites of a sugar-seared rib eye.[57] The doctors are leery about our order of roasted marrow, so they leave us to sample it ourselves.

Truly? My stomach turns a little when the plate is served. There's a big round bone with a gelatinous blob of grayish brown in the middle, paired with slices of bread and a bowl of chunks of Himalayan salt. Tentatively we spread and salt the goo, and with our napkins at the ready, we taste it at the same time.

And then we lose our minds.

The marrow is why meat cooked on the bone is always so much more delicious than its filleted counterparts. Marrow is what gives braised short ribs their flavor. Marrow is the essence of beef and eating it is like biting into a thousand pot roasts all concentrated into one little smear of perfection.[58]

....

[57] Sounds so wrong but tastes so right.
[58] No lie, as I write this description my mouth is watering.

We spend the next twenty minutes saying over and over again, "Oh, that marrow!" It's all we discuss on the way to the theater and it's our main topic of conversation over opera cake and cappuccinos during second intermission. And even though everything about *Carmen* is spectacular, when I look back on this night, marrow is what I'll recall most fondly.

After a drink at the bar, we call it a night. We've got our bathroom kung fu timed perfectly and after a little *Real Housewives*, we're ready for bed.

In the dark, I can tell by her breathing the exact moment Joanna falls asleep, having heard it so many times before. I can't think of a single instance when we lived together that she wasn't out first. I've never been a great sleeper, particularly when I'm not in my own bed, and until I discovered the tiny white miracle called Ambien, it would take me hours from the time I hit the sheets until I dropped off.

I had cocktails earlier in the evening, so I don't take my Ambien because that's a recipe for accidentally ordering an entire new suite of bedroom furniture.[59]

Joanna went down around twelve thirty a.m., but it's one thirty now and I still feel wide awake. I suspect any fatigue may have been counteracted by the coffee I had during dessert. I toss and shift, but I can't seem to get comfortable. At two thirty, I have to employ desperate measures—pillow flipping—in the vain hope that the cool side will help me nod off. It doesn't.

Around three, I feel myself drifting off to sleep FINALLY, only to be awakened five minutes later by Joanna's snoring.

This is new.

....

[59] Trust me on this one.

If she snored as a freshman, we'd have never been together long enough to form a twenty-five-year-long friendship.

I have no problem falling asleep to music and when I was a kid staying at my grandparents' house, my grandfather would blast talk radio all night long. To this day, I adore talk radio because of him and it always makes me feel comforted. Put golf or baseball on the television and I'm out in seconds flat. And whenever I'm on the road, I like to sleep to old sitcoms on Nick at Nite.

But the snoring?

I have a problem with snoring.

Joanna snores lightly, but insistently. Really, it's more of a loud breathing deal and there's no vibrato or anything, but I can definitely hear her.

Maisy started snoring in the past few years, too. Between her and Fletch[60] I find myself sneaking into the guest room more often than not.

I put in my earbuds to see if that blocks her out.

Zzzz.

Nope.

I decide to take a bath, hoping that will put me out.

Zzzz.

Nope.

I push her a couple of times, but feel bad doing so. She probably doesn't normally snore except we talked so much we're both kind of hoarse, plus she's had a night full of cocktails, marrow, and cake. That'd make anyone snore.

So I'm not mad about the snoring. But sleep is impossible.

....

[60] Who also came to snoring far too late into the relationship to break it off.

And then she begins to thrash.

That's new, too.

At four a.m., I can't take it anymore. Because I don't want to wreck her beauty rest, I decide to just go home. As quietly as I can, I collect my things and in the dark I write her a note.

I find out later that my night penmanship is wanting and pretty much the only part of the note she could decipher said YOU SNORE in big, shouty letters. I've come to find in every relationship, one person is inevitably more of a jerk than the other. In the case of Joanna and me, I'm clearly the bigger jerk, but I'm fortunate that we established this long ago, so really, nothing inconsiderate I do now comes as a surprise.[61]

I stop by the front desk to make sure that the whole room is taken care of because I'm not sticking Joanna with the bill, especially as I'm bailing in the middle of the night. Also, I need the valet to bring my car.

Funny thing about hotels that I've found out over five years of early-flight-based departures: no matter how fine the establishment, ninety-nine percent of women sneaking out in the wee hours of the morning are prostitutes.

So as I stand there making arrangements in my sweater set, holding my big pink and green toile overnight bag, makeup off, hair in a ponytail, the desk clerks have no choice but to imagine that I am the oldest, fattest call girl they've ever seen.

Then when I tell them the make and model of car that I'm collecting, they stand there with their mouths agape, faces set in expressions that range from horror to admiration, wondering exactly what kind of freaky shit I might perform.

---

[61] Luff you, sweet JoJo.

As I head downstairs to meet the valet, I swear I hear one of the girls calling, "Teach me!"

This? Right here? Is why people hesitate to embrace new hobbies.

My latest pastime develops so organically that I don't even realize it's anything but a chore at first.

Our house has an unholy amount of built-in bookshelves. Mind you, we own many, many books, at least according to the disgruntled men who had to move them all. Considering I've been reading for almost forty years[62] I can fill ten bookcases. This works out nicely seeing how I own ten bookcases. I was faced with the dilemma of stocking a bunch of naked built-ins because if I placed my collection on the shelves, I'd be left with a bunch of empty bookcases and that would make my house look like it were having a going-out-of-business sale.

Whenever I peruse catalogs, I'm most intrigued by the items that aren't for sale. Like when Pottery Barn displays a lovely bedroom set, covered in a crisp linen duvet and piled up with pillows—inevitably I want the battered silver pitcher that's filled with hydrangeas in the corner of the shot. That's why mass-produced furniture always looks better in print than it does in my living room; even if I were to buy everything on the page,[63] I'm still missing the crucial elements that give the catalog rooms soul.

I keep an eye peeled for estate sales because I heard they can

....

[62] And have a demonstrated dislike for throwing things away.
[63] See: *Ambien Binge, Shopping on an*

be an amazing resource for cheap vintage finds but I hadn't seen any until one day when Joanna and I spot a sign after being out for lunch.

"Look! Estate sale! Are you game?" I ask from the passenger seat of her station wagon.

"Sure! Get your phone out so we can practice navigating! We'll both Google the address and we'll see who gets it first!" Joanna and I are convinced that we'd kick ass as the College Roommates team on the *Amazing Race,* for no reason other than sheer delusion, particularly since I hate to run, solve puzzles, or for that matter, travel.

Also? Not a team player.

Even though I've yet to see a single challenge in which I'd not fail spectacularly, the dream remains alive.

We both dig out our iPhones. Her navigation application isn't working because she can't get a cell signal and I don't have any apps[64] and Google maps is way too small for me to decipher without reading glasses.

After five minutes of swearing and cursing the name of AT&T, Joanna notices that the estate sale sign not only listed an address, but also is in the shape of a giant arrow, pointing in the direction of the sale.

You know those assholes who are always cut the first challenge, five minutes after the race starts? Yeah. Says Phil Keoghan, "I'm sorry, College Roommates, you have been eliminated from the race."

Anyway, the sale items are all way too modern for my tastes, so Joanna suggests I hit some consignment stores to find vin-

....

[64] Don't get me started on the app thing.

tage pieces. We find a local charity shop, I discover a massive footed Waterford trifle bowl for fifteen dollars and thus, a hobby is born.

At first, I'm all about snapping up pieces to fill my empty built-in china cabinets. Although I've been blessed with eight thousand (unmatched) wineglasses, I've never owned plates that weren't basic white diner dishware. We needed money for rent when we were married, not flatware, so we never registered for anything made of crystal or covered in silver plate or designed for the single purpose of holding hot gravy. Plus, we figured we'd be bored of whatever we picked out a few years later.

Fortunately, everyone eventually tires of their fancy, unused, dust-gathering gravy boats and when they do, they take them to the consignment store. I spend weeks scoping out and scooping up beautiful porcelain dinner sets and heavy crystal bowls, paying pennies on the dollar of their original cost.

My hobby morphs into an obsession purely by accident. I find a beautiful silver serving bowl and it isn't until I use it the first time that I notice the engraving. Turns out I didn't nab a fancy five-dollar potato chip holder at all—I purchased a stupid trophy. I still use it to hold party snacks, but I turn the writing side around and butt it up to the wall so no one sees what it really is.

After resenting my purchase for a while, it occurs to me that having someone else's *1967 Division IV Hiring Award* is kind of kitschy. Once filled with potpourri and placed on an empty shelf, it actually seems intentional and *that's* when I realize this is the exact kind of classy shit Pottery Barn uses to make their catalog pages so crave-worthy.

I begin a quest, expanding my search to antiques stores where

I unearth a Bakelite beagle trophy from a 1959 dog show in the thirteen-inch bitch division. I'm not sure if the manufacturer was trying to be funny or if the event organizer screwed up, but it is clear from the beagle's generous undercarriage that *this is no bitch* and a shelf theme is born.

(Do I need to clarify the theme is "trophy" and not "transgender"?)

Six months after beginning the process, I finally collect enough pieces to fill in the empty shelves downstairs, supplementing my trophies with loads of vintage books. Of course, whenever I check out with an armload of novels, the cashier is perpetually delighted. She's always all, "Ooh! You must be a huge reader!" and I never have the heart to tell her that I hand select each novel solely based on their red spines.

I know, I know.

I'm ashamed.

But they match the drapes!

I've slowly been adding pieces to the shelf in the TV room upstairs, too. Even though we're not terribly athletic,[65] I thought vintage sporting equipment would be a fun theme. I envision displays of tattered velvet equestrian helmets and fencing masks and those old-timey leather football helmets, kind of like a fraternity house basement circa 1940, or a T.G.I. Friday's minus the shitty food.

Thus far, I've sourced a couple of vintage baseballs and some scruffy croquet balls, but that's it. The process of unearthing these treasures has been exhausting and frustrating, particularly when I

....

[65] Like, at all.

see something great but it's cost prohibitive.[66] My shelves sit white and open, leering at me.

As always, Stacey shows me the way.

"What about eBay?" she asks.

I grimace. I have such bad memories of eBay. "What about it? I hate eBay. eBay's where I had to sell all my designer stuff back in the bad old days. Far as I'm concerned, eBay sucks. It's nothing but a bunch of crooks in China trying to sell knock-off purses, ruining it for the rest of us by driving down the prices for those looking to unload *authentic* bags to keep their lights on."

Stacey opens her laptop. "What would you like me to find?"

Really?

Do we have to go through this?

"They're not going to have what I want."

"Uh-huh. I'm going to search for . . . 'vintage bowling trophy' and . . . hey. You certainly wouldn't be interested in this." Stacey attempts—and fails—at keeping the smug out of her voice.

I try not to appear interested because I hate admitting Stacey's right, even though that's the case at least ninety-nine percent of the time and the entire basis of our friendship. "What wouldn't I like?"

"A giant silver-handled loving cup from 1917, awarded to the men of Delta Tau Delta to commemorate their second-place finish in the Inter-fraternity Bowling League." She turns the screen to face me.

Oh.[67]

Welcome to eBay.

....

[66] $450 for an old-timey football helmet? No.
[67] Were I to express myself in such a manner—which I won't—this is where I'd say that I got ladywood.

eBay is a fine place to unload your Prada bag when you're in a desperate situation and it's exactly what the doctor ordered when searching for a specific item, say an authentic 1965 edition of the game Mystery Date. eBay is a very, very bad place to go if you're a hypercompetitive asshole with a penchant for spite bidding.

Try to guess which category I fall under.

It all starts innocently enough—like it does—when I spot the perfect old-timey football helmet at an attractive price. I meet the minimum bid and set a reasonable ceiling and then spend a few days watching the nonexistent auction action. But as I sleep, a bidding war breaks out between me and some douche bag named a********7, who wins my stupid helmet for a dollar more than my bid ceiling.

Unacceptable.

At the exact same time, I lose out on a vintage blue ribbon from a horse show as well as a set of leather riding calf protectors that seem like something Ronald Reagan would have worn in a film.

Revolution.

I begin to note auction endings in my calendar and instead of passively going along with the process, I become an active participant. The second the "You've been outbid!" e-mail arrives in my in-box, I'm on it, jacking up my bid ceiling in increments of ten dollars to flush out the lookie-loos.

Yet I still lose auctions.

I imagine elaborate sting operations wherein all the owners of vintage leather catcher's masks band together to create an evil cabal whose sole purpose is to keep me from winning their items. Dicks.

When I spy the potential cornerstone of my collection—a small sterling trophy from the Seawanhaka Corinthian Yacht Club, recognizing Hunky, the 1907 winner of Class Dories competition, shit gets real.

The time has come for spite bidding.

I set my bid ceiling ridiculously high and systematically knock out all the competition. I have no idea who the other bidders are in real life—perhaps a relative of Hunky or a historian tasked with bringing home all the Seawanhaka trophies, but I care not. That trophy is going to sit on my empty shelf, holding a hydrangea blossom when seasonally appropriate, and that's all there is to it. As the time on the auction runs out, it's five . . . four . . . three . . . two . . . one . . .

#WINNING!!!

Once I discover a system in which I get the items I want *and* piss off a faceless portion of the Internet, I'm unstoppable. I win auctions left and right. Vintage hockey skates? Got 'em. Small tin sign indicating where the polo club served cocktails? All over it. Antique Indian juggling clubs? Yeah, baby. Old-timey football helmets? Enough to protect the tender melons of the entire starting line, thank you very much.

Fletch doesn't even balk at what I spend because ultimately a first-place ribbon from the Iowa State Fair for Shorthorn Cattle costs substantially less than shoes, jewelry, purses, or anything purchased on an Ambien high. Plus, I'm working out a lot of aggression by crushing other people's auction dreams. And, if someone out there has to sell her pair of 1952 Wilson Football cleats (with original box!) in order to cover her light bill, I'm happy to pay it forward.

Ironically, what puts him over the edge about my hobby is the packing peanuts. Thus I'd like to present How to Make Fletch Apoplectic in Ten Easy Steps:

2. Spend two weeks spite-bidding on a bunch of random, delicate, heavily packaged items.

3. Accidentally win every single item due to the aforementioned spite bidding.

4. Attempt to open the boxes of shipped items with a tablespoon.[68]

5. Be so excited about the random, delicate items deeply ensconced in packing peanuts that you simply abandon the empty husks of boxes all over the kitchen.

6. Completely forget about the packing peanuts while you arrange your snappy vintage Brownie cameras and croquet balls and cricket bats.

7. Have Fletch fill one entire industrial-sized garbage can with packing peanuts.

8. Suddenly become bored with antiquing on the first sunny day of spring and decide gardening is your new hobby, and thus it's imperative to start planting now, now, now!

....

[68] Hey, it was the most handy pointy thing.

9. Accidentally knock over previously mentioned garbage can while backing out of the garage in your haste to get to Lowe's to buy geraniums.

10. Return home to find white substance spread over 1.2 acres, prompting you to ask, "Did it hail or something?"

11. Bray like a jackass upon discovering those thousands of little blobs are free-range Styrofoam and then wish Fletch a Happy Earth Day.

Fletch has now begged me to reconsider both gardening and antiquing as hobbies, instead opting for something less competitive/messy/expensive.

He suggests sewing.

Sewing?

Huh. That's a thought. I have lots of friends who sew and I love seeing the stuff they create. My friend Wendy is an ace and her basement's so well stocked it's like visiting a tailor.

This . . . might be useful. With some practice, I could whip up some casual, more modern curtains for the bedroom to replace those drapes that look like casket-liner. Plus, I could use the time that I was sewing to listen to opera and that feels really sophisticated and mature.

Yes.

This idea is growing on me.

This could work.

Thing is, fabric can be really expensive, so I'd probably want to start with tiny projects, like napkins or place mats or dresses.

Very small dresses.

Like . . . doll-sized dresses. Really, wouldn't Miss Joan enjoy something comfortable to change into after a long day at Sterling Cooper? Her little purple suit is so stiff and fitted. And those girdles are murder! I bet she'd love a nice, soft housedress. Ooh, better yet—some yoga pants! Just imagine how popular she'd be if she were bendier!

As for Betty Draper—I imagine she's as bitchy as she is because she's stuffed into a girdle all day, every day. All that restricted circulation must angry up her blood. If she had some elastic-waist pants and maybe a loose tunic, she wouldn't be so quick to dismiss Don and then they'd get back together and poor Sally Draper could stop acting out her daddy abandonment issues with all the little boys in her new neighborhood.

If you think about it, by learning to sew, I could (in theory) save an entire (fictional) family.

Plus?

Then I'd have an excuse for playing with dolls!

Reluctant Adult Lesson Learned:

It's not always what you do that makes you a grown-up; sometimes, it's how you spin it.

C·H·A·P·T·E·R N·I·N·E

I Wish I Could Quit You, Gladys Kravitz

In retrospect, the whole spying thing seems pretty childish.

In my defense, keeping tabs on my neighbors' comings and goings was a necessity when we lived in the city. I mean, *someone* had to act as block captain because the police certainly weren't on patrol.

I can count on zero fingers the number of times the Chicago PD responded to 911 calls when we lived in Bucktown, and I'm not talking the usual, *"Hello, Jeannie, who's bothering you today?"* reports about assholes parking in front of my garage.[69]

Squad cars never rolled when we phoned about the sound of gunshots or the knife fight on our sidewalk or when acts of prostitution were committed in the vacant lot next door.

....

[69] Listen, blocking the alley violates fire code and I'm pretty sure that's a crime or violation or at least very annoying every time I had to drive around and park out front.

Yes, the van was rocking but did five-oh come knocking? Negatory.

I'm not sure what the Chicago PD considered *real* crimes in that godforsaken neighborhood, but they included neither drug deals nor domestic violence.

Clearly I had *no choice* but to name myself Neighborhood Hall Monitor,[70] and it's totally not my fault that this dovetailed nicely into my natural propensity for observation. Could I help it if my Constant Vigilance™ occasionally turned up a few hidden truths about my neighbors?

After I spent a full day on Neighborhood Watch, Fletch would return home from work and I'd fill him in on each transgression I witnessed, like which of our idiot neighbors drove her kids around without seat belts and who threw an empty McDonald's bag on my lawn and did he know the McRib was back? Then Fletch would call me Gladys Kravitz[71] and suggest (urge, plead, implore, demand) I find another way to occupy my time.

Every day we had some version of this conversation while he changed out of his grown-up clothes after work:

"You don't understand," I argue, sitting by the window on the bed where I can keep one eye on my husband and the other trained on the street, like one of those creepy chameleons with the swivel-y eye sockets. "It's my civic obligation to note comings and goings."

"What did I tell you about your 'citizen arrests,' Deputy Fife?" he sighs.

....

[70] I should have bought myself a sash and a beret to go along with my whistle, cell phone camera, and good whacking shovel.

[71] Other Notable Nosy Neighbors in Television History include Messrs. Roper and Furley. If you don't catch any of these references, turn on Nick at Nite, like, immediately.

I sigh right back. "That I'm 'not allowed to dole out street justice with a shovel.' *Even though the dipshit who doesn't believe in car seats deserves a solid whacking. Have you ever seen those highway safety videos they used to show in Drivers' Ed? An unsecured baby flies through a windshield like a watermelon launched by God's slingshot! Slam on the brakes once and, ka-blammo! I'm talking front-row seats at a Gallagher show, wiping juice from your cheeks and picking seeds out of your ears.*"

He eyes me curiously. "Don't you have a book to write?"

"That's the beauty of it," *I explain.* "See, I'm, like . . . an amateur detective. As a writer, it's my job to be a quiet observer of the human condition."

"Really?" *he says, poking his head out from behind a bifold door.* "Because I thought your job was to work out with your trainer today and then write up your notes on the Weight Watchers meeting. How'd that go?"

Sheepishly, I admit, "I gave myself carpal tunnel scrolling through GoFugYourself.com so I had to postpone," *punctuating my malady by flexing my sore wrist.* "Hey! Stop that! I can see you smirking! Listen, paying attention to what's happening around us is just as important as exercising for Such a Pretty Fat."

From deep in the closet I hear, "You justify that . . . how?"

"It's my duty to piece together the lives that I observe, like a jigsaw puzzle. It's up to me to fill in the blanks. Example? Remember the people on Superior who had the cameras trained on the doors, bars on all their windows, even the second and third floor, and two perpetually pissed-off Rottweilers roaming the front yard? Why do you suppose they did that?"

"They lived in a shit neighborhood and were tired of getting robbed."

"No! They're ex-spooks. Former CIA, totally. I mean, come on. They'd never make eye contact and the wife sounded like a big-haired Bond villainess. Clearly the guy was an operative who fell in love with his Soviet confidential informant. He left the Agency and now they live here in witness protection. That's why they always cross the street when we're out walking the dogs. They know I know."

"Quite a story. You been watching *Burn Notice* again?"

"No." Yes.

"Then, Special Agent Kravitz, how do you explain that I used to work with the guy back when I was at AT&T in the nineties?"

"Really?"

"Uh-huh. His name is Seth and he's a security consultant. His wife is Zofia and she's from Poland. She worked for AT&T, too. He was her project manager; that's where they met."

That takes the wind out of my sails but I quickly rally. "I'm sure they told you that's where they met. Besides, people in witness protection can have jobs. Wait, they should have jobs. Yes. This makes perfect sense. If they didn't work, what would they do all day? Stare out the window at their neighbors?"

"Are you familiar with the concept of irony?"

"Not always. Point is, my theory holds."

He says nothing but his raised eyebrow says so much. I press on. "I can see you're not yet sold. So riddle me this, Fatman, if they weren't ex–field agents, why would they always cross the street to get away from me?"

"Because you don't have full control of the dogs and Maisy can't keep her tongue off their baby."

Oh. He's got me there. "Well . . . she is affectionate. Whatever, bad example. How about this? How come the old guy on the top floor

of our place on Orchard never once had a visitor the whole three
years we lived beneath him?"

"Because we were busy at our day jobs. Or maybe his friends
were also elderly and couldn't handle all those stairs."

"Bzzt! Wrong. He was anthropologic, which means fear of people and social situations."

"I think you mean anthropophobic. And I used to run into him
with some blue-haired lady at Starbucks all the time, so no, he was
neither anthropologic nor anthropophobic. Still not convincing me
that spying is a legitimate use of your time." He pulls on a polo and
zips up his cargo shorts. "Are we done here? Can we go downstairs
now?"

"No!" I refuse to accept defeat. "If you're so smart, why don't you
tell me why the girl across the courtyard in Lincoln Park moved out
at three a.m.?"

"You mean the moron who left her laundry in the washing machine for a month because she couldn't find a quarter? Her?"

I place my hands on my hips, filling up the doorway so he can't
pass. "Yes. Why do YOU think she moved in the middle of the night?
I suspect she had an abusive boyfriend and had to move to a women's
shelter."

"I suspect she was a dingbat with poor time management skills.
Can I go to the bathroom now?"

"Yes. As soon as you admit that I'm a good detective."

He kisses me on the forehead before wedging past me. "Fine. You
are a veritable Sherlock Holmes . . . in footie pajamas."

I feel vindicated. "Thank you."

"Hey . . . did you shower yet today?"

Obviously not.

Constant Vigilance™ doesn't take bathroom breaks.

In terms of Constant Vigilance™, best thing that ever happened to me was moving into our last house in the Logan Square neighborhood of the city. After we'd been there a couple of days, I noticed all kinds of detritus in the breezeway between my garage and back fence. At first I was pissed off, thinking, "So I've moved into yet another *throw-our-McDonald's-bags-into-your-yard* kind of place, have I? We'll just see about THAT."

While I stomped around picking everything up, I eventually realized that due to a heavy wind, this was just overspill from the construction site next door. What blew in were documents the neighbors had left behind.

As I examined them, I solved the mystery of why no one wanted to rent my pretty house with the huge transom windows. Turns out the vacated-as-of-November-1 place next door wasn't a cute, vintage apartment building. Rather it was a fifty-unit SRO[72] . . . essentially a transient hotel. No wonder the apartment broker remarked on how happy she was that the place next door was going condo.

Because I'm all about urban archeology, I scooped up the wet pile of garbage, drying out the pieces on paper towels lining my counters. And, oh, the pay dirt I unearthed!

I found a letter to an ex-resident from the State Unemployment Office explaining that one cannot *file* for unemployment if one has never actually *held a job*.[73]

Another piece was a bill for six months of car insurance for thirty-six dollars. Thirty-six dollars. For six months. Seriously.

....

[72] Single room occupancy, guaranteed to drop property values for a three-block radius.
[73] Ooh, burn!

What the hell were they driving? A rickshaw? Conestoga wagon? One of those old-fashioned bikes with the enormous front tire piloted exclusively by he-men sporting handlebar mustaches, wearing leotards, and carrying anvils?

I discovered programs from gang members' funerals and receipts for inmate commissary purchases in the Cook County Department of Corrections.[74] Plus there were tons and tons of those tiny zippy plastic bags that my creative girlfriends use to separate beads for when they do crafts. (Clearly the ex-neighbors were running a jewelry-making business.)

Then I found a letter that was like winning the *Gladys Kravitz Nosy Neighbor Memorial Sweepstakes*. Here's what it said:

Dear Pat,

Hey, baby! How are you today! I hope and pray that you and the kids are fine.

Well, this is one of those situations I just won't be able to slick my way out of . . . and *[only]* by chance if I did. By any means, my mind would still be at a blank. Meaning that you're there and whether *[I'm]* in here or out there you and the family is still there. But I ain't mad at ya! Believe me when I say that OK, baby, I'm sorry I took so long writing you. But I just had to find someone— myself.[75] And now that I have done that, whatever life throws at me, I can catch it and run with it.

---

[74] Ask me how much a pack of Kools cost in 1997 at Cook County lockup because I totally know.

[75] I'm going to award him a couple of bonus points here for self-awareness.

Yes, I've gained weight[76] and gotten my health up, smiling and laughing now. But I shouldn't have been so hard-headed. And had to come here to do this. I blame no one but myself for that. If by any chance I lose you or my family, I don't blame you. Please, please don't spin a brother. I can take it in the raw if you're with someone else or talking about getting with someone else, I won't trip.[77]

Stop!! Before responding, play it like it's two thirty in the morning and me and you are having one of those "honesty nights." You do remember that I could be honest with you. I've never lied to you during one of those honest nights. So let's play like we are having one . . . starting now.

Patricia, I love ya, I'll always love ya. I miss my family and everything. I can't imagine myself without you. But you really want to ask me the thousand dollar question. Have I been conversing with Natalie and Regina or Kimberley? Right. You don't have to say it, I know. Well, Kimberley asked me to call her about twenty times but I didn't . . . until today. Regina and I talked about two or three times. Nat I haven't called but Moms relays a message to Ronnell for me, both talking the same old county-jail-shit about how they're going to be there for a brother when I get out. I

---

[76] Oh, honey, who hasn't?

[77] This is where I start to feel sorry for him.

really don't want to hear that, let alone their voices. But a *[very bad word]*'s here and sometimes I get BORED. I'd rather talk to you but at the same time, I don't want to be bothering you too much either . . . I ain't new to this but true to this.[78]

I know how it is when a *[very, very bad word]* gets LOCKED THE FUCK UP. His ass is out and motherfuckers want to spin ya ass like a top. Well, I ain't about to get dizzy.[79] My dizzy days are OVER . . . so I ask you now to be real with me and level with me about your life now.

The last thing I need is for my wife[80] to be lying to me because she feels it's the right thing to do. Not in this case it ain't. Hey, baby, I'll always love ya! But if there's another, let me move on . . .

That's where the first page ended. Fletch arrived home to find me scaling the construction Dumpster with my good whacking shovel in search of the second page because I couldn't stand not knowing what happened next.

Yes.

That was well received.

Not only did Fletch forbid me from additional adventures in

....

[78] I am so stealing this line.
[79] Again, I feel this is a bit profound. He's beginning to win me over.
[80] Hold the damn phone! Wife? WIFE? Pat is your WIFE? So what you're saying is that instead of writing to your wife, you choose to converse with Regina, Nat, and Next Door first? You had me and then you lost me.

urban archeology, but he made me store my shovel in the garage before washing my hands no less than six times.

At his behest, I grudgingly promised to hang up my (figurative) binoculars because we were in a nice house and an up-and-coming neighborhood and he didn't want me to alienate myself exactly like everywhere else we ever lived.

"Fine," I replied. "Then I'll just watch television."[81]

Unfortunately for those of us in the *Gladys Kravitz Anonymous Twelve-Step Program*, this proved difficult not because I lacked the willpower, but because we lived in such tight quarters with the house to the right. Our homes were so close we could hear our neighbors sneeze and the ding of their microwave when their Orville Redenbacher Kettle Corn finished popping. We heard them yawning and watching *American Idol* and running their dishwasher. And the night one of them had a bad egg salad sandwich?

Let's just say there's some stuff you can't unhear.

Our balconies were practically on top of each other with nothing between us but two iron porch rails and a three-foot strip of sidewalk. Such was our proximity that I could identify every legume in their three-bean salad picnic suppers.

Many of our windows lined up with those next door, so the first thing I did upon move-in was to hang completely opaque blinds because I'm a big, fat hypocrite who believes in spying but not being spied upon.[82] However, we had a particularly large set of transom windows over the stairway in that house and they couldn't be covered with anything that wasn't custom-made. We immedi-

....

[81] We all know how that turned out.
[82] I said it so you don't have to.

ately sought out estimates on drapes because my desire to not be seen without pants outweighed my thirst for information.

Due to excessive width and the height, we'd have to pay over a thousand dollars to insure no one saw my underwear as I dashed from the bathroom to the bedroom. I wasn't about to drop that kind of cash on a rental home, so I spent seventy bucks on a pink terry-cloth robe from L.L. Bean. Monogrammed and everything! Problem solved, problem staying solved . . . or so I thought.

Here's the thing . . . if you can see into my house, I can also see into yours. That's how regular glass works. Why the sight of me zipping past in a blur of damp hair and shame didn't spur some flash of realization with the folks next door, I'll never know. Ergo, I felt . . . somewhat justified in seeing snatches of their lives, rationalizing if they didn't want me serving witness, they'd close their blinds. I mean, all I was doing was climbing my stairs—no crime in that, yes?

At first, the window into their home office was a lot like watching the boring bits of *Big Brother*, only with a lot fewer camera angles and no Power of Veto competitions. Due to our proximity, I could read the titles of the books on the shelves. I could tell whether or not the wife had dabbed on zit cream. Like it or not, their world was my (voyeuristic) oyster.

Gazing into the fishbowl of their lives was kind of what I'd expected back in the day when I ordered the sea monkeys advertised in my *Archie* comic books, except they didn't run around in crowns carrying scepters.[83] The best part was that I wasn't spying

---

[83] Anyone else still pissed off about the whole sea monkey thing? They were supposed to hang out in front of their castle and read and be our friends, but all they did was flit about in a bowl of brackish water.

so much as simply walking from the bedroom to the bathroom—repeatedly—and I was able to keep my promise to Fletch. Hey, I'm not spying! I just happen to need to brush my teeth thirty times a day!

A while after we moved in, they rearranged the room and suddenly I could see what was on their computer monitor, too. *Oh, boy! Now it's getting good,* I thought.

The wife was a big fan of Facebook and Zappos and LOLCats. She spent an awful lot of time uploading photos of her dog who had a shockingly large number of embroidered sweatshirts. Every time we saw Pippen, a highly strung Bouvier des Flanders, in the yard with a fresh haircut and a new shirt, Fletch would whisper, "How badly does she want a baby?"

As for the husband's viewing pleasure?

That's where it got troubling, bless his XXX-rated heart.

The (thankfully) odd part is he never seemed to be . . . um, *enjoying*[84] all the bare-bottomed babes on his screen. His actions were never untoward. Rather, he'd simply click through page after page of GIFs for hours in a highly clinical manner, almost as if he were sorting, rather than ogling. He had all the passion of a gynecologist flipping through a bunch of pap smear results. I felt oddly comforted by this.

Now, you fellows out there, I'm not going to judge you if you like to see a little *strange* on the computer from time to time. Because, really? That's why Al Gore invented the Internet in the first place. But I will say this: if you have so much porn on your com-

---

[84] If you know what I mean. And if you don't know what I mean, please don't make me explain it.

puter that it takes months and months to organize your stash, you either need to seek help or turn this into a business.

Perhaps you're not a perv at all; perhaps you're an entrepreneur.

The worst part of all this for me was that the vista was so clear that I could even determine the *era* of nudie photos he most favored. He must have come of age during the Olivia Newton-John Let's-Get-Physical days because he was all about the shots from the eighties. How was I so sure?

The standards of grooming have changed since then.

I haven't been this bothered by anything since I discovered my sea monkeys were essentially water lice. I felt like the universe was telling me, *"Hey, you wanna spy? Oh, I will GIVE you something to spy, missy."*

To put the situation in different terms, you know sometimes when you want a cookie of the oatmeal variety, so you make a batch of them? And you use the recipe from the smiley blue Quaker's drum and it always makes way more than you meant? Like, you wanted enough cookies for a decent snack, yet you wound up with six dozen, even though you got super sick of touching cookie batter towards the end and made the last few dough balls big as baseballs?

And turns out you baked so damn many oatmeal scotchies that all you're doing is eating cookies for every meal because they're right there and you're kind of hungry and, really, you don't want them to go to waste because they took some effort to create? So you eat and eat and eat far past the point of actual enjoyment? And then you spend the bulk of your day in the washroom reading a George R. R. Martin novel because it's the biggest book you can find outside of the dictionary, cursing Wilford Brimley for being the only man on earth who has the time or inclination to process that much fiber? And at some point you're all, *Sweet Baby Ray, I just want a nice steak*?

That's how I felt about the unfettered access to gossipy-type information. Much as I used to enjoy sneaking glimpses of people's lives, this was too much. I wanted three cookies, not ALL the cookies.

I was exposed to so many intimate details of our neighbors' lives that it made me squirmy, primarily when it came to the husband's viewing habits. This guy was on nekkid sites ALL NIGHT, EVERY NIGHT. I figured that every time I climbed the stairs to come face to l-a-b-i-a, *that* was my Greek-tragedy-style punishment for having been nosy.

My life became an inadvertent version of *Rear Window* (minus the wheelchair and telescope) and I began to make my way to the second floor with my eyes clamped shut, muttering, *"We've become a race of Peeping Toms!"*

On top of all the deeply scarring nudity, the wife's mommylust couldn't have been more obvious and clearly no one was in the business of making babies because the guy never left his damn Aeron chair to go to bed already. His habits were tearing them apart and I wanted to help fix them. I wanted to post a sign begging him to PLEASE GET OFF THE INTERNET AND ON YOUR WIFE because I thought it might help.[85]

And even though we were experiencing the most beautiful spring on record, I started keeping all my windows closed on their side of the house because, inevitably, they began to spiral down-

....

[85] Fletch said no because he hates to be helpful.

ward as a couple. Their marriage—which had seemed so fresh and shiny and happy when we moved in—hit more than just a rough patch; it slammed into a bridge abutment going eighty miles an hour in a Smart Car.

As I'd sit in my office trying to organize my notes for my next book, I'd hear the wife screaming at the husband and I'd inadvertently start rocking and murmuring, *"I hate when Mom and Dad fight."*

Every day the hostility got more intense. Although no one ever threw a punch or a vase, the accusations they'd hurl at each other seemed equally damaging. Like it or not, I had a front-row seat to an unraveling marriage. I felt like I was watching a Chekhov play against my will.

When Gladys Kravitz witnessed the occasional confirmation of her suspicions of the Stevens family, she was triumphant. She *knew* there was funny business afoot in that household! Whereas I liked to giggle and speculate about the antics of the amateur Larry Flynt next door, I didn't actually want any of my ridiculous theories to be *true*. Addiction isn't funny.

Every day when they came home from work and the fighting began in earnest, I felt like they were a horrible accident by the side of the highway and the last thing I wanted to see was the carnage. I wish I'd never taken that route in the first place but I had no choice but to drive past.

When they'd start in on each other, I'd head to the farthest point in my house away from them but their words seemed to follow me. I stopped sitting on my deck entirely and took to blasting talk radio on our house's intercom system.

I'd fallen down a rabbit hole and the only way out was to move away.

Fortunately, I won a brief reprieve in May when I had to tour for *My Fair Lazy*. Normally I dread going on the road, not because I don't love meeting fans and doing live events and media, but because I get so homesick. I hate being away from Fletch and the dogs and, to a lesser extent, the cats. I miss them so much when I'm not there. Plus, I'm the kind of person who isn't happy unless I'm sleeping in my bed with my blankets and my decades-old down pillow.[86] I'm so weird about being away that I even bring my own toilet paper because no hotel ever stocks the aloe stuff that I like.

But this year?

All I wanted was to get the hell out of Dodge.

Even on the road, I couldn't escape the drama of their lives. On my first night away, Fletch called to tell me the following news.

"The husband quit his job."

"Wait, are *you* spying now?" I asked. I am the worst influence ever.

"Wasn't eavesdropping. Ran into him in the backyard with Pippen. He was very excited to tell me that he'd quit his job."

"In *this* economy? To do what?" My hope was that he actually was starting a porn site if for no reason other than to justify his extracurricular activities.

Fletch exhaled long and hard before he told me. "He quit his job to pursue his dream. Says he wants to be an actor."

"He was a mechanical engineer!" I protested.

---

[86] Yes, it's as gross as you'd imagine, or would be if I weren't buying fresh pillowcases for it all the time. At this point, the feathers are just little sticks, so it feels a lot like buckwheat. I know it's weird. *I know.* Listen, don't worry about it. If you ever sleep over, I'll put a new pillow in your room, okay?

"And now he's not."

"Oh, God, this is not going to end well," I said.

"Yeah. That's why I bought new headphones."

By the time I returned from book tour, the wife had moved out and the husband had done some redecorating. Specifically, he'd taken sheets and used them to cover all his windows, securing them up to the ledge of the transoms with two-liter bottles of generic diet cola. We never heard anything after that, and thank God, we never saw anything else either. If this guy was so cavalier about what he looked at with an uncovered window and an angry wife lurking about, I haven't any idea what he'd view behind closed blinds.

Not long after that, we found our home in the suburbs. Although we considered a number of contenders in a variety of neighborhoods, ultimately we opted for the one surrounded by the most trees. Except when we're by one particular window on the east side of the property, we can't see or hear anything happening in the neighborhood and that has been a blessing.

The whole first month we lived up here, we used to sit on our new porch enjoying the sounds of silence. Once in a while I'd ask Fletch, "Hey, do you hear that?" When he'd say no, I'd always smile and reply, "Me neither."

After fifteen years of city living, I could not have been happier to let the whole Constant Vigilance™ thing go. I was done being the neighborhood's hall monitor and I was delighted to hang up my good whacking shovel once and for all. Rest in peace, sweet Gladys Kravitz. Rest in peace.

Having spent so much of my life minding everyone else's beeswax, I finally had the chance to mind my own.

And it was bliss.

Until I got bored.

But I'll get to that later.

Reluctant Adult Lesson Learned:

Keep seeking and eventually you'll find what's hidden, whether or not you like it.

The Old Dog Whisperer

*E*very day I feel more and more like a full-fledged adult.

Even though it was (metaphorically) only yesterday I was sloshing in the door at four a.m. after Dollar Beer Night,[87] I find myself with a mortgage, four types of insurance, and a non-laundry-quarter-based retirement fund. Every single one of my bookcases is made of wood, not milk crates, and I don't own a stick of garbage-picked furniture anymore.

Okay, mostly that last bit is because Fletch won't LET me garbage pick[88] anymore. Before I can even finish the sentence, *"Hey, that looks like a perfectly nice—"* he hits the accelerator and we speed away before I can throw open the door and claim my prize. The last time we were driving through Lincoln Park, someone was

[87] Or more accurately, what started as Dollar Beer Afternoon.
[88] What he calls "junking."

tossing out a really luxe, squishy Crate and Barrel–type love seat and I felt a physical ache when he forbid me to lay a mitt on it to see if it was chenille or Ultrasuede. Given no choice, I've stopped junking, yet the desire to junk remains.[89]

Regardless, I've managed to grow up . . . to the point that I'm experiencing the existential angst from having done so. I'm no longer surfing the waves of a Count Chocula sugar high, nor am I kiting checks to the grocery store. Not only do I own the proper glassware for any beverage, but I have seven different kinds of cheese knives. Knives! Exclusively for cheese! Seven kinds!! What kind of bizarre, Dockers-wearing, Kenny G–listening, Williams-Sonoma-credit-card-having alternative universe have I fallen into?

Where I am in life—i.e., coupled up—means I never have to pretend to be interested in techno music or the Golf Channel or, sweet Jesus, NASCAR racing again. Now I'm left wondering, where's the rush I used to get from being a perpetual adolescent? Where's the torment of no one *really* understanding me? Where's the self-righteous self-pity over having to put up with silly rules established by my folks, my school, or my boss? Oh, that's right—by design I've arranged my life in such a way that I'm really only accountable to myself now.

Yet somehow always being able to locate my keys, shoes, and underwear has left a void in my life.

Did not see that coming.

Fortunately the solution to my midlife crisis is sweet and helpless and cuddly with a pink belly, so Fletch and I are adopting . . . a pit bull puppy!

....

[89] Maybe that's why I'm so into antiquing now; it's like garbage picking, only with fewer bedbugs.

Recently we contacted A & S Rescue to discuss a possible dog adoption. Because of Maisy's precarious health, we have to be extra careful whom we introduce to the household. The dog needs to come from a foster home situation, rather than straight out of a shelter because of exposure risk. Our vet said from a safety perspective, buying a dog from a breeder would be best, but considering one out of six hundred shelter pit bulls actually gets a forever home, I could never in good faith do that.

Maisy has always loved puppies, so our thinking is if we bring in some fresh blood, that will rejuvenate her. From a selfish perspective, we understand she's a gift with an expiration date, so we're hoping that if we adopt another dog, he or she will be a little mini-me and Maisy will live on through them.

After an extensive screening process[90] the agency introduced us to a possible new pet. He was a beautiful, energetic, adolescent golden boy with an enormous head and we instantly fell in love with him. With elegantly muscled legs and broad shoulders, he was powerful and handsome and sweet. The rescue organization brought him over to the house and we all went on a long walk to acclimate everyone. The big boy adored us, too. Everyone was on board with the adoption . . . except for the two spoiled, surly middle-aged dogs that live here.

Let's just say the second it came to sharing a water dish, our guys were less than hospitable.

I may have matured, but a portion of our family hadn't.

We adopted Maisy and Loki eight shoe-shredded, carpet-ruined, plant-unpotted years ago. Their adolescence was destructive but brief. Now I'd probably rather they eat the occasional

---

[90] Which I absolutely appreciate and expect, given the breed.

sneaker than the alternative, which is staring at me when they're bored and I'm working. Clearly they've lost any manners we taught them in obedience training when they were pups.

The problem is entirely, one hundred percent our faults. We set the bar for their behavior terribly low. We wanted two sweet dogs that'd coexist with our churlish cats and that'd be friendly towards guests, and oh, boy! Are they friendly! Just ask Stacey about the time Maisy launched herself from one couch to the other so she could show her exactly how friendly she could be. Poor Stacey said it was like being hit with a cannonball. With claws.

Once we achieved the goal of having affable, social dogs, we never pushed them any harder. We wound up with two willful creatures who'd tell us in no uncertain terms when they were ready to eat, potty, and be entertained. If we were lucky, they'd even scoot over enough so that we could sleep on our bed with them.[91]

Apparently this was bad.

Perhaps when our friends made statements like, "You should really read Cesar Milan's books," or "No, seriously, please, watch *The Dog Whisperer*," or "Thank God you don't have kids," we should have taken the hint.

Now I have the clarity to realize we must break the cycle so we've forgone adoption while we bring Maisy and Loki in line. We've enlisted them in a doggie boot camp, which is as much for them as it is for us.

Despite acting like the pronged training collars were killing them dead, splat, the first time we attached them, they've quickly come around. In a few sessions with Elaine, our no-nonsense

---

[91] Years ago we bought a king-sized bed because it was easier than fighting or sleeping on the couch.

trainer from the rescue group, the dogs are starting to learn that everyone wins when they obey our cues. More importantly, Elaine makes us realize that we don't have to live a life where our dogs run the show. In fact, it's our obligation as adults and owners to do so.

Seeing the difference in them is amazing. For example, meal-time used to be chaos with yipping and shoving and jumping. But now we make sure they know we're the ones in charge and they don't get anything until they calmly sit and wait to be served. Through the training process, they've learned that no squirrel tastes as good as discipline feels. Also? It's easier to do what's expected because ultimately the rewards are greater.

Hey . . . that might explain why I finally stopped fighting growing up, too.

When Angie's here for a girls' weekend on one of our regular training Fridays, she wraps her arms around Elaine and says, "Thank you, thank you, thank you!" the second Elaine walks in the door. Elaine, although initially taken aback by being grappled by a stranger, immediately understands because she'll never forget exactly how ill behaved our guys were.

Our progress has been so measurable that the agency believes we're ready to introduce a new dog to the household. The big, golden boy we met was adopted to a wonderful home,[92] so next week we're meeting a puppy. And we're going to begin working with her immediately so she'll grow up understanding expectations and won't ever be stuck in a state of arrested development (like we were.)

Now, if I could only train Jordan and Tucker not to barf in my shoes.

....

[92] Yay!

Then again, there's a reason no one calls themselves the Cat Whisperer.

My friend Gina's mom used to say that everyone needs something to do and someone to love and they'll never be without a purpose.

Of course Gina's boyfriend Lee says in a pinch, all you really need is someone to hate. Hate'll get you through.

Miss Liberty Belle, a skinny brindle pit bull with white feet and enormous brown eyes, has something to do (play with her tennis ball) and has someone to love (Maisy).

As for Maisy?

Her hate for Libby is what's getting her through.

We welcome Libby into our lives on a chilly winter day and we're struck with how angular and bony she is. We always assumed pit puppies were little butterballs like Maisy was when she was small. However, Libby's still recovering from a tragic beginning. First she and her littermates were starved and when they didn't die fast enough, her original owner threw her and her siblings into a box and *hit them with his car.* Only Libby and one of her siblings lived and the other one was so sick she didn't make it.

This is why I'm so adamant about supporting animal rescue. The fact that there are people out there who treat living beings like this makes me weep for humanity.[93]

Anyway, Libby survived, but barely. She was infested with thousands of fleas and she nearly lost her life to parvo. But she

....

[93] And makes me want to dig out my good whacking shovel.

pulled through it all and when she has her clean bill of health and a full set of immunizations, she's placed with us.

I should probably mention that she's the happiest little girl in the world. Dogs live in the now and when Libby looks around, there's nothing about her now that she doesn't love passionately. She doesn't run so much as spring and bounce mountain goat–style and we believe her inner monologue sounds like this: *"Libby! Libby! I am Libbbbbbbbbbbbbbbbbbyyyyyy!"*

Again, Maisy? Not so much.

We thought Maisy would lose her mind with all the mothering she heaps on puppies she meets while out for walks. But I guess street puppies never tried to share her bed or were fed tasty-smelling, high protein, grain-free puppy food in front of her.

All Libby wants is to be Maisy's bestie, but Maisy would like nothing to do with her, thanks for asking. She refuses to play with Libs and she's always shooting sour glances in her direction. Maisy's snarly and unwelcoming and pouts when we make her stop. But somehow, instead of this being stressful and wearing Maisy down, it's lifting her up. We haven't seen her this spry and active since before she was diagnosed.

Gina says Fletch never seems happier than when he's righteously indignant and the same holds true for Maisy.

Of course, Maisy's never come up against the unmitigated joy and determination of a little girl named Libby.

Whereas Maisy's all flinty-eyed and calculating, Libby's face is wide open and unassuming. If she were a person, she'd be wearing pigtails and overalls. Her friendly demeanor is enhanced by her ears which are extra-floppy and project from her head like a set of bat wings. They flap when she runs. She'll often try to put them up Doberman-style when she's outside, but they're too heavy and they just fold over like she's wearing a hat.

Libs never looks at us straight-on. Rather she pulls that nose-down, eyes-up business that buries the needle of the cute-o-meter in the red every time. Even though she's a plush chocolate-caramel brindle, she sports a large white patch on one side of her nose and it's dotted with freckles. I find it virtually impossible to see her snout without wanting to place a kiss on it.

When we first bring her home, I feel like I'm doing something wrong by loving her, even though she's the embodiment of happiness and joy. "Do you think Maisy feels like we're being disloyal?" I ask Fletch again and again.

"I think Maisy wants a cheeseburger and that's the extent of her cognitive abilities," he replies. Of course, Fletch feels none of the lingering guilt because he was smitten the first time Libby curled up in his lap. If there's such a thing as a daddy's girl, Libby is one of them. We actually have to work on this in training because instead of disciplining her, Fletch apologizes whenever she does something wrong.[94] "I wouldn't stress. Libs is going to win Maisy over yet. She'll come around. Mark my words."

It takes two months, but Libby does it. She and Maisy are insepa-rable now and whenever Maisy has a down day,[95] Libby's right there bringing her hot tea, Jell-O, and the latest issue of *Star* magazine.

Of course, everybody is Libby's pal and she brings such a

....

[94] Maybe I spoiled the last two, but I'm doing this one right.
[95] Which are far less frequent since Libby got here.

sweet energy to the room that we're able to have doggie playdates for the first time.[96] Even though Loki and Maisy are lifelong buds, they've never quite gotten the hang of entertaining each other. Maisy only likes to tug and Loki prefers to be chased and they've always looked to us to provide these services. Libby just wants everyone to be together so she tugs and chases and engages all.

If Maisy could, she'd be the older sibling who taught Libby to smoke. Since she can't,[97] she's shown Libby how to bed-hog and counter-surf and beg and she's convinced her that making potty on the living room rug is the next-best thing to relieving herself outdoors.

We have our work cut out for us.

So, we step up our visits with Elaine and buy paper towels in bulk. And offer prayers of thanks to have found such a *good* bad dog to complete our family.

Reluctant Adult Life Lesson:

If you're in the midst of a midlife crisis, you could buy a convertible, have an affair, or upgrade your cup size. But you'll probably be happiest if you save a dog's life.

---

[96] Hello, Tracey's sweet dog Maxie!
[97] No thumbs.

Don't Blame Mii, Japan

When I was in eighth grade, Japan was the coolest country on the planet. With "Mr. Roboto" on the Walkman, *Karate Kid* in the Betamax, and our T-shirts embossed with the characters for "storm sewer" and "dishwasher,"[98] our nation embraced Japanese culture so much that we even tried sushi. I'm sure our Founding Fathers spun in their graves, all, *"Raw fish? Wrapped in seaweed? I'm sorry, did we lose a war or something?"*

Much like Australia and our short-lived passion for Men at Work, Vegemite, and all things *Crocodile Dundee*, Japan's fallen out of favor. One might think Toyota's massive PR FAIL is the root of the problem, but that's just a smoke screen. The real culprit is far more insidious.

....

[98] According to Reggie, our Japanese exchange student who, ironically, came to the U.S. to escape Japanese culture.

I'm talking about the Wii Fit, of course.

If you're Amish and you're reading about this device for the first time,[99] the Wii Fit is a Japanese gaming system designed to get the player moving. Instead of sitting in a stationary position like for traditional video games, participants have to kick their legs and swing their arms in order to boot on-screen soccer balls and return lobs on the tennis court. (I mean, sure, you could kick a ball and swing a racket in real life, but then you'd have to leave your basement.) To me, the Wii Fit seems like a way to work out without actually having to, you know, *work*, so naturally I'm all over it.

Like the rest of the nation on the day after Christmas last year, I knock back my eggnog, brush the cookie crumbs off my lap, and quickly hook up the console.

Ha! Right. As someone who never knew the microwave had any setting other than HIGH, this is way outside my pay grade.

Instead, I task Fletch with the setup.

"It's supposed to be super easy," I tell him. "All the reviews I've read said a thirteen-year-old boy could put this together."

Three hours, a pint of bourbon, and more anguished cries of, "I need a thirteen-year-old boy!" than our neighbors are comfortable hearing, the system is together.

Everyone's always going on and on about Wii Bowling and Wii Tennis, but before I can try my hand at either of them, the game wants to assess my Wii Fit age. I'm not thin[100] but I'm strong and my balance is such that I can navigate a flight of stairs with a basket of laundry and a stack of Pottery Barn catalogs, vaulting over dog-and-cat-based obstacles, never once spilling my coffee.

....

[99] I like your beard.
[100] At all. AT ALL.

I figure the test will more or less reflect my forty-two years. Which it does.

Before adding thirty, thus bringing my Wii Fit age to seventy-two.

Seventy-freaking-two.

That's when I suspect there could be trouble.

I create a Mii avatar and I start playing. I'm totally fine when the other smug Miis gloat every time I go out of bounds and I'm not disheartened when YOU LOSE flashes across the screen in nine-hundred-point font. Frankly, I'm glad there's someone out there today going all Tiger Mother because kids need to learn that not everyone gets a medal. Life is unfair and there are winners and losers, regardless of how much overprotective parents attempt to shield their offspring from reality.

One of my friends is an executive at a large corporation and he had to go through sensitivity training in regard to working with Millennials. Basically he spent three days learning that he was required to heap them with praise and give them plenty of respect, whether or not they earned it. To me? This is unreal.

And yet I begin to struggle with reality myself when using the supplemental balance board. Upon determining my BMI, my adorable avatar in her cute dress with her pink cheeks looks as shocked as I do when she swells Violet Beauregarde–style, turning all lumpy and potato-headed, enthusiastically exclaiming, "You're obese!"

Um . . . thank you?

The first games I try involve the slalom and ski jumping. I believe my spectacular failures here are less a product of shoddy balance and more an issue of a board resting on a thick carpet. My results are consistently worse on every run, to the point that my Mii drops to her knees and begins pounding her head against the ground. Such is her shame I'm surprised she doesn't whip out a Hanwei sword and off herself Samurai-style.

So, fine. I'm not making the cut for the 2014 Sochi games anytime soon. I can live with that.

I switch to the balance fitness test and that's when the machine goes all Regina George. In getting a feel for the sensitive calibration, I biff so many exercises that the Wii notes "balance isn't my thing" and that maybe I'd "enjoy some nice memory games."

Argh.

While I have an amazing memory,[101] I still can't quite master the Wii controller, which gives the impression of being full of a raw, wobbly egg or blobs of mercury. The device is disconcerting and I hate how it feels. Were I born ten years later, I could operate a joystick like it were one of my fingers, but I wasn't so I can't.[102] That's why, despite having razor-sharp recall, I keep selecting the wrong answers. Failing at these tests prompts responses like "Are you usually forgetful?" and "Do you normally have trouble concentrating?"

Too bad the Wii Fit doesn't measure how hard I can kick a TV stand.

The final insult comes when I try Lotus Focus. The goal of this game is to sit still. That's it, just sit. Judging from my four gold stars—the Wii's highest honor—I'm an Olympic medalist in Not Moving.

And *that's* when I realize that "Wii Fit" is actually Japanese for "We fit; you fat."

....

[101] Seriously, ask me anything. First grade teacher? Mrs. White. She wore a wig and smelled like denture cream. Next?
[102] See also: Why I don't text. (Autocorrect can do only so much.)

Japan, if you want to win us back, it'll take more than reengineered acceleration systems. Unless the Wii Fit stops behaving like it's starring in *Mean Girls II, This Time It's Asian*, it's over between us forever.

And P.S.? I hear Paul Hogan's been itching for a comeback.

March 10, 2011

Aw, Japan, I take it all back. I'm sending you the biggest donation I can afford and I'm urging everyone I know to do the same.

I hope that Americans give generously enough to help rebuild your infrastructure . . . even the bits of it that produce insulting games.

Reluctant Adult Life Lesson:

Just because you don't like hearing something doesn't make it not true.

As Seen On TV

*I*f you want me to buy something, include four magic words on the packaging.

I'm not talking about "age-defying," "pore-minimizing," or "lose ten pounds instantly," even though these are all fine qualities.

For me, the only words that matter are *As Seen on TV*.

That moniker alone turns me from a savvy consumer to zealous convert in the time it takes to slap-chop an onion. *"But I've seen this advertised on television!"* I'll say to myself, inspecting the ShamWow or Snuggie on that one weird endcap at Target. *"It must be good!"*

Despite the rational part of my frontal lobe that reminds me, *"Almost everything that's sold in stores can be seen on TV, yet you didn't start squealing and throwing Tide in your cart,"* my brain stem cannot resist anything that's hawked by a pitchman, that ends in ninety-nine cents, or has an operator standing by to double my order if I act now.

I assume this is because what *As Seen on TV* means is there's an infomercial about the product and I could not love infomercials more. When I used to roll home after the bars closed in college, I'd watch them until dawn because I was powerless to turn them off. A special paintbrush that reaches those hard-to-reach corners? A fruit dehydrator? A buzz-cut Susan Powter urging me to *Stop the Insanity*? A tonic used to straighten African-American women's hair that is so nontoxic you can actually eat it? *The Principal Secret?* Yeah, I was in a college apartment that I wasn't allowed to paint, I didn't like dried fruit, I was thin, smooth, and Caucasian, but OMG, yes, yes, yes, yes, and yes! I shall take them all!!

I imagine that because I was young, drunk, and more than a tad stupid, I was the target market for these infomercial makers. They probably lured college students into market research centers disguised as Irish pubs and with banners advertising half-priced drinks. I'm guessing researchers pumped them full of Jameson shots and then monitored exactly which products caused them to lose impulse control first.[103]

Of course, as much as I adore infomercials, Fletch hates them. Between the terrible acting and the exaggerated incompetence, he believes infomercials are an insult to his intelligence. This makes me love them even more because watching Fletch get mad is always funny.

"Who can't crack an egg?" he'll fume.

....

[103] I bet no one could resist the Roly Kit storage containers. They're storage containers! That roll!!

"Blankets aren't that complicated! And it's just a backwards robe, you idiot!"

"Seriously? They can't peel a simple cucumber without stabbing themselves? Seriously?"

"Oh, noes! I can't work this Saran Wrap! Look at my butterfingers! Somebody help me because I'm too stupid to work a strip of plastic!"

We're at the dinner table eating flank steaks wrapped with spinach, prosciutto, and provolone cheese when an infomercial for the Chef Basket comes on. We're both instantly mesmerized for entirely different reasons.

"What kind of half-witted moron can't boil a potato without incident?" he barks.

Ooh, imagine all the potatoes I could cook without incident, I think, immediately kicking into lizard-brain mode.

"Goes right from the pot to the plate . . . dripping boiling hot water across the kitchen the entire time."

I'd never have to wash a colander again!

"From draining to straining! There's no difference! Using two words to say the same thing doesn't speak to multiple functionalities! That just means the intern who wrote this commercial had a thesaurus."

It strains and drains? Is magic device!!

"And the bonus RoboStir? Please."

And the bonus RoboStir! Please!

So enrapt are we with the commercial that neither one of us notices when our eighteen-year-old cat, Jordan, climbs onto the dinner table. As I watch, I hear a quiet *om-nom-nom* in the near vicinity, but it doesn't really register because the dogs are eating dinner behind us and my, God! The Chef Basket handles stay cool to the touch! Finally I'll stop burning my hands whenever I go near the stove!

It's not until the commercial ends that we realize that the cat's not only on the table, but she also just ingested the nine-inch loop of butcher's twine that had held my flank steak together while cooking.

Son of a bitch.

"Did she . . ." I gasp, lifting my plate to find evidence of the string. "She couldn't . . ."

But she had and she did and she's currently smacking her smug, self-satisfied feline chops as apparently I prepare a particularly appetizing string.

I can't believe this just happened. I've spent the past eighteen years trying to keep this stupid cat away from all things dangling, knowing the havoc it would play on her delicate digestive system. I'm so careful that Christmas ribbon is strictly forbidden in this house, as is tinsel and Easter grass. I won't even toss used dental floss in the trash. I wait until I'm ready to take out the garbage and then I collect the used bits I'd safely stashed in my nightstand.[104]

Fletch thinks more quickly than I do in a crisis, so while I pace and try to convince the cat to barf (by describing the oysterlike substance I once saw on a subway platform) he consults both the emergency vet and the Internet.

....

[104] I almost always forget to do this on Garbage Day and Fletch won't go near my nightstand because it's a huge tangled knot of old floss, headbands, uncapped lip balms, free-range antacids, and those tiny silica packets found in shoe boxes for some odd reason. Fletch calls it my Drawer of Shame.

"Good news," he tells me, hanging up the phone. "This isn't such a big deal. We don't have to bring her to the ER. All we need is a tablespoon of Vaseline."

I run to the medicine cabinet to locate the tub I use for my scaly elbows. I scoop up a handful of goo and return to the kitchen. "Okay, what end do I put this in?"

Fletch gives me a Ped Egg–worthy scowl while I wrestle Jordan into position. "Her *mouth*, you ninny. You put it in her mouth!"

"Well, I'm sorry," I scoff. "I've never lubed a cat before."

"You think I have?"[105]

Jordan has always been fairly mellow. She's been a cranky old lady her whole life, but in a passive, sitting-on-the-front-porch-and-exclaiming-into-her-handkerchief-that-those-hippies-need-a-hair-cut sort of way, rather than an aggressive, get-back-here-Bobby-Dylan-and-taste-the-blue-steel-of-my-clippers manner. But the minute I grasp her about the midsection and try to insert a petroleum product in her mouth, oh . . . here go hell come.

There is screaming and there is slashing and there is crying and I believe the bulk of it is coming from Fletch. I quickly witness that two hundred pounds of husband is no match for six pounds of ancient, irate kitty.

My entreaties that I'm trying to save her fool life are for naught and we continue to struggle with her but I can't get the Vaseline anywhere near her mouth. I do, however, get it in my mouth, as well as my hair and my ear and all over the counter, which blends nicely with all the blood gushing from fresh claw marks.

....

[105] Noted.

"Now what?" I wail. The last thing I want to do is take her to the emergency vet because trying to shove her in a cat carrier is the same exercise in futility as attempting to force petroleum into her piehole.

"The doc says if we can't get it into her mouth, we put tiny dabs on her paws and she'll ingest it when she cleans her feet."

I slather handfuls on her front legs. She bolts away from us, but not before spraying every cabinet, appliance, and window with tiny blobs of Vaseline before escaping to the laundry room where every piece of lint we've ever generated clings to her tacky limbs like tiny leg warmers.

"That didn't work!" I shout.

"What part of 'dabs' did you not understand?"

At this point, poor little Jordie's beyond upset and were she capable of registering her discontent online, we'd be unfriended, unfollowed, and in social media jail. She'd be begging Khloé Kardashian to "retweet if you think cat lubers are douche bags" and pinging Angelina and Brad to adopt her because clearly she's being raised by savages.

Despite her anger, we have to get this stuff into her. So I rub down her whole front with Vaseline and, to make it more appetizing, follow it with a smear of creamy Danish butter. Then, for good measure, I apply some of the pan drippings from our dinner. She smells like a fine steak house and her fur stands up in glistening chunks and spikes, turning her into the smaller, more cantankerous feline version of Pauly D. before an evening of fist pumping at Karma. All she's missing is a wee set of Beats by Dr. Dre cans strapped to her melon.

But Jordan, unlike the rest of the *Jersey Shore* crew, is not up for GTL nor is she DTF. Instead she takes off to my closet and spends the rest of the night RAMCLS (Rubbing Against My Clean Lacoste Shirts.)

Fletch takes her into the vet for an X-ray and bath the next morning and the vet tech swears she has to leave the room and laugh for an entirely different circumstance. Right.

The good news is that our labors worked and Jordan is fine. Due to our diligent efforts at greasing her up, things . . . passed smoothly and without incident.

Unfortunately, the vet says the kind of bath they'd have to give her would be too traumatic so we have to rely on a combination of pet wipes and time to get her fur back to normal.

What's a damn shame is that no one's ever done an infomercial about a cat degreaser, because that's the one product that Fletch would buy.

Reluctant Adult Life Lesson:

Unless you enjoy wiping Vaseline smears off of every surface your cat touches for the rest of her natural life, pay attention to your surroundings.

C·H·A·P·T·E·R T·H·I·R·T·E·E·N

Role Models

Once in a while, I question our choice to remain child-free.

It's not that I don't love our pets and enjoy the rich, full lives we've built for ourselves, but there's always going to a small part of me that asks, *What if?* No matter how happy anyone is with their choices, I believe it's human nature to wonder about the path not taken.

If Fletch and I reproduced, I have to wonder—what would our kid be like? We always assumed that our progeny[106] would have my twisted sense of humor and his twisted world view and would thus end up a supervillain, or at the very least, wouldn't get into a decent college because of a piss-poor attitude and problem with authority figures.

....

[106] Holden if it was a boy, and Browning, Caroline, or Phoebe if it was a girl, all of which you're welcome to steal.

After we were married, and at the age it would have been appropriate to have kids, we were broke. Flat broke. *Bitter Is the New Black* broke. Not only did we not have health insurance—we could barely keep a roof over our heads, let alone have the kind of coin to throw around on onesies and Pampers. More importantly, our lives were completely chaotic and we weren't about to subject another human being to our shitty choices and circumstances.

Plus, neither one of us had the greatest role models in terms of how families should operate. Apparently—and I didn't know this until well into my thirties—it's actually *not* cool for families to routinely gang up on one another, nor is gossiping about whoever isn't in the room. Functional families are nice to one another and they understand that pitting one child against the other will only instill a sense of sibling rivalry that can never, ever be overcome.[107]

By the time we had our finances back on track, we both felt too old to bring kids into the mix. (What if I spent the past twenty years on birth control only to find out it didn't matter because I couldn't have kids anyway? I'd be apoplectic!) And I'd be lying if I said a houseful of sticky plastic ovens and Matchbox cars and (having to share my) Barbie shoes holds any appeal.

Yet when I hang out with my friend Wendy's daughters, I'm always smitten, likely because they're almost exactly like me.[108] The last time the girls were here her youngest took a long, contemplative look around the backyard and then said all matter-of-fact, "Jen, when you die, I want your house." Wendy was mortified, but in my opinion, you can't get a better compliment than that.

....

107 Ahem. AHEM.
108 Despite Wendy's best efforts.

Would we be the kind of parents who treat our kid like a status symbol, especially given that we now live in the super-class-conscious, ultra-competitive North Shore suburbs depicted in John Hughes movies? Would I be the mother who'd run the family into financial ruin to make sure my girl had more Louis Vuitton bags and Rock & Republic jeans than any of her classmates so she'd have a positive self-image? I suspect I might.

I bet I'd work hard to expose my child to culture early and often so she wouldn't be the asshat afraid to go out to dinner when her Indian roommate craves tandoori chicken. And if maybe she'd been *more* places and tried *more* things than the rest of her peer group? I'd probably be okay with that, too.

Of course, all my questions are answered the day I meet Margo.

But before I get to Margo, allow me to set the scene. In *Inferno*, Dante depicts an allegorical journey through the nine circles of Hell. Yet if Dante were penning his epic poem today, he'd have included the tenth circle of Hell—the Whole Foods in Deerfield, Illinois.

Nowhere has the motto "abandon all hope, ye who enter here" been more appropriate. Don't get me wrong—the store itself is spacious, clean, and expansive, stocked with the kind of organic, grass-fed, ethically farmed, positive-self-esteem-having products that cause the otherwise sane to take out second mortgages in order to shop here.[109]

The problem is that this particular store is catnip for the clueless. From the parking lot dotted with third-row seating Suburbans

---

[109] Whole Paycheck? More like Whole 401K.

covered in pro-environment bumper stickers to the pacifists who will *cut you* for the last jar of almond butter, it's like entering an arena where irony ceases to exist.

In this Whole Foods, I routinely have to weave in and out of carts where soccer moms block the aisle while prattling into their Bluetooths about babysitters, back to school, and Burgundy while hippies and hipsters alike debate the merits of hemp milk and silly knit hats.

I hate them all equally, but I'm on a mission and I must endure.

I've finally plowed my way through almost all the annoying obstacles between the front door and the deli counter when I'm waylaid by a woman in pajama bottoms yelling at a clerk about a stolen pocketbook. According to the gal whose pants are covered in graphic depictions of Snoopy playing the tambourine, she left her purse in her cart and then "walked away for a little while" and she couldn't find her purse or her cart when she returned.

Although no one deserves to be a victim of a crime, when she's out in public at three p.m. wearing Peanuts pj's, I have to wonder if perhaps she didn't bring this on herself.

Maybe someone like me walked off with her purse. You know, largely honest and law-abiding, but so overcome with the stupidity of abandoning one's bag and being dressed for bed in the middle of the day that they felt this idiot deserved a little tough love.

Or maybe the woman just strolled away and came back to the wrong aisle and her handbag is still sitting there in her cart all forlorn and lonely in front of the Puffins cereal display.

Most likely this store employs the kind of staff who embark on Idiot Patrols to keep their customers from Social Darwinism–ing their way out of existence and her handbag is waiting for her at the customer service desk.

Regardless, I want some damn kale salad and it's my only reason for being here and not the adorable little Sunset Foods market around the corner from my house. Until I learn to perfect their in-house recipe in my own kitchen, I'm stuck in the tenth level with jammie-panted morons.

I finally arrive at the counter and I wait to be served. While I'm standing here, a well-heeled mother and her even better-heeled child of maybe five or six cut in front of me. The kid's clearly just come from ballet practice, judging from her tight bun and leotard. However, her dance outfit is topped in a pair of D&G jeans, which cost approximately what I pay for my student loans each month. She's also wearing Hunter Wellington boots. I know they're pricey because I tried on a pair and ultimately didn't buy them.[110]

The child tugs on her mother's arm, then whispers something in her ear. Then the mom says to the deli clerk, "Margo wants to know what kind of sushi you have today."

Suddenly all the resentment I feel towards this kid and her three-hundred-dollar jeans and fancy boots and pushy mom melts away. How badass is it that a little girl has been so adventurous and open-minded that she's not afraid of a little raw fish? I went three decades before I ever tasted so much as a California roll. And, if Margo has designs on being a prima ballerina, it's admirable that she's already making such healthy food choices.

Margo tugs on her mom's sleeve again.

"Margo wants to know if the rice is extra fresh."

....

[110] More because of my tubby calves than cost, but that's not the point.

Um, okay, not only does Margo appreciate tasty sushi, but she also has an eye towards quality. Maybe once Margo retires from the American Ballet Theatre, she'll become a chef. Her finely honed palate is going to set the culinary world on fire! That's kind of righteous and I'm totally not judging her or her mom, tempting though it may be. In the old neighborhood, I saw nothing but listless kids careening through life without a goal or a plan, so it's refreshing to see a child who's got it going on.

"Margo wants to know if the rice is extra-sticky. The last time it was almost too sticky."

So Margo thinks she's Iron Chef.

Which is fine, and far better than her spending her first six years on earth consuming nothing but hot dogs and chicken fingers. Of course, Margo's refined taste buds are standing between me and my goddamned kale salad, but it's no problem. Really. No problem.

"Margo needs a taste first."

Margo needs to learn how to say "please."

"Margo enjoyed the escolar you carried last week. Margo wants to know if there's any more in the back."

Margo goes to Montessori school, doesn't she?

"Margo wants wasabi but she doesn't like the wasabi you have on display now. Margo wants to know if there's other wasabi that's like wasabi, only less wasabi-like."

And now I'm done.

At this point I'd like to shake both mother and child, shouting, *"What the fuck, lady? MARGO IS SIX! MARGO KNOWS NOTHING! MARGO EATS PASTE!"*

But I don't, largely because the Whole Foods Idiot Patrol is still dealing with the lady in the pajamas. They're probably not prepared to fight a war on two fronts.

Also? Margo's the exact reason that Fletch and I shouldn't—and won't—have children.

But we will have kale salad.

So there's that.

Reluctant Adult Lesson Learned:

Figure out how to do it yourself and you'll never have to tolerate an unpleasant situation again.

Jen's Better Than Whole Foods Kale Salad

1 bunch kale, washed and split with stems removed (the stems are bitter)

Juice of one fresh lemon

2 tablespoons extra-virgin olive oil

2 heaping tablespoons pine nuts

2 heaping tablespoons dried cranberries

Salt, freshly ground pepper, and garlic powder
to taste

*Tear kale into chunks and massage with oil and lemon
juice. Allow leaves to marinate for at least ten minutes.
Toss with nuts, cranberries, and seasonings. If desired, add
crumbled goat cheese, slivers of red pepper, or chunks of
tomato. Dressed salad will last overnight in refrigerator
and is just as fresh on the second day.*

Peer Pressure

*C*ome on.

You know you want to.

All your friends are doing it.

Come on.

You're the last of your crowd to try it.

No, really, it's cool. You'll like it. If you don't like it, you don't have to. No one would make fun of you. Much.

Do it.

DO IT.

Angie does it. Poppy does it. Wendy does it.

You trust Angie, Poppy, and Wendy, right? They wouldn't steer you wrong.

Okay, Blackbird doesn't do it, but she's so cool in other ways that she more than makes up for it.

Come on.

Give it a try. Just this once. It'll be our little secret.

I know you've hesitated in the past, because it's like a gateway drug. Do this, and then who knows what path it might lead you down. But you're strong. You can resist related temptations, right?

Just try it.

One time.

Think of how good it's going to feel.

Do it.

Do it.

DO IT.

You're in the privacy of your own home.

No one will know but you.

And if it doesn't work out, you don't have to tell anyone. You can take that secret with you to the grave.

Come on. You want to. I know you want to. I can see your hand trembling over your mouse as you vacillate.

Just do it.

Click it.

Click it.

CLICK IT NOW.

Before I can change my mind, I press the button and the next minute passes in a blur as I detail my most personal information.

The train's in motion now.

The horse is out of the barn and I can't unring that bell.

This is happening.

This is real.

This is coming.

That's right . . . I just bought my first skirted swimsuit.

Hold me.

The skirted swimsuit always seemed like the pinnacle of adult-hood to me, and not in a good way. I naturally assumed that buying one was the first step to rubber flower-petal bathing caps, orthotic sneakers, and an AARP membership. But over the past few years, I've been noticing more and more of my friends getting hip to the skirt.

When my girlfriends and I spent a long weekend at the beach last year, I was the only one wearing a regular one piece. Every-one else had on cute tank tops with flippy little tennis-skirt-type bottoms.[111] And you know what? They were adorable. In the past, skirted suits have had a Ziegfeld Follies/1920s Miss America Pag-eant vibe, but now they're sporty and really not an object of shame. It's like manufacturers *want* to bring in a clientele who can't remember where they were when Kennedy was shot.

As my friends explained, the skirt's not about hip and thigh concerns. They've opted for extra coverage because of the new and, frankly, unrealistic, hair-removal demands. As they see it they can go skirt, or go Brazilian. They've chosen the route that doesn't involve having your lady parts manhandled by bossy Rus-sian waxers.

While we were at the beach, I admired how they could go straight from the water to walk without having to find a sarong or pull dry shorts on over a damp suit.

....

[111]   Except for Blackbird who was in a bikini. As she's someone who'll hap-pily visit a nude beach, she has no say in this discussion.

I was intrigued by the skirt, yet somehow the act of buying one seemed like defeat. For me the idea of the skirt always felt the first step down the slippery slope of socks and Birkenstocks, four thirty p.m. dinners, and sending angry letters to the editor.

When it came time to buy suits for this year, I opt for my usual—a black Miracle Suit tank with underwire and pink color-blocking on the top for swimming, and a lower-cut black tank with side shirring for tanning. They joined the collection of ten suits I already own in the exact same cuts and colors, each its own degree of chlorine-ravaged. I receive them and I wear them and I like them, yet there's a tiny part of me that wonders, *What if . . .*

Maybe it's because of the suit sale, maybe it's due to the Ambien, or maybe I, too, am weary of maintaining unrealistic standards of grooming, but when I see the darling blue-and-green-dotted swim dress on LLBean.com, I take the plunge.

When it arrives a few days later, I make a big production of showing it to Fletch, waving that dotted Lycra flag like I've just been liberated.

He nods and says, "It's very nice."

I guess *some people* don't recognize the beginnings of a revolution.

For me, I feel like I've entered a new phase as I throw off my clothes and slip into my skirted suit. This suit represents the Next Big Step in my life. The skirt embodies everything about who I'm going to be. Women who wear skirted swimsuits are mature and regal and they do cool stuff like patronize the arts.[112] They know who they are and what they're about and they're not afraid to tell the world exactly what they think.

....

[112] Does that sound right? I don't mean they mock the arts.

You know who wears skirted swimsuits? Serious women. Important women. Women who rule. I bet you anything that both Margaret Thatcher and Queen Elizabeth embrace the swim dress. You think Golda Meir or Indira Gandhi ran around in tankinis? Think again.

I admire myself in the mirror, noting how even though the skirt only skims the very top of my thighs, the dress conceals a variety of ills. I mentally kick myself, wondering why I resisted its siren song for so long.

Yes.

I'll say it.

The swim dress is genius.

The swim dress is full of win.

I head outside with my book, planning to bask in the sun until I get hot enough to want to dive in; it doesn't take long.

As I ease into the water, I notice the skirt doing something . . . odd. There's a whole underlining that hugs my body like a regular suit, but the dress part has separate material that starts at my bust line. The longer I'm in the water, the more the suit seems to expand. The fabric around me begins to swell and bloom, as though I were clad in a giant tampon that is currently sucking up all the blue pool water.

The entire time I'm in the water, I'm enveloped by wads and wads of superfluous cloth. It's . . . disconcerting and I feel waterlogged. While I swim, I have the distinct impression that my bathing suit is trying to drown me.

When I get out, the sodden suit material now reaches my knees and is so heavy that I have to hoist myself up the steps, staggering under its excess weight.

Then as I settle into my chair, I'm swaddled in mounds and

mounds of damp bathing suit. Within minutes, I'm shivering despite the eighty-degree temperature because I feel like I'm trapped under a load of drenched sheets.

I last another five minutes before I go inside, step out of this soaking wet albatross, and step back into one of my unliberating, unforgiving, thigh-revealing tank suits.

And I have to wonder if the great ladies in history couldn't have accomplished a little bit more if they weren't weighed down in thirty pounds of swim skirt.

My girlfriends have come to my house for our annual long weekend. I'm here in my thigh-revealing tank suit and they're all done up in their adorable, flippy swim skirts. I watch as their suits engorge around them, and they're suddenly surrounded by circles of sodden Spandex.

When we get out of the pool to eat lunch, the complaints begin in earnest.

"*Jesus Christ, it's freaking cold out here,*" says Angie.

"*I feel like I'm wearing a wet diaper,*" says Wendy.

"*There's just so much fabric, I can't seem to dry off,*" says Poppy.

One by one, they peel off to put on regular clothes to finish their lunches.

And there I sit in my girlish one-piece, smug as a bug in a rug.

Oh, tank suit . . . I shall never forsake you again.

Reluctant Adult Lesson Learned:

"Everyone is doing it" was a lousy reason to go along with the crowd in eighth grade and it's a lousy reason now. If the whole carpool wants to jump off a bridge, then demand they drop you off at the office first.

How Do You Talk to Girls

"*You know I feel so dirty when they start cooking cute; I want to tell her that I love her but the point is probably moot.*"

I finish dicing the last of the celery for the mirepoix while I wait for the pancetta to finish browning. Oh, crispy pork fat, you're the most delicious pork fat of them all.

As I survey the rest of my *mise en place* ingredients, I'm overcome with a sense of satisfaction. A couple of years ago, I was content just to shove a couple of naked pork chops under the broiler, splash on some preservative-laden barbecue sauce, and call it a meal. But now? I'm creating a culinary masterpiece, slowly building flavor one layer at a time. In two hours, this is going to be the most beautiful Bolognese sauce anyone has ever seen, and that is not an exaggeration.

"'*Cause she's watching him with mirepoix!*"

I giggle and toss the celery in the pot.

"And she's lovin' him with that carrot, I just know it!"

There go the carrots.

"And he's sautéing golden brown late, late at night!"

And finally, the onions. I grab my spatula-microphone to belt out the next verse. *"I wish that I had Bo-lo-gnese! I want Bo-lo-gnese! Where can I find a fresh sauce like that?"*[113]

My interest in cooking neatly coincided with buying my first iPod. Turns out I don't get so bored with all the scrubby-peely-choppy tedium if there's music involved. Yeah, we have a decent stereo, but Fletch has a tendency to overcomplicate home electronics, so the path from "off" to "The Smiths" requires a master's degree in sound engineering. Also, I'm far too impatient to listen to a whole CD at a time and I tend to go all MC JazzyJen,[114] and having to switch artists every three and a half minutes is exhausting. Cooking's one of the few situations in which I can multitask[115] and I'm totally over eating cereal for dinner, so it's all worked out nicely.

As I stir and shimmy and slaughter the lyrics, I feel a presence. I glance up to find Fletch frowning in the doorway.

"What's up?" I ask, removing my snappy new replacement earbud.

(Libby ate the last set.)

(Libby, bless her heart, is kind of an asshole.)

He looks grim. "Did you know Rick Springfield is dead?"

What? No! Noooooo! Not Rick Springfield! Rick, also known as Dr. Noah Drake to *General Hospital* fans, was my first real musical love. Before he came along with his velvet-revolver voice,

---

[113] What, you don't change the words when you sing?
[114] My DJ name.
[115] Notable failures include driving while talking to passengers, swimming while cocktailing, and running while breathing.

feathered hair, and stunning assortment of Members Only jackets, my interest in music was strictly secondhand, an offshoot of my brother's esoteric band du jour.[116] Much as I tolerated the Marshall Tucker Band and Jethro Tull, nothing about their songs really spoke to me.[117]

Rick Springfield's one-two punch of talent and good looks had me smitten. I'd sit in my bedroom, tape recorder at hand, listening to Kasey Kasem's *American Top 40*, ready to hit RECORD the second I heard the opening notes of his melodic stylings. And every week, I'd buy *Tiger Beat* or *Teen Beat,* basing my purchase decision on whichever magazine featured more pictures of him, and, please, Jesus? Let him be shirtless.

I found out recently one of my friends harbored the same kind of crush on our boy Rick. Except she grew up in Beverly Hills and she and her wealthy friends would pool their allowance to hire a limo driver to cruise past his house whenever they could. To this day, she can recite his old license plate number. I thought I was a committed fan when I framed his *Working Class Dog* album cover, but clearly not. Also? I suspect her allowance was higher than mine.

"Jessie's Girl" was one of the first videos I ever, saw, too, and Rick tore out a piece of my tender thirteen-year-old heart every time he smashed the mirror with his guitar neck in utter frustration. *No, Rick, no!* I'd shout. *Not Jessie's Girl! You don't want Jessie's Girl! You wish that you had Jen-ni-fer! You want Jen-ni-fer! As I'm only thirteen, I don't have a real concept of what*

....

[116] With a brief but intense dalliance with Andy Gibb. But I was only in fourth grade back then. No one really understands true love until middle school.

[117] The flute doesn't rock as hard as one may think.

statutory rape entails, but that's not the point; I should be your girl.
You should spray-paint MY *name on that brick wall. My parents*
won't mind.

The pinnacle of my young life was when my friend's dad drove
a carload of freshmen girls up to South Bend to see Rick perform
at our first concert ever.[118] Of course the minute I discovered a re-
cording artist who was sure to return my love[119] I was totes over
Rick, but for a brief moment in time he was my pink heart, yellow
moon, orange star, and green clover. To this day, every time I see
a bull terrier wearing a short-sleeve dress shirt and a skinny tie, my
heart beats a tiny bit faster.

"I can't believe it! He was fine last week—I mean, I just saw an
interview with him about *Late, Late at Night*.[120] What happened?"

Fletch's lips get all white and puckered. "Your singing killed
him."

Nice. I swat at him with a saucy spatula but he manages to
dodge me. "If you're going to come in here and be all critical while
I'm slaving over this gorgeous Bolognese sauce, *you* can have
Lucky Charms for dinner."

"Jen, I could hear you over the sound of my power tools. In
the basement. At first I thought the ungodly screeching was one of
the cats caught in the drill press, but then when I really listened, I
realized they wouldn't howl to the tune of 'Jessie's Girl.'"

After an (insincere) apology and a promise to tackle the dishes,
I grudgingly allow Fletch to have my Bolognese for dinner and it *is*
spectacular. The trick is adding a quarter pound of diced mort-

---

[118] My friend Poppy's first concert was the Rolling Stones and Blackbird's
was Led Zeppelin. Yet when I told them mine, they were jealous.
[119] George Michael, of course.
[120] Kudos for whomever titled his memoir.

adella (with the inset pistachios if you can find 'em) and slow heat for maximum flavor concentration. And don't even get me started on the importance of using San Marzano tomatoes!

While we're eating, I reflect on my first concert experience. Now that I'm an adult, I have a whole new appreciation for how much bourbon it must have taken Mr. Moon, my girlfriend's poor father, to wash the sound of a station wagon full of shrieking freshmen (and the stench of Aqua Net and Love's Baby Soft) out of his head. Yet here I am thirty years later and the night's as vivid in my memory now as it was then and so I'm thankful he afforded us the experience.

"Hey," I say, the kernel of an idea forming, "we should take Joanna's daughter to her first concert. How fun would that be?"

Fletch deliberately sets down his fork. "By 'we' you mean you and Joanna, right?"

"Um, yeah. Considering the last concert you saw was Ministry, I'm thinking Taylor Swift isn't quite your jam."

"Then I wholeheartedly approve."

In *Atlas Shrugged*, Ayn Rand stated that there's no such thing as real altruism. She espoused the principle of ethical egotism, meaning that a person's moral obligation is to promote their own welfare.

Translation?

I still have the musical sensibilities of a teenage girl and I kind of want to see a shitty pop concert in the guise of doing something nice for my pal's kid, so I need to find a way to make it happen.

Not long ago I asked for some upbeat, treadmill-worthy iTunes suggestions and I ended up downloading the super-sugar-pop playlist of your typical eighth grader, full of glitter and Katy Perry and Lady Gaga and Justin Bieber. Despite an almost pathological desire to douse that kid with a can of mousse, I've played "Baby" more times than I care to mention. So the idea of taking Joanna's daughter to see him wasn't without appeal. More importantly, I could write off the cost of my tickets in the name of research—win, win!

Joanna threw a wrench in the works, however. "Anna doesn't like Justin Bieber. She says he's for younger girls."

Fine.

I have the musical taste of a tween.

We can still work around this.

Joanna buys four tickets for the Chicago leg of the *Glee* tour and her daughter Anna loses her freaking mind when she finds out we're going. (Joanna doesn't let her watch the whole show, but she gets to see the musical numbers and I guess that's enough.)

I make sure Anna's aware that it's me who masterminded this whole idea because, for some odd reason, it's important for this kid to like me. I've never been one to win a child's favor before, but this is Joanna's daughter we're talking about and I want to be her Auntie Jen, largely because she's a fine young lady and her parents have done an amazing job of raising her. In fact, at her last birthday party, she asked for donations to the local animal shelter in lieu of presents. How cool is that?

Anna's favored me more since she came swimming here last fall and I made some decent headway with a marshmallow-scented Philosophy gift set and the *Monster High* book, but I've ground to cover still.

You see, our last big outing together was kind of a misstep. During Christmas break in 2009, Joanna and I had the bright idea to take Anna to the museum and then to high tea because Joanna's mom and her friend did this when she was Anna's age and she has such fond memories of that day.

However, our edited-for-tween-listening college stories did nothing for her,[121] nor did the Matisse exhibit.

I'm not sure how to say this next part because the last thing I ever want to do is offend Joanna. I adore her and her daughter so much, and yet I need to get it out . . . Little girls ask a lot of fucking questions.

For two hours we trudged through the museum, and, to her credit, Anna's behavior was exemplary. But she was relentless about gaining an understanding of stuff we had no idea how to answer, like why this particular artist worked in the medium he did, what's the deal with all the tiny dollhouses and who came up with the idea to miniaturize everything in the first place, and how come everyone's naked in that portrait? Good Lord, my dogs drive me to drink and they can't even talk. I can't imagine the lush I'd be with the barrage of questions all day long. Were I to hear "Hey, Mom? Hey, Mom?" that many times in a row, I'm pretty sure I'd hang myself.

Anna didn't care for much of what we saw[122] until we came upon this massive painting featuring hundreds of amoeba-looking blue circles hanging over the staircase leading down to the first floor.

Anna stopped to gaze up at it. "What's this called?" she asked.

"Oh, *liebchen*, I don't see a placard so I'm not sure," Joanna replied. "Let's try to find out."

We spent fifteen minutes looking for some sort of guide or

....

[121] Even at ten and a half, she didn't buy that we were reading the Bible with all those Sigma Nus.
[122] Likely because we're shitty docents.

description or replication in the gift shop, and failed to turn up anything. However, Anna was on a mission. She found some art that spoke to her, damn it, and we were going to find out its backstory.

Or die trying.

Another ten minutes of interrogation later, I realized that A) Anna has a brilliant career in litigation ahead of her, B) I should buy better museum shoes, and C) I need to nip this question foolishness in the bud.

I snapped my fingers. "Hey! Wait, I totally remember! The artist is Von Rizcheck and it's called *Ebb and Flow*, like those iceberg pieces you see in *National Geographic* specials about Alaska. Notice the darker blue parts around the circles? That's the Antarctic Sea and the painting is the artist expressing his concerns about global warming."

Seemingly satisfied, we finally moved on.

Above Anna's head, Joanna mouthed, "Von *Rizcheck*?"

I shrugged and replied, "Maybe?"

And there in the Art Institute, I learned a valuable lesson that will surely change the course of history because I'm the first person to have discovered it:

Sometimes lying to children is the path of least resistance.

That's my gift to you. You're welcome.

Anyway, Anna eventually found out the real story behind the painting[123] and now perceives me to be full of shit, so this concert is a prime opportunity to work on my image.

Speaking of my image, what do I wear to impress a twelve-

---

[123] It's by Georgia O'Keeffe and is called *Sky Above Clouds*. I would have gotten away with it if it weren't for your fine, meddling school system, DuPage County!

year-old? Joanna's going to the show in full Coach Sue Sylvester gear but A) I don't have an Adidas track suit and B) no. I've been all about the beachy-preppy-tunic-and-long-white-shorts thing this summer, but I'm not sure the kids are into J. Jill and I bet their math teacher wears polo shirts, so my usual Lacoste is out, too.

I settle on a funky white T-shirt and some stupid pants with silly stitching and sparkly side panels I bought while in a panic in Pittsburgh after spilling an in-flight Bloody Mary on my good travelin' trousers. (Lousy turbulence.) I loop a lightweight Burberry scarf around my neck and throw on some wedge sandals. To curry extra favor, I wear the necklace Anna made for me out of a domino and some glitter paint. When I'm donning the pants, I notice the button is one enormous rhinestone and I wonder exactly how drunk I was when I got off the plane and headed to the mall. A lot, I think.

I'm meeting the gals at Allstate Arena. When I park, I pay special attention to being as close to the exit aisle as possible. The last place I want to be is trapped in this parking lot for an hour with twenty thousand little girls all hopped up on Vitamin Glee. What's surprising is given the audience, I thought I'd be in Minivan Central, but most of the vehicles around me are all shiny and new and sporty. Weird.

Anyway, I'm excited for the concert! I've adored *Glee* since the premiere episode, which lives on my iPod. Every time I take a flight longer than an hour—which is almost daily when I'm touring—I rewatch it. I normally have distaste for pilot episodes because they're almost uniformly terrible with stilted dialogue and awkward exposition, no matter how good the show is once it hits its stride. The problem is a pilot episode has to establish the why here/why now aspect, as well as providing enough character development to make the viewer invested, so they tend to be all words and little action. Rarely are pilots anything less than painful.

However, the first episode of *Glee* was the best I've ever seen, from the second Mr. Schuester stepped out of his crappy old Honda to the final chorus of "Don't Stop Believing." Everything about it was perfection, which is why I feel it's my job to voice my displeasure on the Internet every Tuesday night after yet another disappointing episode. My constant constructive criticism is exactly what the show's writers need to get back on their game.

Again, you're welcome.[124]

I find Joanna, Anna, and her friend Morgan easily. Joanna's stocked my seat with a large beer and a cold water, unsure of which I prefer.

She's a keeper.

As we survey the crowd, I'm surprised by the demographic. I'd envisioned Rick Springfield, Take Two, except there are people here over the age of fifteen. A whole bunch of them, in fact. And they're not all chicks. At least half the audience is comprised of gay men. Guess that explains all the fancy cars in the parking lot.

Of particular interest is the couple sitting directly behind us. I'd guess they were in their sixties and don't have kids or grandkids with them. We're not sure why they're here. We're trying to figure out their story when the lights come up and a shaggy-haired break-dancer appears onstage. When the roar of the audience dies down, I hear the gentleman ask his companion, "Is that Justin Bieber?"

Turns out they're not sure why they're here, either.

---

[124] And P.S., Very Special Episodes are a privilege, not a right, and aren't meant to air every damn week. Ryan Murphy, I love you, man, but enough already.

After the opening act, we have a short respite before the main event and that's when Anna and Morgan ready their signs. They spent the afternoon perfecting their artwork and I step back to admire their craft.

"'Anna + Artie = love'?" I ask Joanna. Although Artie's character is adorable with his nerd glasses and wheelchair, I kind of thought the girls would go for more obvious choices like Finn or the blond boy with the lips.[125]

Joanna beams with pride. "She's sensitive."

The lights come up again and the opening notes to "Don't Stop Believing" play. And that's when I hear The Noise.

The Noise is like nothing I've ever heard before and probably nothing I'll ever hear again. Were one to try to replicate it, one would need to set off an atom bomb in a bubble gum factory or perhaps burst a Hello Kitty Macy's Thanksgiving Day Parade balloon with a unicorn horn.

The Noise sucks all the air out of the arena.

The Noise causes dogs three states away to bark.

The Noise could simultaneously cure and cause cancer.

The Noise refers to the collective gasp coming from twenty thousand twelve-year-old girls and gay men, jointly sucking in their breath at the same time before screaming themselves apeshit, ratfuck, banana-sandwich crazy over cute little Chris Colfer.

I'm probably going to need a second beer.

Two songs into the performance, I've lost a large portion of my patience as well as most of my hearing to the screaming. So when the small, tidy, peevish Asian man in knife-creased khakis taps

---

[125] Or, if you're Team Cougar, Puck.

me on the shoulder to say something, I'm in the mood to rumble. I can't make out his words the first time, so Joanna leans in to listen when he repeats himself.

"Listen, ma'am, I paid a lot of money for my seats and your little girls are blocking my view. It's not fair for me to have paid all this money and then all I see is the back of their posters."

Seriously, dude? You're what, fifty? And you're surprised that there are kids here ruining the performance for you? What is this, Ravinia? Tanglewood? A night at the opera? Give me a break, pal.

When I was the girls' age, we were vaulting over dividers and shoving security guards out of the way to get closer to Mr. Springfield. If we had to, we'd have slit people's throats and ridden their bodies like toboggans down from the balcony if it got us six inches closer to the stage. Plus, you're sitting down, asshole. Of course you can't see over the signs. You don't sit down at a concert! What the fuck is wrong with you?

As I'm drawing a breath to explain to the gentleman that he need just bend over and I will find a new home for those posters immediately, Joanna jumps in. "Girls, put the signs down. Sorry, sir!" Then she smiles and he returns to his seat.

Oh.

I guess that's another way to play it.

Good to know.

As it turns out, the kids don't bother me at the show, but the adults are making me nutty. There's a woman across the narrow aisle from me whom I would very much enjoy punching, as much for the ear-piercing screams that erupt from her piehole every ten seconds as for her "dancing," which is really more of a full-body contact sport. Even though we're six feet apart, she's nailed me in the back three times with all her flailing.

She's been pantomiming the words to most of the lyrics, e.g., raising her glass during the Pink song, putting an L on her head during "Loser Like Me," and waving her naked ring finger around for "Single Ladies." She's doing the kind of emoting that makes me want to kick my television during *Idol* auditions. Also, she's my size, yet did not get the Very Important Big Girl Memo about bras never being "optional."

Having already been deafened, I swear if I'm robbed of my vision by one of her free-range ta-tas, I'm going to wear her skin as a coat.

"I'm going to shove the bitch down the stairs," I tell Joanna. The only reason I haven't is because I don't want to make a bad impression on Anna.

"Oh, come on, she's just really happy."

"No, she's obnoxious. That's a subtle but crucial difference. I hate her. Everyone sitting around her hates her. The world hates her."

Always the optimist, Joanna replies, "The guy with her doesn't hate her. He must be her boyfriend."

"She doesn't have a boyfriend; she has a *cat*."

"How do you know?"

"Because the guy started crying when Chris Colfer sang 'I Want to Hold Your Hand.'"

Joanna's face arranges into the kind of wry expression that speaks of an entire afternoon of dealing with "Hey, Mom! Hey, Mom!"

Okay, okay, message received.

I'm on my best behavior for the rest of the show. I experience a surreal moment when Finn performs his version of "Jessie's Girl" and every twelve-year-old in the joint loses her fucking marbles.

With the wailing and crying and rending of garments happening all around me, I can't help but recall that similar night thirty years ago when another young rock star filled a similar arena. I'm simultaneously shocked and thrilled at how every girl in the joint knows every word.

Maybe someday they'll be grown-ups, singing in their own kitchens, making their own Bolognese sauces, and recalling what was, to that point, the greatest night in their own lives.

Yet I can't help but comment to Joanna, "Rick Springfield is currently performing at Indian casinos. How mad is he right about now?"

I slip out after the first encore. Though I'd like to see the much-hyped production number when Artie finally stands up from his wheelchair and safety-dances, my desire to exit the parking lot expediently is stronger.

When I get home, I tell Fletch all about the show and he's the one who insists we raise a glass to my friend's dad Mr. Moon.

Even though it's thirty years later, he's still earned it.

A month later, I find out one day too late that Rick Springfield himself played my little town's fireworks celebration on the Fourth of July.

Part of me kicked myself for not reading the local paper sooner, and part of me was glad to have missed it.

I wonder, would I have still swooned at the sight of him, willing to commit a very public homicide just to stand closer to him? Or would I have just felt so damn old seeing him after all this time?

Ultimately, the idea of my first rock god performing for a pittance on a small festival stage breaks my heart.

Yet knowing that his songs—or at least the most important one—can still bring an entire arena to its feet, makes me feel better.

Still crazy for you, Dr. Noah Drake.

Rock on.

Reluctant Adult Lesson Learned:

Speak with an investment advisor about planning for your retirement, because, really? You never know what the future holds.

Ring of Fire

"*I*'ve got it!"

I dash down the stairs to the door, shoving pushy, barky dogs out of the way before grabbing money off the bookshelf.

I slip out the door to trade the cash for a brown paper bag from which exotic spices emanate. The restaurant must be busy tonight; the owner usually delivers the order himself, largely because his young daughter is in love with Libby and she likes to ride along. But that's no surprise; every little girl loves Libby.

Physically, there's not much difference between Maisy and Libby—they both have strong, stocky bodies and big, square heads. Maisy with her super-smiley face and tan and white coloring actually looks less foreboding than Libby, but Maisy isn't nearly as popular with the Elmo set. Being around Maisy is like strolling a Moroccan souk—one second, you're minding your own business, innocently perusing a lovely display of woven wicker baskets, and the next, BAM! A cobra pops out ninja-style and attaches to your face.

Granted Maisy's a kisser, *never* a biter, but it's really hard to explain the difference to a wailing kindergartner.[126]

Libby's equally enthusiastic, yet more gentle. Earlier this summer my friend Becca was over with her family. We kept the dogs inside for a while because we knew her little girl was terrified of them. Flash forward an hour and an introduction—instead of swimming, her daughter spent the afternoon leading Libby around with her finger looped through her collar, while Libby obeyed every command given to her.

What can I say? Libby's a charmer.

Of course, later that night, Libby counter-surfed herself a packet of lightbulbs, chewing everything to shards on the kitchen rug.[127]

The next day I received a thank-you note from Becca reading, *"My daughter wants a dog. Your dog. Beware a preschooler in princess shoes scaling the fence to dognap."* So it's no surprise that the daughter of the Thai restaurateur always wants to see the puppy. Libby has that kind of effect on kids.

The Thai place also knows us because it's pretty much the only delivery we order. When we lived in the city, we could get every possible variety of ethnic foods, from Afghan to Vietnamese. But the unfortunate trade-off for safe streets and an outstanding

----

[126] We give families an extensive briefing before they're even allowed to meet the dogs. Regardless of warnings, the kids are always, "I love doggie kisses!" but they fail to anticipate the French part.

[127] She was fine. The only one who ended up bleeding was me when I cleaned up the mess.

public school system is that there are almost no decent restaurants. We tried ten different, disgusting delivery joints[128] until we found the Thai/Japanese place and now we're frequent fliers.

I bring the bag upstairs because we're allowed to eat in the TV room only on delivery nights. Granted, the worst that can happen is a small soy sauce spill, yet we've created an elaborate system of carpet-saving checks and balances, largely because Libby's wreaked such havoc on them. When we first adopted her, we called her Whizzy Libby and The Bladder o' Doom.

With a lot of training—A LOT—she's better about holding it. However, the more she learns to control her elimination, the more she acts out in other carpet-hating ways. Like eating pens. And magic markers. And bottles of Lincoln Park After Dark nail polish.

I settle in and queue up the DVR. "*Burn Notice* okay?"[129]

"Definitely," Fletch replies, systematically unloading the bag. He first lays out packets of soy sauce, napkins, and chopsticks before opening containers and inspecting their contents. "What'd we get? Tempura—mmm, Pad Thai with chicken, that's me, some jasmine rice, and . . . no. Jen, what is wrong with you?"

He's referring to the Panang Thai Curry, otherwise known as my kryptonite.

The thing is with Superman?

He knew he couldn't handle kryptonite.

He hated kryptonite.

He actively avoided kryptonite.

He would never willingly order kryptonite because he was

---

[128] Although it's difficult to ruin a pizza, it can be done.
[129] If you haven't already figured it out, Michael Westen is so the new Jack Bauer.

smart enough to know that kryptonite would cause him to spend the entire night crying on the toilet, cursing the state of his bung-hole. Week after week after week.

That's when Libby dashes into the room, proudly carrying a plastic toilet brush in her mouth.

"It is truly impossible for you to learn, isn't it?" he asks. Whether he's directing this comment to me or the dog is yet to be determined.

I don't reply. Instead, I take the brush back to the bathroom while Libby trots along beside me. Then I point to the brush and tell her, "Leave it!"

What I don't mention is that Mama's probably going to need this later.

Panang Thai Curry seems innocuous enough because it's mostly coconut milk and there's barely any chili powder in it. Plus, it's indescribably delicious because of the basil and red pepper, with a hint of lime. The addition of fish sauce sounds grotesque, but that's what gives it such depth of flavor.

The first time I ate it I tried to use a fork and I dripped it all over the place, which is one of the reasons we[130] instituted the We Eat Upstairs Only on Delivery Night rule. Also, when I finished I was covered in broth. Fletch said I looked liked I'd been through a curry car wash.

I ordered the dish because it sounded like a little adventure for my mouth. Plus I could secretly congratulate myself for moving so

....

130 Read: Fletch.

far away from the cheeseburger-and-orange-soda comfort zone of my youth. Through college and my early professional years, I didn't have the budget to improve my palate and enjoyed many, many presweetened-cereal-based meals. But after almost passing out in Target after yet another blood sugar spike, I had to accept that there's more to life than empty carbs.

Also, I've talked enough smack about the employees at the Elston Target and it's not in my best interest to be unconscious around them.

Almost as soon as I discovered a deep and abiding love for Panang Thai Curry, I discovered that I can't digest it. Maybe I don't have a tolerance for so much spice or it may be that I ruined my colon from years and years of running Artificial Red Dye #7 through it. Regardless, I need to cease and desist with the Panang Thai Curry because I'm murdering myself from the inside out.

And yet I can't stop myself from stuffing it in my mouth, much like Libby can't help but chew up my cordless mouse every time I accidentally leave my office door open.

It's a problem.

For both of us.

Panang Thai Curry chooses you last for kickball.

Panang Thai Curry asks you to sit with her at the cool table at lunch specifically so she can mock your *Flashdance* sweatshirt.

Panang Thai Curry snaps your bra straps.

Panang Thai Curry won't stop you when you've tucked your prairie skirt into your panty hose.

Panang Thai Curry tells the boys on the bus you have your period.

Panang Thai Curry invites you to the Huey Lewis concert but never shows up with the tickets.

Panang Thai Curry "accidentally" mentions you smoke to your mom.

Panang Thai Curry has sex with your ex.

Panang Thai Curry thinks you're fat.

Panang Thai Curry lets your inside cat out.

Panang Thai Curry "forgets" to pay you back.

Panang Thai Curry cancels out your vote.

Panang Thai Curry uses a metal utensil on your Teflon pans.

Panang Thai Curry tapes over your unwatched *Bachelor* season finale.

Panang Thai Curry sticks you in an orange bridesmaid dress.

Panang Thai Curry ate the last piece of pie.

Panang Thai Curry steals your status update.

Panang Thai Curry doesn't put the cap back on.

Panang Thai Curry finishes all the milk and doesn't leave a note.

Panang Thai Curry swipes your top-secret baby name.

Panang Thai Curry shows your puppy exactly where you keep your gel pens.

Even though you'll probably never get it through your thick skull (or sensitive colon) PANANG THAI CURRY IS NOT YOUR FRIEND.

But your husband is.

So when he instructs the restaurant owner to never deliver Panang Thai Curry ever again, you are not allowed to divorce him because he's only trying to save your dumb ass.

Literally.

Now if he could keep the dog from pulling up the carpet in the family room, you'll all be in excellent shape.

Reluctant Adult Lesson Learned:

Being a grown-up means not staying in an abusive relationship . . . even if it's just with your colon.

Bond, Jen Bond

When I thought about adult life when I was a kid, I imagined cool stuff, like gambling in the casinos of Monte Carlo, zipping around winding mountain roads in my Aston Martin convertible, and taking top secret meetings in underground lairs.

Basically I thought all grown-ups were James Bond.

At no point did I realize the pinnacle of my own personal quest for maturity would entail this: sitting across a real dining room table in an actual dining room, debating the merits of whole versus term life insurance.

Talk to me five years ago and I'd have laughed at the thought not only of voluntarily inviting in the insurance agent but sitting in a room with him where—by design—it's impossible to eat dinner and watch *The Real Housewives of Beverly Hills* at the same time.

The agent explains, "They used to call it 'death insurance' but that bummed everyone out." Yeah, I could see that. Yet that's exactly what this is. As Fletch and I debate payout amounts, we eye one another warily, having come to the mutually horrific realization that we're both more valuable dead than alive.

I tell the agent, "Of course Fletch should be taken care of if I kick it first, but I'm not sure I want my legacy to include a boat that sleeps twelve." Fletch's stipulation for me is that I can pay off the mortgage, but not have enough cash left over for the Jocelyn Wildenstein–level of plastic surgery I'd need to rope in a new mate.[131]

There's nothing like putting a price on your own mortality to make you reflect on your life. Yeah, I'm only in my early forties now, so it's not like I'm just sitting on a plastic-covered couch by the front door with my purse in my lap, waiting for the clock to run out. However, the window for, say, auditioning for the Dallas Cowboys cheerleaders has firmly closed. Unless of course I lose Fletch and go for the full Montag. Then I'd also have to learn to dance and embrace the pairing of boots with hot pants, so this may all be a nonissue.

Anyway, after our meeting where the core message is YOU ARE GOING TO DIE, I begin to wonder if I'm living life to the fullest. Sure, I'm happy, but I was a whole lot happier before I realized I'm putting a bounty on my own damn head.

Am I accomplishing everything I want? Maybe? My books have hit the bestseller lists[132] and I've sipped wine with Hoda and Kathie Lee on the *Today* show. (Try and guess which one I'm more proud of.) But in terms of milestones, I can't come up with any and

---

[131] Granted, I'm mostly fine the way I am, but if I lose Fletch, I plan on going full-on cougar, so I'll need a number of nips/tucks to attract Taylor Lautner.

[132] Thank you for reading!! And did I tell you how pretty you look today?

my old goal of starting a Twitter war with a Kardashian seems a little juvenile now.

I wonder, do I need to create a bucket list? Do I need to spell out what I'd like to experience before I check out?

As I research other people's bucket lists, I see that "Go on an African safari" is pretty popular. Sounds exotic, yes? I'd be fascinated to experience the cradle of civilization from atop an elephant. The minute Africa rids itself of all their venomous spiders, black mambas and puff adders, and automatic weapon–toting warlords, I'm sure my insurance company will be delighted to extend coverage while I visit.

Some bucket lists reflect a desire to be more active. I see entries about swimming the English Channel,[133] running a marathon,[134] or climbing Mount Everest.[135] While I congratulate others for setting such lofty goals, I'm someone who will drive the fifty feet between Costco and Ulta rather than park somewhere in the middle so I can't imagine I'd like to add anything particularly sweaty to my list.

Adventure factors high on a lot of bucket lists and it seems like everyone wants to skydive, run with the bulls in Pamplona, and swim with sharks.

Let's break this down, shall we? Folks either want to voluntarily jump out of airplanes, take a jog in front of thousands of pounds of angry, charging bulls with nothing to protect themselves save for a bandanna and a pair of Air Nikes, or splash around with a bunch of creatures who have "man-eating" as part of their name?

....

[133] Too cold.
[134] Too hard. And too many annoying marathon runners.
[135] Too much carrying stuff and too much possibility for an avalanche and you just know I'm going to be the one everyone wants to eat.

Um, A) *you* are not James Bond, and B) is *everyone* desperate to nullify their insurance policies? Come on, people! Hazardous activities are not permissible under standard coverage![136]

Also, you don't think that sometime soon M plans to have a sit-down with one Bond, James Bond so they can renegotiate his long-term care coverage? That man is an actuarial nightmare and he's costing the British taxpayers a mint!

What's a shame is that I can't put "not die" on my bucket list, but perhaps I can invite the insurance agent over again, because the hour we spent discussing net premium earnings truly felt like an entire lifetime.

I've tabled the thoughts of my bucket list because my more immediate concern is going through this stupid insurance physical. The only upside is when you opt for private insurance, they come to you, instead of vice versa. We've been sitting at our kitchen table for an hour with a nurse, recounting every single health-related detail of our combined eighty-plus years on earth. This wouldn't be so bad except she hasn't drawn samples yet so we can't have coffee.[137]

For the most part, I've been a paragon of health with zero surgeries, actual diseases,[138] or broken bones, although more through a fluke of sturdy genetics, rather than decent planning or effort. I've only had one hospitalization and that was for pneumonia in

---

[136] Please, I beg you to make sure the purveyor of such activities has liability coverage before you strap yourself to a bungee cord and take a leap of faith.

[137] As I'm always one step ahead of Fletch, I volunteer to go first.

[138] Save for all the ones I self-diagnosed on WebMD.

sixth grade. I didn't even have to be admitted, but we were moving out of my dad's little temporary apartment and into our first house in Indiana that week. Frankly, the whole hospital thing was easier from a logistical standpoint. Really, this shouldn't even count and I tell the nurse as much.

However, her ears prick up when I mention that this summer my doctor thought I might have a pulmonary embolism. I was just off of twenty-one days of consecutive flights and I had tightness in my chest. Turns out it wasn't a blood clot at all. Rather, everything was stress-related due to trying to buy a house and move, but we didn't know for sure until I was tested.

The nurse consults her chart. "You had an MRI?"

"Yep," I reply. "The doctor didn't like my d-bagger levels—"

"Jen, I think it's D-dimer," Fletch interrupts with a smirk.

I glower at him from across the table. "Oh, you're helpful *now*. But on the day that the doctor said I needed an MRI immediately, *you* made us stop for coffee first. I might have been DYING but *you* needed an iced latte."

He shrugs. "Please, Starbucks was in the lobby of the professional building. We had to pass right by it to get to the car! And Dr. Z's an alarmist. She humors you by checking for everything, or do you not remember the parasite incident?[139] You were fine and on the slim, slim chance you weren't, I figured we'd be at the hospital for a long time and then I'd really be wishing I had coffee."

I tap the table with my index finger. "Please make a note in his chart that my husband is a jerk. Also, he's addicted to caffeine."

The nurse scratches more notes on her pad. "So this happened in June?"

....

[139] Don't ask.

I shoot Fletch another look. "Yes."

"What was the date of your last mammogram?"

I shift in my seat. "Never?"

"You've never had a mammogram?"

"No."

"Even a baseline reading?"

"No."

She peers at me from over the top of her paperwork. "Why not?"

Um, the same reason I didn't pay State of Illinois taxes back when I was unemployed? Because it seemed annoying and definitely not something I'd enjoy doing? Because I was behaving like a child? Because doing so seemed unpleasant and in weighing risk versus reward, procrastination came out the winner?

None of these seem like answers that should go in my permanent record, so I tell her I'll schedule one immediately. Then she draws my blood and I pee in a cup, followed immediately by washing my hands and starting the coffeemaker.

While Fletch does his interview, I sit across from him and remark about how particularly rich, smoky, and delicious the coffee tastes today.

Iced latte, indeed.

Scheduling my mammogram takes all of two minutes.

That is, after eight months of putting it off.

I know, I know, but I'm here now, okay?

I made the appointment yesterday for the first thing this morning so I wouldn't have the chance to chicken out or get distracted again for three seasons.

I check in at the Women's Center in the Lake Forest Hospital and the first thing I see is the plaque with John Hughes's and his wife Nancy's names on it. Seeing his name in this community makes me so happy that I forget to be nervous. First, John Hughes helps me make sense of high school and now he's here to make sure I don't freak out at this very adult experience? Sir, your legacy lives on.

Anyway, the only downside so far is that I can't wear perfume, deodorant, or powder, but I've got all of the above in my purse and can put them on the second I've finished. From what I've been told, the mammogram isn't painful so much as it is uncomfortable.[140]

I change into my gown and exit to a waiting area that's full of coffee fixings and Quaker Chewy Granola Bars. But before I can choose between chocolate chip and peanut butter chocolate chip, I'm whisked down the hallway into the mammogram room.

The tech explains how I'm supposed to stand while the big plastic plates clamp me into place. As I remove my gown and the tech guides me into position, I realize what a prime opportunity this is.

"Excuse me, since we're here, can you please take a moment and look at this contrast? Like, as a medical professional?" I point to the white part of my side boob, holding up a forearm whose color can best be described as Rich Corinthian Leather. "I mean, I have the best tan of my life and outside of my husband, no one

---

[140] I bet it's less of a pain in the ass than the whole-body MRI with that weird vein dye they inject that makes you feel like you've just wet your pants.

ever sees me with my shirt off so they don't understand how naturally pasty I really am. *This* is a tan."

The tech nods. "That *is* impressive."

"Thank you. You may proceed."

The process . . . is not comfortable. Actually, it sucks. The act of turning each appendage into a pancake is like the worst purple nurple ever, but it's only twenty seconds per pose and I imagine it's a lot better than breast cancer. My friend Stacey says when she goes in, they have to switch to the big plates so I feel it's a minor victory when I only have to use the regular ones.

I clock the whole procedure from entry to exit and I'm back in my car twenty minutes after I arrive. I'd have been here a minute sooner, but I was pawing through the granola bars.

I have to admit, out of everything I've done so far, *this* feels like the most adult decision I've made in my life and the process was remarkably easy. The gearing up for it was hard, but now that it's done I'm kicking myself for resisting for so long.

What I'm learning is the process of becoming a fully fledged grown-up isn't anything like I imagined as a kid, but each step I've taken has been a necessary one. Nothing that I've done has been glamorous, yet there's comfort in knowing that even James Bond gets his prostate checked.

Reluctant Adult Lesson Learned:

YOU ARE GOING TO DIE. Probably not today, but you'll feel marginally better about it if you get your shit together first.

The One About the Monkey

There's an expression that goes, "A friend will help you move. A good friend will help you move a body."

I'm exceptionally fortunate to have a group of girls[141] in my life that would absolutely help me move a body. Of course, Stacey wouldn't move it herself, but she'd give me the name of a guy who moves bodies for a reasonable fee and has tons of excellent references and in fact, did I know he used to move bodies for Sammy "the Bull" Gravano?[142] And after the guy and I are done moving the body, she'll happily provide tea and cake at her place so we can do a conversational postmortem on who needed a killing in the first place.

Gina might not be so keen on, say, physically wrapping a body

---

[141] Doesn't matter if we're over forty—we can call ourselves girls if we want.
[142] Quoth Stacey: "We're Jews. We have a guy for everything."

in a rug with me, either. I mean, she would, but she's busy running her empire during business hours. At any point in time, Gina's doing work for six clients, armed with no less than three cell phones, two laptops, a personal Wi-Fi hot spot, and a power strip. However, she'd be unbelievably helpful in negotiating with the owner of the place where we'd dump the body, in supporting my decision to have offed the body in the first place, and in finding an even better rug afterward, because she knew how well it tied the room together.

As for Tracey, she's the kind of person who'd check if I also required assistance with the stabbing/shooting/poisoning to create the body needing moving in the first place.

My friends are the best.

I hook up with these three gals every week for lunch in the city, even though I live thirty miles away now. I've never left a date with the 2-Live Lunch Crew without a throat sore from laughing. My favorite lunches ever were back when Tracey dipped her toe into the online dating pool. For two blissful months until she got too creeped out, Tracey reigned over lunch with the funniest stories.

"Check this one out," she said one day last spring. She pulled up a photograph of an elderly suitor on her iPhone. "Got this through Chemistry.com. Says he's thirty-seven."

Gina barked with laughter before passing the phone. "I'm sure he *was* thirty-seven . . . thirty-seven years ago when this was taken."

Stacey inspected it next. "No, he's not thirty-seven. He's clearly dyslexic. What he meant to say was that he's seventy-three."

I studied the photo when it was my turn. "Did any of you notice that he looks exactly like Ronald Reagan?" And then none of us could eat our breakfast burritos because we couldn't stop pinging Tracey with one-liners about winning one for the Gipper. It was beautiful.[143]

I didn't meet any of these gals until I was in my late thirties, so anyone who says it's impossible to make friends after college is dead wrong. The fact that they aren't old friends has no bearing on the quality of those friendships. Maybe the four of us don't have twenty years of shared history, but we will fifteen years from now.

Although I'm generally loath to hold up *Sex and the City* as a good example, the show was a testament to women's relationships with each other. If Carrie didn't have Charlotte, Miranda, and Samantha, would she even have been Carrie at all?

I feel like I'm a better me—quicker, funnier, more trusting—having these women in my life. I don't care how happily married you are or how deeply enmeshed you are with your children and family and career—every woman needs a couple of chicks who'll break out the sangria just because you need to vent. If you're hesitant to put yourself out there by being open to meeting new girlfriends, please take the risk because it's worth it.

Anyway, because Tracey is who she is, I knew she'd participate in my latest scheme. When I got to lunch last week—and after everyone politely entertained my usual five-minute rant on why every driver on the road (except for me) is stupid—I said, "I have two words for you that are going to change your life: *Banana Derby*."

"Do I want to know?" Gina asked.

"I do *not* want to know," Stacey stated.

All Tracey said was, "I'm in."

---

[143] More of Tracey's (barely fictionalized) dating adventures can be found in *Off the Menu*, by Stacey Ballis, in stores July 2012!

How awesome is she?

For some quick background, I make it a habit to scan the local online newspaper because it's always filled with gems like *"Lake Bluff Family Gains Approval to Raise Backyard Fence"*[144] and *"County Questions Mental Health of Man Who Exposed Himself at Walker Brothers Pancake House"*[145] and *"Lake Forest Shakes off Federal Credit Downgrade Worries."*[146] Recently they posted the article *"Two Dead after Tollway Driver Goes Wrong Way"* underneath a picture of a little girl riding an alligator, which garnered a number of complaints. (Actually, I was glad to see that I wasn't the only asshole who felt bad about inadvertently laughing at the juxtaposition.)

Anyway, I read about how the Lake County Fair was starting soon and that surprised me. I didn't realize I lived in the kind of rural area where county fairs existed. There are farms up here? I mean, within five square miles of my house, there's a Saks Fifth Ave store, two Williams-Sonomas, ten Starbucks, and a Maserati dealership. But farms? Who knew?[147]

The county fair was an institution when I lived in Indiana. All year long my classmates in 4-H would prep their livestock to show. I remember being astounded at prices their animals fetched at auction; I'm talking thousands of dollars for a prize steer or sow. For months before the fair, kids toiled away on their art and sewing projects and I vaguely recall someone talking about mixing seeds to create a new corn hybrid.

....

144   Quite a story, but I'll probably wait for the movie.
145   Listen, that shit may fly at Denny's but NOT at Walker Brothers.
146   Bless their denial-loving hearts.
147   I guess it stands to reason that the guys at the Farmers' Market on the square come from somewhere, though.

Honestly? I didn't get it.

Before we moved to Indiana, I lived in urban areas. I grew up going to museums and theme parks, so I thought I was far too cool to slum around some stupid barn full of hand-stitched apron displays and of pies you couldn't eat. Plus carnies manning death traps masquerading as Ferris wheels and Tilt-A-Whirls?

Thank you, no.

Okay, fine, I still went because what else is there to do in Huntington, Indiana?

But grudgingly. Oh, so grudgingly.

What I'm noticing is the more time passes, the more I appreciate anything nostalgic even if I hated said bit of memorabilia at the time. Like a few weeks ago when I was cruising around in Fletch's car, windows down and sunroof open, collar popped, and Def Leppard came on satellite radio. I immediately cranked it up. When I caught a glimpse of myself in the rearview mirror, my first thought was . . . *If it were still 1983, I would be the coolest person ever.* Then my second thought was . . . *Since when do I like "Pour Some Sugar on Me"?*

The befuddled excitement over Def Leppard was exactly how I felt at the thought of attending the fair, so I pulled up their Web site for more information. Back in the day, I equated the hours random high school boyfriends spent dragging me around the stinking, dusty fairgrounds with visiting the dentist.[148] Painful, but necessary. But now? I saw the potential for camp and kitsch all over it, so I was intrigued.

And when I read about the Banana Derby? Sold!

"What's a Banana Derby?" Gina prompted.

....

[148] FYI, guys? This is why I didn't put out.

"Picture this, if you will," I said. "Imagine a couple of capuchin monkeys, all dressed up in colorful jockey silks. Now imagine dogs wearing saddles. Put the monkeys on the dogs and have them race each other around a small track. Bingo! Banana Derby! Monkeys! In costume! Racing dogs! Believe it! Now which of you naysayers other than Tracey is in for the ride of your lives?"

"I have to work that day," Gina said.

"I'm out of town," Stacey added.

"You don't even know when it is yet!" I protested while they had the courtesy to at least appear sheepish.

"Jen, if these two don't want to have a good time, then we don't need them," Tracey said. She and I made plans to meet up while our fun-hating friends talked amongst themselves.

It's a week later and Tracey, Fletch, and I have just arrived at the fair. We pay our entrance fee and the second we walk in the gates, we're overwhelmed by the smell of fair food.

Oh, fair food.

I forgot about fair food.

Everywhere we look, there are lurid neon booths selling the kinds of magical concoctions that can be crafted only by a carnie's skilled hands. I'm instantly torn between every single vendor's siren song and I can't figure out what I want to stuff in my mouth first.[149]

I practically salivate as we pass the vendor boasting roasted pork chops on a stick.

Food on a stick!

Yes! Genius!

Everyone knows that anything can be made better by placing

---

[149] This must be how every red-blooded American frat guy feels when set loose in Amsterdam's Red Light District for the first time.

it on a stick. I mean, pork chops: lovely on their own, but served on a skewer? Whoa!

An apple? Meh, okay, I guess.

An apple covered with a nonnutritive sugar varnish and presented on a tiny wooden stake? Heck, yeah!

Corn on the cob? Very nice, thank you.

Corn on the cob, dunked in a vat of butter and slapped on a stick? OH, SWEET BABY RAY, YES!

While we scurry to the Banana Derby (post time is at one p.m. sharp) I make mental note of my dining choices. I go all Mr. Microphone commercial on the vendors—*"Hey, good-lookin', we'll be back to pick you up later!"*[150]

We're running a little late because the fair's physical address is different from what was posted online, because, yes, I imagine anyone who pulls up the Web site does so because they plan to send the Lake County Fair a letter and not, you know, visit, so it makes sense to bold the mailing address in lieu of the address needed for GPS navigation. Argh. We found this out when we first arrived at a small roadside fruit stand and Fletch commented, "I thought the fair would be bigger."

Anyway, I'm distracted by all the choices while we dash to the track. In my peripheral vision, I spy lemon shake-ups and elephant ears and cheese curds! Pizza and burgers and barbecue! Cotton candy! Snow cones!! Popcorn and soft-serve and funnel cakes! This spawns a rather heated discussion about the difference between funnel cakes and elephant ears. Turns out I'm Team Elephant Ear, while Fletch is firmly Team Funnel Cake. We vow to buy both and

---

[150] In retrospect, does that portion of the commercial seem a bit date-rape-y to anyone else?

make Tracey our tiebreaker and I may or may not pledge to eat my way across the fairgrounds à la the rat in *Charlotte's Web*.

We arrive at the Derby and the stands are already full with spectators, so we find a wide-open spot next to the track. Almost immediately a family of vaguely thuggish rednecks muscle their way in front of us, despite there being a ton of standing room all around us. The group seems somewhat indifferent to the concept of personal space (or personal hygiene) and they sport matching tattoos of a wrongfully imprisoned family member on their forearms.[151] We determine the matriarch of the group is the gal with the homemade dollar sign inked behind her ear.

The clan's clad in matching West Coast Chopper gear and I count sixteen different earrings on the lot of them, none of which is located in the actual lobe. However, they're all shorter than your average Homo sapien so we can see over them just fine.

Also, I'd be hesitant to start shit with them because, frankly, they look like biters.

I silently mock them for a good five minutes until I start to feel bad about it. Given the fact that out of anywhere in the world I could be right now, I've chosen to be in the exact same spot as these folks speaks more to my own lack of judgment than anything else. Plus, none of them have a pink ribbon tied around their ponytails. I probably qualify for an ass-kicking for that alone.

While I try to peaceably coexist, the first act begins. We watch a trained dog doing almost every imaginable trick while standing on his hind legs. The pup gets a ton of "attaboys" and a million Snausages and I'm pleased to see he's being positively reinforced.[152]

....

[151] Because neck tattoos are for baby names. Duh.
[152] Before we came, I did a check to make sure the show didn't have any history of animal cruelty.

After the opener, two big dogs come bounding out, astride by teeny monkeys in racing breeches gripping the dogs' bridles, which is quite possibly the most adorable thing I've ever seen. As they parade around the track, the monkeys look like they're having the time of their lives. I turn to Fletch and say, "They're available for private parties. If you don't hire me some Banana Derby for my next book party, you're dead to me."

Then the race begins and the dogs tear around the track twice while Tracey and I shout ourselves hoarse cheering them on. The monkeys' tiny faces are wreathed in joy, with wide eyes and big openmouthed smiles. To look at them, you'd think they were born to ride dogs. In my research I learned they were trained as helper monkeys but flunked out of the program. How one makes the logical jump from helper monkey to dog rodeo is anyone's guess, but they seem genuinely happy to be doing what they're doing. Serendipity, I guess. If life hands you tiny saddles, make dog-horses.

After the race, fans can have their picture with the monkey for ten dollars and I'm shocked that no one stampedes the booth. Other than the Manson family in front of us, we're the only takers.

"This is going to be the greatest ten dollars I ever spent," I declare. Tracey opts out, so it's just the two of us. While we wait our turn, we watch the Manson family have their portrait taken. As they pose with the monkey, I can't help but notice the similarities.

Fletch grimaces and leans into us. "You said this is going on our Christmas card? Well, *that* picture is going over their mantel."

When it's our turn, one of the Russian girls helping the handler tells us to *"make nice pose wis monkey"* and we attempt to place him on our lap. But the monkey doesn't want to make nice pose wis us; he wants to go home with us. He keeps climbing up Fletch's arm, hugging his neck, and gazing into Fletch's eyes as if to say, "You have dogs and I have a saddle—we can make this work."

We're sad to leave the monkeys, but there's so much more fair to be seen and tasted. But as we walk away, I notice raised red bumps on all the places the monkey touched me and give myself a vigorous scratching.

Fletch coolly appraises me. "And *that's* where Ebola comes from."

After bathing myself in hand sanitizer up to the elbows, we're ready to begin our dining odyssey.

As an appetizer, I opt for a corn dog drenched in mustard, washed down with cherry limeade, and chased with a few bites of Fletch's sausage and peppers. While Tracey enjoys a barbecue sandwich,[153] I dive into some waffle fries, topped with a generous dollop of gelatinous orange cheese, scooped from the bubbling vat at the back of the tent.

We split popcorn, fudge, and a dipped soft-serve cone on our way to the exhibit hall, while Tracey texts enormous fibs to her personal trainer about what she's eaten. "Just water so far!" ranks right up there with whoppers such as "I have a wide stance."

We veer into the exhibit hall—mostly because it's next to the lemon shake-up stand—and the first display is of roses grown by 4-H participants. "Pfft," I say, pointing at the blue-ribbon winning hybrid. "You call that a spiral? And that centerpoint? Weak sauce. My roses are way better than these, so where's MY ribbon?"

The roses in my yard are the one thing in my garden that I outsource to a professional. When we looked at our house, I was hesitant about the roses all around the back side of it. I knew they were

....

[153] Barbecued what? We don't ask and they don't tell.

difficult to grow, having had terrible luck with them in the past, and I was afraid as soon as we went into escrow, our new yard would be a thorny, barren wasteland. Our Realtor simply said, "You will have Mike take care of them,"[154] and that was it. Now, for the price of a fresh-cut bouquet each week, I have dozens of roses blooming in my backyard every day from May until November, producing such an intoxicating scent that it almost masks the smell of dog poop.

Almost.

"What you're telling me is that the roses grown by children aren't as good as the ones you pay a guy with thirty years' experience to tend?" Fletch asks with a wry grin.

I nod. "Exactly."

"By all rights, the children's roses should be much better. They have those little fingers that can really get in places. That's why they make such great sneakers in third-world countries," Tracey explains. "Small hands are much better at creating detail."

I reply, "See? Tracey gets it, that's exactly—wait, you're both making fun of me, aren't you? You know what? I'm not sharing my elephant ear with either of you."

We cruise the length of the hall and when we get to the photography display, I'm suddenly a lot less smug. Some of the pictures taken by the kids are magazine-worthy. There's depth, nuance, and professional composition and for a second I feel like I'm in a gallery and not a big old barn. I'm not entirely sure how photography relates to farming, but I'm glad 4-H embraces the artistic as well as the practical and we leave the hall on a high note.

More likely the high note is my excitement over getting an elephant ear.

....

[154] Talk to Roses & Roses & Roses in Wadsworth. They're the best!

I'm already taking my first bite of the hot, crunchy, sugary confection while Fletch waits for his funnel cake. See, the funnel cake is a much more complicated undertaking. With an elephant ear, the dough is stretched like a pizza crust before being placed in hot oil, so it cooks up to a uniform crispness.

Funnel cake batter is placed in the oil via a squeeze-y ketchup bottle, so it comes out in ribbons, thus creating a more doughnut-like treat. The key—and the reason that elephant ears are far superior to the funnel cake—is the butter. Hot elephant ears are slathered in hot, melty, golden goodness before the cinnamon-sugaring, whereas funnel cakes just get a dusting of the powdered stuff. With funnel cakes you have the option to top them with cherry pie filling or chocolate sauce or candy apples, but that's like slapping a spoiler on a Rolls Royce—totally unnecessary.

I try to tell Fletch exactly why he's not enjoying his funnel cake nearly as much as I am my elephant ear, but he's stubborn and refuses to admit defeat. I'm sure he licked his fingers afterward out of spite more than pleasure.

Tracey, of course, agrees with me. Butter makes it better.[155]

When we reach the point of nausea, we decide it's time to go, but on our way out, we're lured in by a carnival game. The barker points out that all the seats are empty and if we play, one of us is guaranteed to win.

I like those odds.

In this particular challenge, the goal is to shoot so much water into the clown's mouth that it bursts a balloon. Whoever breaks it first wins a prize. Easy-peasy. Unbeknownst to Fletch or Tracey, I

....

[155] Don't believe me? Then ask Paula Deen.

happen to be a whiz at this particular challenge, having spent many summers on beach boardwalk arcades perfecting my game. And although my finger hasn't touched a trigger in thirty years, I'm confident that I've still got it.

The key is to line up your sights and have the trigger pulled before the water comes on. Those extra few seconds gained while opponents struggle to hit their mark are the difference between winning and losing.

Between them, Fletch and Tracey have more than a decade of military experience and both have had combat weapons training. But they should have practiced shooting clowns and not terrorists because I whip their asses in record time.

Twice.

The two wins are all I need to claim the stuffed bulldog I'd been eyeing, so I lay down my weapon, victorious. Fletch grumbles all the way to the exit, claiming that I somehow rigged the competition.

"How could I have cheated? Do you think I was in cahoots with the carnie?" I ask.

"She was deliberately putting thinner balloons on your clown," Fletch insists.

"They did seem thinner," Tracey agrees. "Fletch, I'm pretty sure your balloon was more full than either of ours."

Encouraged, he continues. "The sights on my gun were off— way off. Otherwise I'd have won."

"Yeah," I reply, "if you can't trust a carnie to properly calibrate a water pistol, who can you trust?"

He's still suffering from extreme sore-loserism when we get to the exit, so much so that he won't lend me eight dollars so I can get a cup of deep-fried alligator bites, having blown through the remainder of my cash at the cotton candy stand.[156]

Tracey offers to buy them for me but then my stomach lurches in a manner that suggests any deep-fried reptile ingested will make a reappearance on the way home. But next year, gator nuggets . . . bank on that.

Fletch and I opt for a dinner of chicken noodle soup and Alka Seltzer instead of the pork roast I defrosted when we left for the fair. When Tracey e-mails the photos, I find out she's having saltines and ginger ale.

As I look through the shots, I marvel at how skilled she is with the camera and how she captured all the best moments. I'm so happy she came with us because she made the whole experience more fun.

As much as I love being with Fletch, there's something to be said for introducing another personality to the dynamic once in a while. Although usually she's Team Jen, she's Team Fletch enough to be fair and we both appreciate that.

But mostly she's just Team Help You Move the Body.

And that? Is worth its weight in waffle fries.

Reluctant Adult Lesson Learned:

You are not too cool for the Fair, but you are too old not to practice moderation.

---

[156] There are ATMs but somehow using one at a carnival seems like an engraved invitation to identity thieves.

C·H·A·P·T·E·R N·I·N·E·T·E·E·N

It's Not Like Texas Didn't Warn You

Singer/songwriter/philosopher Jim Croce said it best when he warned people not to tug on Superman's cape, spit into the wind, or pull the mask off that old Lone Ranger.

By following the spirit of his sage advice, which I interpret as "avoid that which seems like an overwhelmingly poor choice no matter how you slice it,"[157] I've lived a primarily happy life. Yet at no point in my tenure as a reluctant adult did it occur to me that asking for big hair in Dallas, Texas, could possibly violate Croce's dictum.

To backtrack, when my friend Stacey Ballis's new novel *Good Enough to Eat* was about to come out, she asked me if I was game and I was, so I helped her with a book contest. Anyone who preor-

---

[157] Examples include taking rides from strangers, ever letting your drink leave your sight in a college bar, and jeggings.

dered her novel was entered into a drawing in which Stacey and I would come to wherever the winner lived and take her and her best friend to lunch. We were crossing our fingers for New York because we have a number of mutual friends there but were delighted when the contest took us to Dallas instead because I happen to adore Texas.[158]

Stacey and I arrive on a Tuesday in late March and we immediately lose our minds over the gorgeous weather. It's at least fifty degrees warmer here than at home and we contemplate shedding our pants and rolling around in the grass in front of the hotel. However, Dallas does not seem to be the kind of place that tolerates a lot of pants-less nonsense,[159] so we opt for dinner alfresco instead.

We have time to kill before our reservation, so to thank me for being an excellent sport, Stacey treats me to a service at a hair place called Drybar where their motto is No Cuts. No Color. Just blowouts.

For thirty-five dollars, they'll give you a full blowout in a salon that boasts iPod docks and big-screen televisions broadcasting a never-ending series of rom-coms starring Kate Hudson, Sandra Bullock, and Jennifer Garner. Sweet! There's champagne available and adorably bagged snacks, too, and the whole place is bright and lively. Plus, you can choose the type of blowout you'd like via a "cocktail" menu—for example, the Manhattan is super-flat-ironed NYC chic, whereas the Mai Tai is more about beachy waves.

While we wait for our appointments, I don't hear a thing Sta-

....

[158] Maybe it's all the gun racks? So when they say don't mess with Texas, they're not kidding.
[159] Please see previous footnote.

cey says because all that runs through my mind is, "How do I invest in this place?!"

Stacey insists on getting us the extra ten-minute scalp massage, too. Yay! However, I can't enjoy mine because as I start to grab my handbag, the stylist says, "No, no, no, leave that here. You'll be much more comfortable without it," but this goes completely against my nature. He pretty much insists that there'll be no issues with my leaving my bag up front before ushering me into the area with the wash sinks.

This does not sit well with me.

"I assure you I'd be much more comfortable with my bag," I tell him as he wets my hair. "I'd like to go get it now."

"It's fine," he promises me, squeezing a generous amount of shampoo onto my scalp.

"Yes, you say that, but what if it's not?"

He's supremely confident. "It is."

I realize that my overbearing attitude is exactly why people in the South[160] call me "Yankee," but I can't stop myself. "What if it isn't?"

I'm a neurotic enough traveler that I always have a spare credit card and some cash stowed in my carry-on bag (along with extra lipstick) but that's not the point. The point is I want my damn bag in my damn lap and leaving it unattended is the kind of stupid risk I never take, even if there is a receptionist sitting right next to it. What if she's crooked and wants to steal my dental floss or my lucky yellow paper clip or my identity? What then?

....

[160] I know Texans don't consider themselves the South, but in cartography terms, they really are.

"Don't worry. Are you enjoying the massage?"

Normally during a scalp massage I turn into Loki when he gets his back scratched, all wiggly and leaning in and kicky-legged, but that's not the case right now. "I'd enjoy it more if I were holding my purse."

"Ha! You're hysterical!"

Yeah, you'll see exactly how hysterical I can be if my purse isn't there upon my return.

However, he's right and my bag is perfectly safe. I surreptitiously check for my paper clip and it's right where it should be, so I unclench a little.

Stacey is smirking in the chair next to me. "How'd that bag thing work out for you?"

I flash an obscene gesture before picking my style off the menu. I opt for the Southern Comfort because it has lots of gorgeous, Brigitte Bardot–type volume. There's a nice amount of fullness at the crown and the sides sweep back gently in a bouncy, face-framing fashion.

After a five-minute monologue on exactly what I like about the do Brigitte Bardot made famous, I finish by telling the stylist, "I can normally get my hair to go like that for about five minutes before it flattens back out. Maybe we need a little extra volume?"

"Oh, honey," he says. "This is Texas. We know big hair. Are you game?"

This is the point where if my life were a movie, the music would become more urgent and you'd see the first fin circling the boat.

Mind you, the last time someone asked me if I was game, I nodded and ended up eating a diver scallop served on a bed of sautéed BEEF HEART while Fletch, who was decidedly not game, watched in utter horror.[161]

"I'm totally game."

I mean, he was right about the purse, yes?

Stacey and I chat over the whir of the blowers and by the time we're dry, she looks exactly like the girl on the Straight Up page of the menu. Her Breck Girl hair is silky without being flat and it's swingy and glossy. Her stylist tells her she can wait in the chair while they finish me.

I'm underwhelmed with my results thus far. I appear to have the same blowout I came in with and if I can do it myself, why pay thirty-five dollars for duplicate results? I mean, I like Sandy Bullock and I root for her[162] but there's no reason to fork over that much cash to see a movie she made ten years ago while someone may or may not be stealing my lucky paper clip.

"I'm going to use the curling iron now," the stylist informs me.

Ah, there's your pro-tip, I think. I bet that's why my hair always falls—I'm too lazy to lock in the body with a curling wand.

While Stacey takes a call from her fiancé, I read my e-mails and catch up on a couple of blogs.[163] She finishes before I do and when I finally glance up, I see her staring wide-eyed at my reflection, her mouth positioned in a perfect O.

And that's when I finally notice the stylist's interpretation of the Southern Comfort. There's no elegant back-combing going on

---

[161] FYI? There's a reason you don't see a lot of heart on the menu.

[162] Seriously, no one is Team Jesse James. No one.

[163] I'm obsessed with the girl who blogs about her morning oatmeal every day. Even though my day-to-day life is uneventful, she makes me feel like Kim Kardashian in comparison.

here, no sexy tousling, and I don't look like I've just rolled out of bed after a three-martini lunch with Don Draper on the set of *Mad Men*.

Instead, I appear to be making my debut on the child pageant circuit.

My hair has been forced into a tight series of sausage curls and seems to be a solid four inches shorter than when I arrived here thirty minutes ago. Seriously, it was shoulder length and now it's barely past my ears.

The hair is not "big" so much as it is "wide." With a perfectly level crown, it's so flat on top that one could land a tiny helicopter up there before the hair shaft bends at a ninety-degree angle in a cascade of bizarre ringlets. The entire effect is that of a cubed Afro. There's an eighties hip-hop duo dying for this look, I can feel it.

Stacey's sputtering with barely suppressed laughter and sneaking photos of me in the mirror. However, I'm an ace with a round brush, so I don't panic. I mean, when I did my friend Angie's hair on our last girls' weekend, she looked exactly like Phil Spector until I did the final comb-out and then, voilà! She was all Katie Holmes Interprets Jackie Kennedy Before All the Unpleasantness and it was FAB. What's going to happen here is he's going to give my tresses a few flicks of a rattail comb and then Stacey is going to be VERY jealous.

The stylist gives me a few flicks of a rattail comb and . . . now I'm ready for the swimsuit competition on *Toddlers & Tiaras*.

What the hell?

"This is more 'Shirley Temple' and less 'Brigitte Bardot,'" I tell him.

He assures me, "It'll loosen up while retaining volume. Give it a few minutes and tousle it with your fingers."

I tousle the ever-loving shit out of it while Stacey pays and gets us a cab, but all that does is make my fingers tacky from product. When I try to separate the curls, they don't loosen up and give me big, sexy volume. They instead splinter into smaller, angrier, more aggressively springy curls.

I'd have been a big pain in the ass about this if I were paying, but it's on Stacey and the whole experience was fun, so I gather my hair-snakes into an elastic band and we ride back to the hotel. I spend most of the trip sticking my head out the window, but thus far thirty-five miles an hour of wind hasn't made a dent in the do.

While Stacey rests before dinner, I assemble my hair-fixin' tools—dryer, conditioning spritzer, round brush, comb, travel-sized flat iron, and the kind of silicone-based serum that takes even the most unruly tresses from Shakira to Gwyneth in seconds flat.

I spend the next thirty minutes alternately squirting my hair and pulling it taut with a brush, but every time I release the lock, it sproings back into an enormous spiral.

Why is this happening?

The more I tug and spritz, the bigger and stickier my hair gets.

I feel like David After the Dentist. I keep looking at my head and asking, "Is this real life?"

I finally give up and rinse, assuming that if I start from scratch, I can turn this hair-don't back into a hairdo. However, since I'm only using Dallas tap water and not, you know, holy water, it is almost completely ineffectual.

I remember one time I watched an episode of *Jersey Shore* where Pauly D. went swimming and his coif stayed perfectly in place. At the time I thought this was some sort of trick photography, but now I realize he must have employed the same kind of witchcraft as my stylist today.

When Stacey and I meet up in the lobby, she asks if I took a nap instead of dealing with my Medusa. When I tell her no, she clamps her lips together and her eyes water, but she makes no further remarks. Yet the entire time we're on the patio enjoying our dinner, her gaze keeps falling on my barely restrained hair-bush.

I scour my hair in the morning to no effect and it's not until I wash it on Illinois soil that I finally get it looking normal again.

I don't know why I was so surprised by all of this because with a motto like "Everything's bigger in Texas," it's not like they didn't warn me.

But going forward, trust me, I will never mess with Texas.

Reluctant Adult Lesson Learned:

The phrase "Are you game?" is an enormous red flag. Heed it or eat beef heart. Your call.

Quickbooks, Quicker Shovels

*N*ever hire the cheapest accountant you can find.

This dictum doesn't have direct bearing on what happens next, but it's an important rule that Fletch and I learned the hard way; ergo it bears repeating.

Speaking of business, last year, Fletch quit his job to manage the corporate end of my writing career full-time. I realize this sounds like we're very fancy and important, but that's not the case.

Frankly, I needed someone to get my lunch.

Between what Fletch spent on multiple daily Starbucks runs, monthly parking at the Sears Tower, dining out, and dressing up, his salary was kind of a wash. You know how some moms quit their jobs because the child-care costs are killing them and it's cheaper for them to stay home with the baby? In this case,

Fletch is the baby with a taste for custom-tailored shirts and indoor parking.[164]

Also, after putting in years of sixty-hour weeks at jobs he hated in order to earn enough for me to pursue a writing career, I kind of owed him. That's not to mention how I kept screwing up the business end of things by stuffing important corporate notices in drawers because they looked boring and I was busy *creating*.[165]

So we decided he would become my assistant.

Turns out he's kind of terrible at it and I would fire him in a minute if he weren't particularly conscientious about providing a noncereal-based lunch. Since we've started working together, I've yet to waste a single afternoon recovering from a sugar crash. Yay, Fletch!

We're eating our Fletch-fetched lunch in the kitchen today—Jimmy John's Beach Club, a perennial favorite of mine—when Libby leaps to her feet and begins to glower at something outside the sliding glass door. Her entire ruff goes up, too.

"That's weird," I say. "What's with her?" It's unusual to see her like this because there's absolutely no one and nothing she doesn't like. Case in point, this morning she finagled her way onto a chair I didn't fully push in, climbed on the kitchen table, and swiped and ate a banana (peel and all) and most of an overripe pear.[166]

We follow her gaze all the way to the back of the yard where we spy . . . something gray with a pink tail.

....

[164] Fletch just read this and says it's me who's the baby in this scenario and he's the caretaker. He is wrong.
[165] Fletch made me add this whole paragraph. And he rolled his eyes at the "creating" part.
[166] Actually, yes, we do go through a ton of antibacterial spray in our house. Why do you ask?

"That is the biggest freaking rat I've ever seen!" I shriek.

"Jen, it's a possum," he replies between bites of his Billy Club sandwich. "You really need to have your vision rechecked."

Darkly, I reply, "I would . . . if my assistant ever made me an eye doctor appointment."

"I'll put it on the list."

Don't get me started about The List.

I hate The List.

I want to punch The List.

Every time I need something done, Fletch says he's going to put it on The List but at this point, since nothing in the history of ever has actually been accomplished on The List, I don't believe The List even exists.

The List is a Lie.

I scrub at my eyes and squint at the distance between me and the possum. "What's he doing?"

Fletch peers out the window behind him. "He appears to be eating dog shit. That's what they do; they consume waste."

This is so wrong.

I drop the salt and vinegar chip I'm about to eat. "So, what you're telling me is this possum *is* a giant rat, only with a better PR department. Are you going to call the doody removal service now? Please?"

Recently we had a few warm days when the snow in the yard melted and all the dog crap that magically disappeared in the winter magically reappeared. The guys who mow our lawn are supposed to take care of this but we won't see them until spring. Also, their usual preferred method of "removing it" entails driving a riding mower over it, chopping it into a thousand shards, and then nodding enthusiastically when I inquire if it's gone. The whole thing turned into a bit of a Mexican standoff[167] and we need a better long-term solution.

He nods complacently. "It's on the list."

I grit my teeth. "In the interim, we're just going to have the possum take care of it?"

He takes a thoughtful chew. "We'd probably need to bring in more than one possum for that to be an effective solution."

This? Right here? Is why he's a terrible employee.

But if I fired him, I'd have to pay him unemployment.[168]

I make the executive decision to find a waste removal service my damn self and it turns out we can get weekly poop-removal for eleven dollars! Eleven dollars!! I can't imagine how the company possibly makes a profit by only charging eleven dollars because the time needed to pick up the dogs' deposits is not insignificant.

Maybe we use the same accountant?

I hope they're up-cycling the waste somehow and selling it as fertilizer so it makes financial sense because I'd like for them to stay in business so I never handle dog poop again. Last year we had a tiny yard and a lot of snow, so in the spring it fell to me to do clean-up as Fletch was busy at his job drinking lattes and wearing shirts with fancy cuffs. A sudden thaw left us with a backyard that looked like the open sewers of Bombay and even though I was wearing protective rubber boots up past my ankles, let's just say they weren't high enough. As I sloshed through the SlushPoopy™, I would have happily paid someone ten times eleven dollars. When I finished my gruesome mission, I stripped everything off from the

---

[167] In the figurative sense, not the pejorative.
[168] I checked.

underpants down and threw it all away. That I didn't somehow catch hookworm is nothing short of a miracle.

After lunch I snap a photo of the possum and post it on my Facebook page. People write on my wall telling me that if we're seeing a nocturnal animal in the daytime, he's likely ill. When I relay this information to Fletch, he replies, "How do you know they're sick? Was he in his bathrobe? Did he have a tiny cup of tea?"

So now I have yet another furry creature to worry about. Poor little Libby almost died as a puppy because of starvation, which is why I never give her too hard a time when she steals food. We didn't get her until she was perfectly healthy, but I still have trouble letting down my guard. Both my cats Tucker and Jordan seem happy enough, but at seventeen and eighteen respectively, they're thinner and less energetic than they were back in their heyday.

Of course, Maisy has her issues and even though she's doing well, particularly because of Libby, I perpetually fret over the *"what ifs."*

I don't quite know what to do with a sick possum or how I might go about having him treated. If I could even get my hands on him, I'd probably have to take him to a different vet because I'm kind of embarrassed about my last visit when I took Tucker in for date rape.

Yeah.

Talking about *this* visit at lunch is fun.

"What do you mean your cat is a *'date rapist?'*" Gina asks, while Stacey and Tracey gawp at me, trying to form questions.

I set down my grilled cheese because I probably can't recount the story without hand gestures. "You know how Libby had a little adjustment period when we first got her? Everyone was jealous and there was some aggression. We'd keep them from fighting and in turn Loki and Maisy would get frustrated so they'd hump each other."

Everyone's witnessed this at my house at one time or another and it's a sight to behold. Maisy's always been the main culprit and what's so weird is she's female and generally opts to hump the wrong end.[169] But she's also kind of fat and a little slow, so her victim generally escapes and then she's left with all this pent-up energy and she, for lack of a better description, air humps.

I call it her Elvis impersonation and it is hilarious.

I brush crumbs off my shirt and continue. "Sometimes when Maisy couldn't catch anyone else, she'd hump Tucker. And because Libby worships Maisy, Libby thought, 'Hey, that must be what we do,' so *she* started humping Tucker. Our trainer Elaine has basically told us we're morons and we have to stop this behavior, and we did, but it's too late. Poor Tucker has apparently snapped and now he's doing *things* to the other cats. Dirty things. To the other *male* cats, that is."

"Like . . . prison?" Tracy asks.

"Like *Welcome to Oz*[170] things?" Stacey adds.

I nod. "Exactly. I'll be asleep and I'll wake up to this godawful howling and Tuck will have the other cats pinned and he's . . . kind of going at it. He's been fixed for, what? Seventeen years? But apparently there's some muscle memory. We've done our best to eliminate all the humping from every creature and we thought everything was copacetic. Then Tucker started doing this

....

[169] It's a dominance thing.
[170] HBO, not Judy Garland.

weird squatting thing so we rushed him to the vet because we worried that he had kidney failure."

"Poor guy!" Gina coos.

I take a swig of my iced tea. "Um, no, he's fine. Three hundred and fifty-two dollars later, we come to find out there's nothing wrong with him and he's just a dirty old man, trying to lure kittens into his panel van with saucers of milk."

Stacey's still confused. "Wait, does he have syphilis? What is the test they administer to find out if your cat is a date rapist? Did they check him for HPV?"

I wave her off. "Not anything specific like that—they just ran a ton of blood work to eliminate all the other possibilities and they determined there's absolutely nothing wrong with him. He's just a pervert." I lean back in my chair and sigh. "It's the cycle of abuse."

Stacey processes this and then says, "So what you're telling me is they didn't do a swab under his claws or anything."

"Right."

Tracey interjects, "Now are the other cats . . . is it a big humpfest? They're just taking it?"

I run my hand over my ponytail, forgetting that it's probably greasy from my sandwich. "No, they're kind of sad and withdrawn . . . you know, they're not on Facebook anymore and they're not really seeing their friends."

"They're probably not going to go back next semester?" Stacey adds.

"Yeah, they're probably not going back," I laugh.

That's when I launch into possum updates and I mention how Fletch, bless his Appalachian-American roots, has offered up what he finds to be the most elegant solution. "He wants to shoot the poor creature to put it out of its misery, to which I responded, 'We're not shootin' us some possum in Lake Forest.'"

Seriously, would you hire this man?

Regardless, the possum thing ends up being moot because I don't see him for a couple of days. Perhaps now that we've hired the poop patrol, he's off to greener, more vile pastures. Plus, it's since snowed again and I don't see any signs of him having come in the yard.

I'm getting ready for bed and the dogs have had their final out of the evening. That's when Libby decides it's time to wrestle and afterward everyone inhales a gallon of water. Even though "final out" is Fletch's responsibility because he tends to be clad in real shoes and not just slippers, he went to sleep early and the task falls to me.

As Libby's still working on the "come" command, we keep her on a very short leash. In fact, the few times during the day that we don't walk her, we clip her on a long lead within the backyard so she's always in our sight when she does her business. We have a small hole in the fence by the pool mechanicals and we have it blocked off, but this dog's got the flexible exoskeleton of your average city rat,[171] so we're extra careful.

In terms of being smart, Libby is very, very pretty. She's sweet and trainable but she's not much of what you'd call a "critical thinker." This is evidenced every time she clotheslines herself at the end of a long lead, which is every time she's on it. She's yet to figure out where her personal force field ends and her wipeouts are both spectacular and frequent. No matter how many times

....

[171] Or possum.

we slowly and deliberately demonstrate her reach, the lesson never seems to stick.

Loki, on the other hand, understands the "come" command, but he could give a good goddamn about it when he catches the scent of something in the wood line, which leads to me having to traipse through the snow in my bathrobe and slippers to retrieve his yappy ass. So now, I'm choosing to save myself some aggravation by clipping Loki to the long leash. Libby's always sucking up to him and I figure if he's confined to a fifteen-foot radius, she won't go anywhere.

I figure wrong.

Immediately Libby takes off for the other side of the yard and I find myself bounding through snowdrifts in Crocs and a robe. Then we play a long, freezing game of hide-and-seek, which culminates in Libby spotting the hole in the fence. We both make a mad dash and reach it at the same time. Libby, however, has the good sense to not trip over the small grayish object right in front of it.

I am not so lucky.

And by the way? Apparently the possum had returned at some point earlier in the day.

To die.

As I brush snow off my knees and scramble for the puppy, I have a choice: I can avoid hypothermia by keeping my robe shut, or I can remove the belt, tie it into an ad hoc leash, and drag the frisky puppy away from a serendipitous snack.

I pick the option that doesn't include a midnight emergency vet run.

Mind you, none of this would have happened if Fletch

hadn't gone to bed in anticipation of rising early for his class in the morning. As figuring out how to take care of our business record-keeping must be on some list other than The List, Fletch signed himself up for a two-day QuickBooks class.

When I come inside, and after I defrost, I wake Fletch up to tell him I found the possum and that he needs to bury him. He mumbles something about property taxes and Animal Control and promptly goes back to sleep.

Typical.

I spend all morning taking the three dogs out on leashes[172] because I don't want them getting close to the tasty, tasty, disease-infested possum. When I finally reach someone at Animal Control, they tell me they don't pick up dead animals in people's yards and that I should simply double bag him as though he were a pound of hamburger and toss him in the trash.

How much would that suck if you had a deer croak in your yard?

Regardless, not only does this feel unspeakably sad. I also don't want to piss off the kid who drives the little golf cart to pick up our trash. I've barely gotten over past lectures on the proper disposal of cat litter and his impassioned soliloquy on *Recycling and You—Our Partnership for Greener America, Or, Really, Lady, Is It That Freaking Hard to Put Your Empty Wine Bottles in the Specially Marked Bin?*

Point? I decide a proper burial is required.

I e-mail the following note to Fletch:

Where is my good buryin' shovel?

Since we moved up here, I've had very little use for my vast

---

172 And cursing what should be an assistant's job.

collection of shovels-cum-weapons, largely because it's safe and boring up here.

Fletch doesn't respond to my note, so I poke around the basement and garage until I find the pointiest shovel in our vast collection. I don my warmest and most somber coat and set to my task.

I feel like the possum would be happiest being laid to rest in the woods but I quickly determine that this isn't an option. Funny thing about the ground in Illinois in January—it's rock solid. No wonder Chicago's underworld is always dropping bodies in the river; it's so much easier on the back.

As I scout the landscape from my spot in the woods, I spy all the places where Libby's been digging on the side of the house. I figure the ground must be warmer there as she's able to displace a good deal of dirt in a fraction of a second, before dashing inside with muddy paws to dance all over clean bedspreads. I find a lovely resting spot directly beneath the window on Fletch's side of the bed. I dig down some and figure this to be a sufficient amount. I mean, I'm not burying a human body, so there's no need to worry about going down six feet, right?

Then I steel myself for the worst part of the task—moving the possum. I walk over to where he is and I gently attempt to lift him with the business end of my shovel.

The little bastard is frozen solid to the ground.

For two horrifying minutes I attempt to pry him loose until I finally free him. And if I never have to witness the sound and feel of dead marsupial being wrenched from the frozen earth again, that would be aces with me.

I want to be gentle and respectful but mostly I don't want to break off any bits because I'm pretty sure Fletch doesn't want me showing up at his class shrieking about possum parts.

Then, cradling my good buryin' shovel, I bring him over to his hole in the ground, quickly tossing scoops of dirt on and all around him.

I say a few words over him and try to sing "Sunrise, Sunset" but realize I don't actually know most of the words.[173]

Then I step back to admire my handiwork and just as I'm congratulating myself for a job well done, I have a terrifying thought—what if he's not actually dead and he's just "playing possum?" I mean, he seemed pretty stiff and never flinched a bit when I poked all around him, or stumbled over him for that matter, but maybe that's all part of his defense mechanism?[174] While I'm working it all out, a flock of geese flies over my head, squawking, and I practically jump out of my skin.

I take some twigs and fashion a small, tasteful cross to adorn the mound of dirt which, frankly, looked a lot easier when Pa Ingalls did it on *Little House on the Prairie*.

When I get back inside, I e-mail Fletch again:

Possum buried. Shovel still outside because you might want to rinse it first.

Then I begin to wonder if I dug his grave deep enough so I do a quick Google search.

Way off on that one.

For future reference, should your feckless assistant ever be off at a class learning to operate QuickBooks and you find yourself alone and needing to bury a marsupial, I suggest you do the Google search first.

Fletch finally has a break in his stupid class and sends me a

---

[173] I suspect I may be remembering the "Where is the little girl I married?" line wrong, too.
[174] The possum and his ability to plant, or nature's little Ann Veal.

note where he uses the word "biohazard" no less than three times, to which I reply:

Listen, if YOU don't want me accidentally creating biohazards, then perhaps you should be a better assistant.

Fletch doesn't respond and we will definitely discuss this at his next performance review.

Since there's nothing for lunch,[175] I run errands. As I'm checking out at the grocery store, the clerk asks how my day is going.

Listen, if you're not prepared to hear the response, "Not bad, but I buried a possum," then I suggest you not ask such leading questions.

Anyway, I fear this story may not be over, due to the nature of shallow graves and Libby's propensity for digging, so perhaps one day we'll see the possum again.

Until then, please join me in a moment of silence for a marsupial I called Chewie.

Godspeed, my friend. Godspeed.

Reluctant Adult Lesson Learned:

You should never hire the cheapest assistant you can find, even if you are married to him. Also, and I can't stress this enough, buy yourself a good shovel, because you really never know when you'll need it.

---

[175] We'll just add this to your file, too, honey.

I Know Why You Fly

I'm terrible at a lot of things.

I mean, really just awful.

Hear me sing and you'll accuse me of killing music.

Watch me dance and you'll pray for a return to the rhythmic stylings of Elaine Benes.

See me run and you'll make a mental note to buy a new sports bra.[176]

Challenge me to add one-fourth plus two-thirds and observe the circuitry in my brain melting.

I can't thread a needle, cut a straight line, or convince my dogs it's not cool to crap indoors. I can't hold my breath for more than ten seconds, remember any numerical sequence longer than four digits, or open a jar without first stabbing airholes in the top of it.

---

[176] And some diet soda.

I can't apply fake eyelashes without looking like my eyeball's grown a beard.

I can't ride a bike. I mean, I could thirty years ago, but I haven't tried since then and I guarantee those skills have deteriorated. I won't even opt for the regular exercise bike at the gym because I'm afraid I'll fall off. It's recumbent bike or nothing at all.[177]

I can't play Sudoku. I can't play cards. I can't play chess. I can't play checkers. I can't play tic-tac-toe. (Or, at least I can't win at it.)

I can't inhale.

I can't read in the car.

I can't fold a fitted sheet.

I can't keep a secret.

And I'm fine with all my failings because I do one thing better than almost anyone.

I can fly.

On planes, I mean.

If air travel were a sport, I'd not only be pro, but I'd have my own endorsement deals. Despite having no control over the vagaries of weather, mechanicals, and air traffic control, I rock at all other matters flight-related. I can pack for a week on the road—and not just to a beach vacay. I'm talking outfits for media appearances and book signings and scrubby stuff to wear in hotel rooms between events—using nothing but carry-on luggage.

The key is color coordination. With a few simple solid dresses, plain cardigans, Capris, alligator shirts, and a couple of cute print scarves, I easily cram a week's worth of looks in the overhead compartment. I'm sure Rachel Zoe wouldn't approve of my immensely

---

[177] That I can't drag myself to the gym with any sort of regularity anymore goes without saying.

boring personal style, but I don't approve of those hairy vests she wears, so we're even.

Also, if you take more than a pair of flats, a pair of heels, and a pair of flip-flops or sneakers, you're doing it wrong. And you won't get scabies if you wear your nightgown more than once between washings.[178]

Because I inevitably pick up more stuff along the way, I leave enough room in my suitcase to accommodate for those things. Traveling is the best time to get rid of your ratty underpants, old socks, and spray-tan stained bras.[179] By leaving worn undergarments in the trash, you won't feel guilty for tossing them out and you won't be stuck with a ton of dirty laundry upon your return home. Win, win!

The benefits of carrying on are practically unlimited—first, the airline doesn't get to wallet-rape you on checked bag fees. Also, if you carry on, the likelihood of you ever seeing your suitcase again rises to one hundred percent from approximately three percent. Plus, you never know what's going to happen to your plane once you get past security. Recently I had a flight canceled because of a missing crew member. We passengers were all, "Missing? Missing how? Like late for work missing or like call-*CSI*-missing?"[180] As airlines have strict policies about separating travelers from their bags, if you haven't checked anything, you're a lot more nimble if there's the inevitable flight cancellation or change.

I find the lighter I pack, the quicker I move. I recently topped

....

[178] Again, been tested.
[179] Okay, those may just be mine.
[180] Although rumor has it this is airline bullshit for "didn't sell enough seats on the plane so we rebooked all of your sorry, inconvenienced asses."

my previous personal best at Washington Reagan Airport by getting from the curb through security at O'Hare in less than two minutes. Two minutes! No exaggeration! That's because on the way, I always put all my jewelry in the zippy part of my purse, and when I step out of the car, I've already got my boarding pass, license, Kindle, iPad, and quart bag in my hands, ready to be thrust in a bin the second I get to the conveyor belt.

Over the years I've flown enough to earn medallion status, which means that sometimes I get to go through the priority line. I love the priority line. I live for the priority line. The priority line is *bank*. I will do unspeakable things to access the priority line.

If you have any say in the matter, you want the priority line because it's filled with road warriors, the folks who fly every Monday morning and Thursday evening, every week, every year, until they get divorced or promoted. They've done this a million times and it's a point of personal pride to cruise through security quickly. This line is for pilots and flight attendants, too, and you know they're on top of it. Once in a while, you'll see a bona fide jet-setter in this line.[181] They want to get in and out as fast as they can, due to the extreme mortification of being spotted flying commercially.

The priority line is for pros.

No one travels in their pajama bottoms in the priority line.

No one brings the pillow from their bed in the priority line.

No one requires an explanation that "no metal" includes coins in the priority line. No one tries to plow through anyway, despite carrying enough quarters to feed an entire city block's worth of meters for a week.

No one has to get the full-on-plastic-gloved-how's-your-father

....
[181] They're always carrying Louis Vuitton luggage. Always.

after failing the metal detector because they had the good sense to remove their n-i-p-p-l-e ring before they got to the airport in the priority line.

More likely, they never got it pierced in the first place.

The priority line fills me with the smug sense of self-satisfaction that is almost wholly lacking in other areas of my life, due to my inability to manage many of the basic aspects of living.

Sometimes when I'm in the priority line, I like to predict who's going to be trouble in the regular line. You, who I just witnessed buying the enormous water bottle? Try not to look surprised when security removes it from your bag. And you, I'm wagering in thirty seconds you're going to be bitching about you had no idea you couldn't bring a half gallon of shampoo, likely because you haven't watched the news in ten years.[182] And you, with the purse, the backpack, the suitcase, and the shopping tote—the "limit two carry-on items" business is not simply a suggestion.

One time I watched an otherwise normal-looking woman holding a bunch of bananas in the security line, which . . . what the *fuck*? Where was she going that bananas don't exist? Sure, I could see wanting to have a banana on the plane as a snack, because they're fairly tidy and there's no annoying crunch factor and they're self-contained. Plus, personally, I have a pathological need to never throw bananas away.[183] But six bananas? For a lady traveling alone? I had to cover my mouth to keep from laughing when the TSA guy explained that unless her bananas were in a bag, they counted as a carry-on piece. And then I watched as she ran the

---

[182] I also predict you cut your hair yourself. Often, these qualities are soup and sandwich.
[183] My freezer is a testament to this. Oh, and if anyone needs one hundred thirty-seven overripe bananas to make bread? Call me!

bananas through the conveyor belt and then how all the TSA guards gathered around the screen pointing and asking in incredulous tones, "Are those *bananas*?"

I posit that travel can make the very best of us a little stupid; for those who blithely stroll through the metal detector with a dinner-plate-sized belt buckle, maybe they're just having an off day. What I don't get is why airline travel causes people to forget very basic manners, but it does and they do. When I had to catch a connecting flight in Memphis recently, I was overwhelmed by the heady smell of all the rib joints in the terminal. To me, airport food is a necessary evil. I try to stick with reliable standbys like McDonald's or plain turkey sandwiches or bags of almonds due to my penchant for avoiding airline bathrooms.[184] But one whiff of Memphis barbecue and I was ready to throw my rigid travel rules out the window. Unfortunately, I had only five minutes to get to my gate and what was I going to do, suck on a pork bone while jammed between everyone else flying coach?

Apparently I was one of the few who didn't make this choice. I watched in horror as passenger after passenger boarded with stacks of short ribs and sampler plates and burnt ends. Although not seated directly next to anyone tonguing up a mess of ribs, I was fortunate enough to have a visual on a man one seat up and over cleaning every scrap off of his order, before neatly storing the naked bones in the seat-back pocket in front of him.

Previously I thought I couldn't hate anything more than flying out of the United terminal in O'Hare where passengers load up on

---

[184] How do people join the Mile High Club in there when I have to open the door to bend over and pick up a paper towel?

Nuts on Clark's cheddar and caramel popcorn. I've spent many an unpleasant flight next to egregious finger-lickers, but in terms of lip smacking, nothing compares to being seated near someone enjoying the Neelys' slow-fired finest.

And yet if I were to express exactly how much they were annoying me, *I'd* end up on the terror watch list.

So not fair.

I believe my purpose in life is to be the World's Manners Monitor and I hate when my efforts are thwarted.

The travel portion of my book tour this year concluded in Seattle. Can I tell you something about Seattle? Everyone there is a filthy liar. They're all, "Don't move to Seattle—it's so rainy!" And yet every time I've been there, a tiny amount of rain falls before the whole sky explodes into rainbows and sunlight. Seattleites mean to hog up all the stunning vistas and good coffee and flowering bushes for themselves. Bet on it.

Anyway, I finished doing Seattle media very early in the morning so I had the day to shop and explore. My friend Joanna traveled to New York with me to work as my "assistant" for the day and I wanted to buy her a present. On the way to Pike's Market, I found a Finnish store full of Marimekko goods and I got her some stuff I knew she'd love.

My policy is to never buy more than I'm going to dispose while on the road, but it was my last city and I figured the world wouldn't end if I checked my bag. So I stocked up with confidence before inhaling my own weight in crepes and espresso.

I spent the rest of the day on the hotel's deck watching tugboats dock enormous container ships, while listening to some blowhard yammer into his phone about how he bought one thousand copies of his boss's book in order to keep him on *The New York Times* best-seller list, which, OMG! I've yet to figure out who he was talking about but when I do . . . BUDDY, I'M ON TO YOU.

Point is every part of my Seattle visit was amazing, from the media to the weather to the food to the event at Third Place Books to the shopping.

Naturally, shit was going to fall apart on the way home.

That's just how it goes.

Part of the reason that I'm an excellent flyer is that I'm an early arriver. When the airlines tell me to arrive at least two hours before my scheduled departure, I do. Once in a while, this allows me to catch an earlier flight. A lot of times this means I spend a couple of hours camped out at the gate if there's no Admiral's Club. Give me bored and early over stressed and late anytime.

A few years ago I watched my friend Poppy slip a skycap a twenty dollar tip and he slapped a Priority tag on her luggage so fast it was almost as if it had always been there. When it comes to travel, I learn quick and whenever I'm forced to check a bag, I follow her example and I've never not gotten the magical tag. Said tag not only insures that the bag will be the first unloaded, but also that at no point will my luggage be used as a football.

When I get to the airport, my driver pulls up right behind a bus. "Oh, no," he said.

"What's the matter?" I asked.

"Cruisers."

"Police cars?"

"No," he sighed. "Cruise people. One of the ships must have docked this morning and now you're going to be behind all these morons. From the looks of them, it was an Alaskan cruise. Good luck, ma'am. You'll need it." Then he handed me my bag and drove off, rather quickly now that I remember it.

But the line for the skycap was only a few people deep so I figured it couldn't be so bad, plus the kiosks were mobbed inside, with the line of passengers snaking down the length of the terminal and back up around.

As I waited behind two couples, a harried-looking chauffeur kept making trips back and forth from a big passenger van. Although the number of customers in front of me didn't get any larger, the amount of baggage they were checking grew exponentially until there were five massive pieces of luggage for every hunched old person.

When I say massive, I mean it. I've never seen such enormous suitcases. An adult could have easily zipped him- or herself inside and still had more room than your typical airplane bathroom. Seriously, I'm talking massive towers of bags the same size (and floral fabric) of those overstuffed couches that were all the rage in the eighties. Although I wouldn't say I'm a clotheshorse, I have a decent-sized wardrobe, yet I assure you everything in my closet would fit in three of these bags.

I didn't get the full measure of exactly how heavy the bags were until the older woman in front of me knocked one of them onto my foot and spilt my toenail in half. I haven't felt pain like this since a horse stepped on me in college. As I howled, clutching my shoe and hopping around one-legged in pain, the woman merely turned around, looked me up and down, shrugged, and then turned back around without picking up her fallen bag.

Wait.

What?

Oh, bitch . . . it is *on*.

For the first fifteen minutes in line, I was too focused on my throbbing digits and roiling rage to notice that the line seemed to have stalled. But fifteen minutes after that, I began to wonder if there wasn't a problem, as neither of the two couples in front of me had moved. As I looked up and down the white unloading zone, I saw that every other skycap was surrounded by tiny old people and mass amounts of baggage.

And this? Right here? Is why I'm never moving to Florida.

The beleaguered skycap was whizzing around, at least in spirit. He was banging on his computer keys and printing out long, sticky bag claims before wadding them up and trying again. I couldn't figure out the problem, but he seemed enormously distressed and it wasn't until he staggered out from behind the counter that I noticed he had a terrible limp, too.

Fucking cruisers.

Eventually the first old couple finished their business. I noticed that they were responsible for only four pieces from Mount Samsonite, so that meant the couple ahead of the rest of us in the line was in charge of the remaining sixteen. While we waited, a few random old folks shoved their way in front of me to talk to the Toenail Assassin, and then they'd meander away again, so she must have been responsible for checking everyone's bag in addition to ruining my pedicure.

None of us in line could move up, though, because the lady refused to scoot any of her bags closer to the desk. At one point she said to me, "Why don't *you* move those?" and I pointed to my savaged piggy toe saying, "I can't. I'm crippled." So she left them.

Forty-five minutes into the wait, the rest of us in line got to know each other, forming the kind of bonds forged during war or hostage situations or freshman year of college. I had a deeply meaningful chat with Bernie, who was headed out to DeKalb to spend some time with his fiancée's family. Yeah, it took him a while to come around to realizing that he wanted to get married, but hey, how often is he going to meet a cool gal like Casey? So he took a leap of faith and it totally paid off and I hoped to dance at their wedding. If I could ever walk again, that is.

After quite some time, Bernie decided he'd take another leap and try the terminal inside because clearly this line was never moving. He promised to come back for us if it was any better inside, but we knew he never would. At some point, self-preservation kicks in. We all sorely felt the loss of Bernie; he was kind of like our mascot.

At this point, the woman in front of me knocked her suitcase over again, but I was able to hop out of the way. When she wasn't looking, I gave it a solid kick with my good foot.

The Lopezes were very excited to see their grandson for the first time and maybe going to the top of the Sears Tower if they had the chance, and please, God, let their kids have gotten a new sofa bed so it didn't mess up Jose's back again. That thing was going to be the death of them!

Bill and Brian were ecstatic about their wicked pissah meeting at Microsoft, although they were dreading the long flight back to Boston in coach. Maybe if they landed the deal, their boss would let them do business class next time. Bloody Marys were on them if our crew ever made it inside to the bar.

And then there was Bubbe Bernbaum, who announced she was not about to spend the few years she had left in this fakakta line and what the hell was wrong with the meshugenah with all the fakakta luggage? Then she rammed some of the offending pieces of luggage with her wheelchair. Bubbe Bernbaum raised such a stink that eventually another skycap came out to assist, fifty-four minutes after I arrived.

Bubbe Bernbaum is the only reason that I'm not currently standing in that line today.

The kicker is that after taking up an entire hour of the skycap's time and, most likely maiming his foot, too, the woman gave him a five dollar tip. Five dollars! At that point, airport security be damned, I couldn't take it anymore. I shouted after her, "Hey, lady! I've got your five dollars right here! Bend over!"

She shrugged and then turned back around.

ARGH.

Of course, everyone in line clapped for me, but hey, that's what friends do.

I didn't want to engage the skycap too much when I got to the counter so I was extra-prepared with my ticket, license, and big tip. "I can't believe after all that, she only gave you five dollars."

All he said in response was, "Cruisers."

Security also took forever, largely because three TSA agents spent ten minutes pawing through every single item in the Toenail Assassin's carry-on bags. When it was my turn to have my license checked, I pointed and told the agent she was a problem outside, too.[185] Last I saw, she was being escorted to one of the little rooms off of security.

If there is a God—and I believe there is—she received a full cavity search.

Bet they found five dollars up there.

I arrived home four and a half hours later and without further

....

[185] Congratulations to me for being a walking, talking piece of the Patriot Act!

incident. I stumbled going up my front step and that night I needed Fletch's help to get the television off whatever weird button I'd accidentally pressed and back on my TiVoed copy of *American Idol*. Then I spilled a bowl of grapes and we had to move the couch to find them all.

We were laughing as we chased down all the shiny green orbs and in so doing, I knocked over my glass of wine, and almost soaked the cheese plate. "My God, it's like I can't do anything."

Then I remembered my three weeks of smooth sailing through airports as I crisscrossed the country.

So I amended my statement.

"I mean, *almost* anything."

Reluctant Adult Lesson Learned:

Play to your strengths. (And remember, there's no shame in taking the bus or the train if air travel perplexes you.)

That's the Night That the Lights Went Out (in Lake County)

We are the kind of people who are prepared in this house.

Always prepared.

Utterly prepared.

Of course, the manner of preparation varies according to each member of the household. The cats, for example, have a bead on the cabinet where their food's kept, and at least ten times in the night—every night—they pry open said cabinet to feast on the exact same kibble located in their endless feeding bowl one foot away from the scene of the crime.[186]

As for the dogs, they've stashed no less than eight thousand bones and tennis balls throughout our home, thus assuring the human members of the household frequently twist their ankles

---

[186] We eventually have to install baby locks.

stumbling over said objects in the dark when they're roused to check on the cats' banging.

Fletch says this is the dogs' way of preparing for impending doom. He figures if the balloon[187] goes up, the dogs' plan is to hobble us so we're easier to catch and eat. Considering these same dogs spend the majority of their day barking at their reflections in the window and tossing their own salads, I'm hard-pressed to believe they're capable of this level of vigilance.

I, on the other hand, *am* that kind of capable. Seriously, you've never seen anyone so ready for some shit to go down; all you need to do is take a peek inside my purse.

If you've ever rushed a sorority or worked with a skilled wedding planner, you're acquainted with the magical bag of tricks these ladies[188] carry. Now I'm not talking your garden-variety bag containing mints or a couple of Kleenex (which, of course, they have.) Rather, the level of preparation contained within their satchels is an art form. Did your clumsy new spouse accidentally step on the hem of your dress during your first dance? Did your drunken sister-in-law-to-be spill her red wine in the limo? Did your monthly bill arrive right before the Alpha Phi open house? No worries! A good rush counselor/wedding planner has everything needed for a quick fix from sewing kits to stain wipes to every kind of tampon manufactured in North America designed to staunch any flow from spotty to tsunami.

Because I pack my purse for my own eventualities, my emergency supplies are a little more personalized. For example, I'm never without at least one extra string of pearls, earrings, and a

---

187 Or is it the bubble? I can never get this expression right.
188 Or the occasional fancy gent.

bracelet. Because I'm concerned about squint lines[189] I always carry a spare set of contact lenses, eyedrops, and at least two pair of sunglasses. Depending on what kind of hair day I'm having, I can simply smooth out my tresses with the brush, yank it back in a ponytail holder, tame an unruly bit with bobby pins, get more sun on my face via pearl-adorned or tortoiseshell headbands, or coax my bangs back into shape with a single pink Velcro curler.

My smile's guaranteed to look its best due to ample supplies of floss, gloss, balm, liner, and three shades of lipstick, which I apply depending on my mood and state of my tan. Should I want longer eyelashes, I have lengthener mascara and if I want them thicker, I have thickening. Although I hope the circumstances never arise, I'm also carrying enough concealer to camouflage a black eye or blemish up to and including the size of Mount Vesuvius.

Do I keep sparkle powder on hand?

Oh, honey, please.

Do you prefer iridescent pink or shimmering gold?

In more practical terms, I never need to make awkward conversation in a long line at Costco because I can busy myself with my iPhone, iPad,[190] and fully charged Kindle e-reader.

Should my feet get cold, I have a spare pair of socks and if I ever find myself in shoes that aren't one hundred percent comfortable, I'm packing Band-Aids, anti-rub blister stick, and the cutest little black bow-topped ballerina flats that not only match everything I own but also curl up to the size of a Honeycrisp apple.

My Leatherman tool allows me to open wine bottles, turn screws, snip wires, and, if needed, cut a bitch.[191] I can start fires

---

[189] Botox can do only so much, you know.
[190] Complete with earphones.
[191] To this point, I've only used it for wine, though.

with my matchbook and cure anything from anxiety to acid reflux to shoulders strained by lugging too much with my ample pharmaceutical stock. I can even secure all the items in my bag with my ever-present gym lock!

On top of the extras, I port the basics, too, like credit cards, writing devices including at least one Sharpie in case anyone wants an autograph,[192] a checkbook, a compact, a handkerchief, and four kinds of nail polish.

Ironically, I never seem to have more than about eight dollars of cash on me, but that's not the point.

The point is we like to be *ready*. I suspect this compulsion stems from when we were unemployed and practically destitute back when the dot-com market crashed. We were caught at such unawares that we vowed to never be taken by surprise again. I mean, if you've ever dined on a faux pizza made with stale hamburger buns, tomato paste, and nonfat mozzarella cheese because that's all you have, you never, ever forget it.

And now, while this whole author thing seems to be at least semipermanent, I've yet to get rid of the clothes I wore when I worked temp jobs because my perpetual state of "what if" never permits me to let down my guard.

I liken us to the older generations who lived through the Depression. No matter how good and bountiful their lives are now, they can't forget what it was like to want or need. Because of that, they stockpile resources. Grandma Daisy isn't showing signs of senility when she cans every wormy peach she plucks off the tree before her driver drops her off for lunch at the country club; she's hedging her bets.

. . . .

[192] So far no one's wanted one, but when they do, I'll be all over it!

Fletch's preparedness veers more towards the dramatic. He believes the eventualities for which we might prepare are a bit more apocalyptic. Maybe it's his military training or perhaps he watches too much *it's-the-end-of-the-world-as-we-know-it* Discovery Channel programming. But for whatever reason, he's concerned a major catastrophe will occur in our lifetime. When it happens, he assures me we'll be all over it.

Bless his tinfoil-hat-wearing heart.

As soon as we moved to the suburbs, Fletch converted our basement to a veritable army surplus store. Tucked between plastic tubs of ancient sorority sweatshirts and framed photos of me from a spectacularly big-haired[193] time period, Fletch has been squirreling away everything from water purification tablets to Arctic weather–grade sleeping bags.

He promises nothing will catch us off guard. Like, if a riot breaks out on the mean streets of Lake Forest? Perhaps in the main square by J.Crew or the Talbots? Across from the farmer's market where they sell those magnificent heirloom tomatoes? Then his grenade simulators will disperse any crowd!

Chemical attack? No worries! Fletch's premeasured sheets of window-sealing plastic and industrial-strength duct tape are located on the shelf marked Zombie War next to the box containing my Christmas nativity scene. (He's very helpfully drawn an arrow towards his arsenal, so I won't confuse his thousand rounds of ammo with the Baby Jesus figurine.)

And if the Russians ever invade à la *Red Dawn*, trust me when I say it will be Fletcher shouting, "Wolverines!" and leading the counterattack.

....

[193] And small-assed. Sigh.

If being prepared is a virtue, then he's Mother-freaking-Teresa.

Like I said, we pride ourselves on being ready for whatever happens next.

Or so we thought.

We're upstairs having post-dinner ice cream[194] and watching *White Collar* when I notice the sky has turned the same shade of purple as my dessert.

"That doesn't seem right," I comment.

"I'm sure it's fine," Fletch replies, eyes fixed to the screen. I suspect someone may have a big boy crush on Tiffani (formerly Amber) Thiessen.[195] "Besides, if the weather were really bad, we'd be seeing an alert."

We're at the point in the summer that we pretty much ignore inclement weather warnings. I swear that some sort of alert goes on every damn day and I've yet to see an episode of *So You Think You Can Dance* that isn't at least partially obscured by a map of the tri-state area and rolling crawl announcing the possibility of wind in a bunch of counties of which I've never even heard.

Seriously, there's no reason for the hyper-enthusiastic Storm-TeamSix folks to break into whatever I'm watching fifteen times an hour to tell me I'm going to get wet if I go outside. Um, yeah, guys, that's why I choose to live *indoors*. When it starts raining frogs, feel free to interrupt our regularly scheduled programming. Otherwise, I need to be able to hear whether or not Mary Murphy's putting Caitlynn and Tadd on the Hot Tamale Train for their interpretation of the cha-cha-cha, so stuff a prepacked sock in it, why don't you?

....

194 Try Graeter's Black Raspberry Chocolate Chip—you'll thank me.
195 Oh, Kelly Kapowski, your legacy lives on.

We continue to watch the show, although I do keep stealing glances out the window. The sky's the exact color of the bruise I got when that horse stepped on me in college. Stupid horse.[196]

"Trees are getting kind of bendy," I comment.

His eyes don't leave the screen. "It's fine."

The downside of Fletch's level of preparedness is that he tends to not sweat the small stuff. Me? I'm all about the small stuff. I mean, a zombie war may happen once in a lifetime, whereas I apply lipstick many times a day.

The wind begins to howl so loudly that Fletch has to adjust the volume. I say, "What's happening out there is the opening scene of *The Wizard of Oz*. I just saw an old lady knitting in her rocking chair go by, plus a cow, an antenna, and a couple of guys rowing a dingy."

"There's no alert on the screen," he counters. "It's fine."

I know something's particularly wrong with the weather because Loki, who fancies himself a lone wolf, is presently trying to climb inside my shirt.

When the wind hits so hard the second floor shakes, I finally realize what's happening. "Um, honey, we're watching a cable show on TiVo. If there's a weather alert, we're going to miss it."

We switch over to network programming to see that not only is there a tornado warning, but it's pretty much *over our damn house right this minute*.

We dash down to the basement, sweeping up cats, dogs, and ice cream in our wake.[197] Although the cats weren't so much "swept

---

[196] This is, what? My fourth mention of the horse? I must really be holding a grudge.

[197] If I'm going to die, then I'm finishing my dessert first.

up" as "dragged kicking, screaming, and clawing the ever-loving shit out of us" as we wrestle them to safety.

And that's where Fletch's superior preparedness skills come into play. We immediately herd everyone into the most protected corner of the basement, where there's a cushioned area large enough for us all to wait out the storm in comfort and safety. He's staged emergency lanterns about the area, has a battery-operated NOAA radio at the ready, and we're hunkered down next to enough food,[198] water, and medical supplies to last a nuclear winter. He tosses me a headlamp, an emergency whistle, and some antibiotic cream to take care of Gus's scratch marks. I apply the salve to my gaping chest wound right as we lose power.

We're under an active tornado warning for another half an hour and while we sit there in the dark, rapidly warming basement with the sound of a hundred freight trains going on overhead, the dogs aren't the only ones shaking. The crackly, computer-generated messages on the NOAA radio make me feel like we're among the last survivors on earth. As we hear about all the marine warnings, I say a little prayer for anyone on the lake who was caught by surprise.

When the tornado warning ends, we tentatively make our way upstairs. I half expect to see huge tree limbs poking through our roof, but for the most part, everything appears normal. Dark, but normal. Fletch patrols the yard with his flashlight, but other than a bunch of smallish downed branches, there's no appreciable damage.

"Okay, that was terrifying," I admit. Fletch and I are standing

....

[198] Human and pet varieties.

in the kitchen, illuminated by each other's headlamps. "What do we do now?"

Fletch knits his brow. "Now we wait for the power to come back on. I'm sure it won't take long."

When we were looking for houses, our Realtor mentioned that losing electric is an occasional cost of living in a suburb known for its trees. We have so much old growth up here that when one strong breeze hits an ancient limb the wrong way—boom! No air-conditioning or *Price Is Right* for you!

Early in our home search, we saw some listings that had built-in natural gas–powered generators, capable of running the entire electrical grid. The preplanner in me thought this was the ultimate in being prepared, but Fletch disagreed.

"If there's a cataclysmic event, you really think North Shore Gas is going to keep the methane flowing into the house? A generator may work in the short term, but if we're going to invest in anything, we need the capability to defend ourselves," he reasoned.

And at the time he made a lot of sense.

But now that I'm standing here in my hot, dark kitchen? Not so much.

I grab a couple of lanterns, a flashlight, and something to read. I decide to station myself on the back porch where I might catch some cross-breeze. Even though we've been without power for only an hour, the house is already sweltering.

As I settle in with my Kindle, I can hear Sergeant Fletcher poking around in the back of the house gathering supplies. He returns a few minutes later with a Navy SEAL-type apparatus strapped to his leg. In the wan light, I make out a sidearm, a small bayonet, and a high-powered Maglite. Although it's dim out here, I have no trouble seeing the smug look on his face.

"See how good it feels to be prepared?" he crows.

"What?"

He repeats his statement, louder this time. "I said, *'see how good it feels to be prepared?'*"

"Oh, honey, I'm sorry," I say. "I can't hear you *over the roar of the neighbors' generators.*"

Our porch sounds like we're surrounded by dozens of riding lawn mowers going full tilt or ten million angry African bees. The ground is vibrating from the omnipresent hum. Although most of our views into their homes are obscured because of the trees, I can still make out lighted windows and, in one case, the ambient glow of a television. "Look!" I shout, pointing east. "They're watching *Burn Notice!*"

Fletch waves me off, patting his thigh apparatus. "Please, they've got the TV on. Big deal. This is a tiny, tiny inconvenience. A blip, really. How are they going to protect themselves from looters? How are they going to disperse a riot? When the grid goes down, who's going to be laughing then?"

I take a moment to consider his comment. "So . . . what you're telling me is that we're prepared for looting, riots, and zombie wars and if we need to, we can take the neighbors by storm?"

"Bingo."

"And yet, despite our superior firepower, in the short term, I can't blow-dry my hair or run a load of laundry, and in the morning, I'm going to have to throw out our mayonnaise."

He shrugs. "I stand by our choices. Long term, baby. Long term."

I grit my teeth. "Then I'd better eat the rest of the ice cream."

"I'm sure the freezer will be fine for now. Your average fridge stays cold—"

"I SAID I'D BETTER EAT IT."

We sit in as much silence as the neighboring generators will allow. Our house is normally a hermetically sealed seventy-two degrees, so Libby and the cats are reveling in the excitement of roaming the screened porch in the sultry evening air.

The older dogs, on the other hand, are tense. You see, we were back on our feet financially when we rescued the cats a couple of years ago. Their lives are nothing but belly rubs and store-bought treats. Neither they nor Libby know of the days when we'd lose electric or heat due to nonpayment. They're completely unaware of the daily low-lying tension that used to envelop our lives like a fog that never quite lifted. They have no idea why we sometimes still inadvertently flinch when the phone rings. But the older dogs? They remember. Maisy rests her head on my lap, searching my face with her liquid brown eyes, as if to say, "Are you idiots poor again?"

When we go to bed, I'm completely restless. I'll doze off for a minute and then wake up, expecting the power to be back. We're trying to retain what little cool air is left from the air-conditioning, so we keep the windows shut. The house is deadly silent, so much so that I decide to use up precious iPad battery life to run the ambient noise app I'd downloaded for book tour travel.

"Flanders! My socks feel dirty. Give me some water to wash them," Fletch says, quoting *The Simpsons* episode where Homer uses up all the canteen's contents for grooming purposes while lost at sea.

"I don't care to be mocked," I reply darkly.

"What's the problem? You in a mood because the lights are

out? Big deal. It's not the end of the world," he says, attempting to comfort me.

"Oh, no," I agree. "We're ready for the end of the world. Just not for the end of the night."

Fletch smiles and shakes his head. "This is because you can't watch your stories, isn't it?"

My stories.

My secret shame.

Or rather, my *Secret Life* shame.

When Stacey and I went to Dallas, we'd lost our voices by the time we arrived at the airport on our return. To save our throats, we opted to watch our various handheld electronics instead of chatting.

Despite wearing earbuds, I couldn't help but notice Stacey's reaction to her iTouch in the chaise across from me. From exasperated gasps to the snorts of derision, something was clearly bothering her.

"What on earth are you watching?" I probed.

"Only the stupidest show on the face of the earth. It's called *The Secret Life of the American Teenager* and it's about a moronic fifteen-year-old who gets knocked up and then spends all day moping around her house, hugging her knees in a sweater with exceptionally long sleeves," she replied.

"Isn't Molly Ringwald in that?[199] And wasn't it supposed to be critically acclaimed?" I asked.

Stacey sighed and rolled her eyes towards the ceiling in the Admiral's Club. "Yes, and I thought so, too, but clearly not. Seri-

---

[199] Do I even need to mention how I feel about Molly Ringwald at this point?

ously? The writing on this show makes *7th Heaven* look like *The Wire*. It's corny, it's cheesy, it's ridiculous, the acting is atrocious, the dialogue is completely wooden and"—she paused to meet my gaze—"*you'd* probably love it."

As I had plenty of shows already programmed on my iPad (of course) I didn't get a chance to tune in for a while. But the minute I started, I couldn't stop. The show is exactly as corny and cheesy and ridiculous as Stacey claims. *Secret Life* is part telenovela and part after-school special and that's what makes it so good. I mean, have you ever seen a show where the Christian girl claims that her dad[200] was killed in a private plane accident because she lost her virginity? Or that the character played by the kid with Down's Syndrome is a raging asshole? Or that the writers are clearly being paid every time the actors say "had sex" and never once use a different euphemism for said act?[201]

In the past month, I've viewed almost five and a half seasons and watching this show is my nighttime ritual. I'm at the point where it's not really bedtime until I find out the latest haps in the Ben-Amy-Adrian-Ricky love square. It's killing me that without power, we don't have the bandwidth for Netflix to work on my iPad.

That's why I can't sleep.

Of course, I don't admit Fletch is right because he'll laugh at me.

Ironically, Stacey hasn't even told her shiny new husband, Bill, that she watches the show because she's mortified. She waits until he's out cold and then pulls out her iTouch all silent-like in the middle of the night.

....

[200] Played by John Schneider, aka Bo Duke!!
[201] I've since learned that there are drinking games based on this show.

After a fitful night of dozing in half-hour increments, I finally rise for the day. I spend the next three hours fishing foliage out of the pool with a big blue net and hosing a billion fallen leaves off the patio. I don't get a full idea of how bad the storm was until I notice that one of our forty-foot pine trees is listing at a forty-five-degree angle. The wind pulled it right out of the ground and half its tangled roots are visible at the base. Whoa!

Later, Fletch pries the electric garage door open and goes out to buy ice. We've already lost the contents of the fridge, but I'll be damned if we're going to waste my stockpiles in the freezer. I've spent a year loading up on extra cuts of meat so in case we ever find ourselves in a lean time, we won't want for protein. I've easily stored hundreds of dollars' worth of rib roasts and steaks and pork loins, well aware of how much better these items taste than hamburger-bun mini-pizzas. Fletch returns home with a cooler the size of a coffin filled with bags of ice and we're able to save all our frozen goods.

Although we have every resource available from cash and credit and plenty to eat and shelves of books I've been saving for just this kind of occasion, I can't seem to unclench.

I'm furious that for all my worrying, for all the ways that I plotted and schemed to make sure we were never without again, here we are in a situation that's completely out of my control. In my head I know I'm in my own home with a mortgage that's paid in the gracious green suburbs, but in my heart, I'm standing by the back window of my shitty rental apartment, watching the repo men wheel away in the car we can no longer afford and waiting for the eviction notice.

Funny how one tiny power outage can bring me back to the

very worst time of my life, triggering every fear and insecurity about not being ready.

Fletch, who's been diligently tucked away in his office all month reconciling our bank statements from 2010, is delighted to have a Mother Nature–induced day off. While he was out, he picked up a chain saw and related protective gear and has been happily hacking away at downed limbs and overgrown brush. To him, this is, like, the best snow day ever!

But for me? I can't stop fretting about my stupid wavy hair and pacing around in the vicinity of the television. I try to read but nothing holds my interest, likely because I'm up and fooling with the dial on our battery-operated radio every ten minutes trying to get an update on ComEd's progress. I just need the lights to come back on so I can remember that it's 2011, and not 2002.

When I go to use my iPhone to order a pizza, I burst into frustrated tears when I find the battery drained because it always gets bumped on in my overcrowded purse. Fletch senses I need some cheering up. He challenges me to a board game, something I always suggest, but rarely get to play. But instead of being thrilled at the opportunity to finally whip his punk ass at Worst Case Scenario,[202] I fret and pout through the first two games.

Due to a couple of clever guesses on my part in regard to grizzly attacks, I'm in the lead when, out of nowhere, the room is flooded with light. I spring from my seat, dashing over to the power strip where I charge everything.

"I wouldn't get so excited," Fletch says. "They may be work-

---

[202] How does Fletch know so much about shark bites?

ing on the line and we'll probably go out again before we're back on."

We have two blissful minutes of illumination and I get to whiz with the lights on for the first time in twenty-four hours, and poof! Just like that, they go out again.

"NOOOOOOOOO!!!" I shout.

"Yeah, figured that would happen. Sit down, it's your roll," Fletch says.

We return to our game and I'm energized by having the lights on again, even if it was only momentary. But that's really all I need to get my head back into the present.

As we play, I'm reminded of my seemingly endless stretch of being unemployed. Although things were pretty bad at the end, it occurs to me that at no point while I was out of work did I ever think to enjoy having the time off. I never once gave myself the luxury of relaxing. In retrospect, I probably would have gotten a job a lot quicker if I hadn't gone to my interviews so tightly wound. I'm sure I came off ten times more intense than I actually am.

I'm not saying I'm unhappy with the way things turned out— far from it. I have a career that I love and a life that's full of joy. But I wonder if I wouldn't have created a happy ending just a little bit sooner if I'd ever allowed myself to just *be*, to appreciate the freedom of not being tied to a corporate life that I'd hated, to realize that in a world that's constantly go-go-go, sometimes it's nice just to turn everything off and spend a little quality time across the table from the man that I adore . . . while beating his pants off at a silly board game.

The lights come back on about twenty minutes later, as we're halfway through with the rubber match determining the World Champion at Worst Case Scenario. Instead of bolting out of our chairs to throw in some laundry or run the dishwasher, we stay seated, enjoying the game and one another's company. And even though I lose the game, I still end up with the feeling of Charlie Sheen–grade #WINNING.

Later, after straightening my hair and running the vacuum, I happily climb into bed. Before I even get to the part where Molly Ringwald sings *Secret Life*'s theme song or the cats open their first cabinet of the evening, I fall into a deep, blissful slumber, glad to be out of the past and back in the present.

My not-so-secret-life is good.

However, I do plan to shop for my own generator.

Because if the world does come to the end? I'm going out with the lights on.

Reluctant Adult Lesson Learned:

Being prepared in life is good, but living life in the moment is better.

The Five Stages of Grief

"*Gotta go! Close up shop!*"

Two minutes later.

"*Did you not hear me? We've got to go!*"

A minute after that.

"*Jen, the 'Internets' will still be there when you come home. Move it! Don't want to be late!*"

I sigh and log off, hustling down the stairs to change out of my robe and into some clothes. We have an appointment to talk to the bank about refinancing our home today. The rates have dropped and because Fletch and I are all grown-up now, this is the kind of thing to which we pay attention.

Or I normally would . . . if I weren't so distracted online watching the melee between a bunch of bloggers arguing over whether or not some fighting unicorn-shaped dessert served at their convention seemed "racist."

Don't misunderstand me—racism is still a problem in this country and I'd never discount how tragic and unfair that is. However, I posit the best way to combat ignorance and intolerance is not by sending passive-aggressive tweets to those who ate the cake in the first place.[203]

On my way out, I stop in the kitchen to grab my iPad. If the whole cake thing turns ugly, I intend to have a front-row seat.

Fletch pauses before we head to the garage. "You look nice."

"Thanks! Did you expect to see me in my bathrobe? Or did you assume I'd put on yoga pants and a stained Champion T-shirt?" To be fair, that is my standard at-home, go-to outfit.

"Sort of," he replies. "New shorts?"

I nod. I'm clad in an adorably fitted pair of knee-length, white Not Your Daughter's Jeans denim shorts,[204] wedge sandals, and a sheer floral tunic with a stretchy tank underneath. I threw on one of my fancy bras, too, and not my usual ones with the tatty lace and spray-tan stains. I figure if part of it peeks out from underneath my Spanx top, it should seem intentional and cute and *Hello, Sailor!* and not, you know, pathetic. I don't want the banker to be all, "Oh, honey, stop worrying about rates and get yourself to Victoria's Secret STAT."

I tell Fletch, "I thought I should look 'breezy,' like we don't care whether or not we get refinanced."

Fletch glances down at his khakis and gingham-check shirt.

....

[203] But what do I know? I wasn't even invited!
[204] Wearing white bottoms for the first time in thirty years . . . thank you, perimenopause!

"Am I breezy?" I nod and then I fill him in on CakeGate all the way to the bank. His only response to my story is, "These are adults?"

I shrug and that's when I notice that FancyBra is a bit tighter than I remember. Also, because it's underneath one of my scuba-suit tank tops, the whole thing is compressing me in a not entirely comfortable manner. I shift a bit and try to move the band out of the ridge it's already creating in my skin.

The bank's door has a sign posted about all the items that aren't allowed to be worn inside, like sunglasses, ball caps, and hoodies with the lid up, especially when paired together. As I read the sign I remark, "If the Unabomber wants to refinance here, he's going to be sorely disappointed." I give FancyBra a tug for luck before entering the lobby. My sunglasses are resting on top of my head, holding my hair back, but I suspect that's okay.

Our banker ushers us into a conference room and then we begin to Talk Seriously about Important Banking Matters. Or, Fletch and the banker Talk Seriously while I concentrate on Shrugging My Shoulders in a Way That Might Provide Some Relief. Apparently upon sitting, I've angered FancyBra and now it's going all boa constrictor on me. Every time I breathe in, it tightens its grip on my rib cage.

I swear this thing fit this morning.

Breathe and squeeze.

Although . . . it *was* at the back of my drawer.

Breathe and squeeze.

This bra is still new and fresh-looking and doesn't have those weird orange half-moons on it from the VersaSpa booth at Palm Beach Tan, which is way better than the Mystic one. The Versa does terrible things to brassieres, but it gives my skin a very healthy, natural red undertone as opposed to the full Oompa Loompa/Snooki hybrid of the Mystic.[205]

Anyway.

Breathe and squeeze.

Why *haven't* I been wearing this bra in my daily life, which entails an occasional trip to the spray tanner? How come it's not all sad and flaccid and comfortable like the rest of my collection? Is it possible that this is the bra I always put on and then immediately tear off again because OWIE OWIE OWIE?

No. I wouldn't do that. I'm too smart to do that. I'm too *grown up* for that! I would never willingly keep an uncomfortable piece of clothing around because that's ridiculous. Although . . . I still do wear those crippling Burberry ballet flats that I got at a fraction of the original cost because they may or may not have been mis-sized. And the last time I had them on, despite my moleskin bandages and Dr. Scholl's anti-rub stick, they still filled with so much blood that I left O. J. Simpson-esque tracks all through Neiman Marcus.

I fear I've made a grievous error.

Today's lousy with pollen and that makes me sneeze, which gives FancyBra the chance to reposition its grip. NO! Stop it, FancyBra! I hate you! You are the worst bra I ever owned! Your job is to lift and support, not dig and bruise! No wonder I never wear you. I don't *like* you. None of the other bras do. They told me so at the big party we threw without you, where we ate nonracially problematic cake. Suck on that, FancyBra.

....

[205] I realize this problem could be neatly eliminated if I spray-tanned topless, but let me tell you something. Gravity, like Panang Thai Curry, is not your friend. I'd rather deal with orange half-moons on my bra than the white ones beneath my low-hanging fruits.

FancyBra interprets "suck on that" literally and tightens up even more. The pain makes me gasp, which in turns causes me to sputter and have a coughing fit.

The gentlemen turn to look at me. "Do you need some water? Are you okay?" the banker asks.

No, I am most decidedly *not* okay, but what am I going to say? I bought the wrong-sized bra and now it's trying to assassinate me before we can get this whole refi-thing done? Come on. I want to demonstrate how I'm businesslike and professional and adult and not someone who can't even dress herself because she was so busy with an Internet girl fight.

So I make the one statement that will clearly express all of the above.

"Oh, I'm fine. I just . . . choked on some spit."

Fletch and the banker pause for a moment and, finding themselves at an absolute loss for words, proceed like it never happened. The banker clears his throat and Fletch neatens up the pile of file folders he removed from his bag a few minutes ago. They continue their conversation and I reach the bargaining stage of grief over this horrible, horrible bra.

I'm sorry I haven't been laundering you in FancySoap from the FancyBraStore and that I used FancyMeshBag only the one time because it was a pain in the ass and the zipper kept getting caught. You, FancyBra—you're special and I realize that now.

You're the thoroughbred of bras and it's my fault that I've been treating you like a plow horse. Loosen your grip and I swear I'll spoil you! I'll treat you right, baby! I'll wash you in a crystal bowl with bottled water—no, sparkling water! Yes! And I'll never let that nasty old Maytag dryer touch you again. I'll construct a special line so you may bask in the summer sun, clipped onto the natural hemp rope with clothespins carved from trees in the Amazon rain forest! It'll be great, I promise! Just please, please let me go.

FancyBra responds by ratcheting up the vise around my chest one more notch.

That's how it's going to be, FancyBra? You call the shots now? And I'm just the chunky chump in a tank top willing to take whatever abuse you heap on me?

FancyBra, I bet you're an object lesson on why I should mind my own business. I probably deserve this pain. Doesn't matter. Nothing matters. In fifty years you'll be in a landfill and I'll be in the ground so who even cares.

I guess that's how it goes, circle of life and all. One day you're young and firm, and the next you're fighting a feckless battle with two nylon cups and an unforgiving swath of elastic.

And so it goes.

And so it goes.

I'm slumping down in my seat, accepting my fate that Fancy-Bra will, in fact, end me when Fletch and the banker rise from the table and shake hands.

Huzzah! All is not lost!

I'm within thirty seconds of being able to escape to the car where I can free myself from this Iron Maiden and ride home in unencumbered glory!

Yes!

I am safe!

I am free!

I am almost home!

"Hey, there's a couple of folks I'd like you to meet in the office," the banker says.

Fletch starts to say, "Sounds great," when I interrupt him with a noise best described as a high-pitched keening. Everyone in the lobby looks at me like I just donned a ski mask and I begin coughing again. Fletch shifts his computer bag to the other shoulder and says, "I think what Jen is saying is that she's meeting her friends for lunch today and she has to go."

Mutely, I nod.

The banker bids us good-bye and tells us he'll be in touch.

As we walk to the car, Fletch says, "Well, *that* was interesting. I assume there's some explanation as to why you lost your mind. Was it the cake?"

I fill him in on the terrible things FancyBra had done to me and he's surprisingly understanding, likely because of his whole stream of "pants feel like paper bag" e-mails he sent me from work a few years ago. I remember the time he cried about how his linen shirt made him feel like a sweaty Bedouin wrapped up in sheets, too. He *knows*. He's been there.

The second we hit the car, my hands are in my shirt, unsnapping my shackles and pulling the harsh mistress out of the bell sleeve of my tunic all *Flashdance*-style before we're even out of the parking lot.

Sweet, sweet, sweet relief.

When we get home, I toss The New Hotness in the trash and find one of my Old 'n' Busted bras before heading to lunch. Every time I breathe or laugh without being stabbed or asphyxiated, I am grateful.

In entirely unrelated news, our refi hasn't come through yet.

I'm sure it's just a paperwork snafu.

Reluctant Adult Lesson Learned:

If the glove doesn't fit, you must a-quit wearing it if you want to take advantage of the new, lower interest rates.

C·H·A·P·T·E·R
T·W·E·N·T·Y-F·O·U·R

Generator X

I'm in bed when it happens again.

We're hit with a small burst of rain at some point before my alarm sounds. I knew a storm was looming because Loki woke me up earlier when he tried to wedge himself underneath my pillow. Then the other two dogs followed suit, burrowing under the covers with us and immediately inflating to twice their size. Squeezed out, I left to sleep with the cats in the adjoining bedroom.

When I entered the cats' camp, Odin glanced up at me with his one good eye to confirm that I wasn't "scary monster." Odin's partially blind and generally thinks everyone's a monster because he can't quite see them. I'm the only person from whom he doesn't hide.[206] I have friends who visit weekly and have never met him.

---

[206] He likes Fletch but Fletch is tall, which, often in Odin's world, equals monster.

Satisfied that I'm on the buddy list, Odin stretched out so that I could rub his tummy. Then as I lay down, Chuck Norris and Gus wrapped themselves around either side of my head. Their purring immediately put me back to sleep.

I'm kind of amazed with what we've accomplished with these cats. When Gina, Fletch, and I rounded them up two years ago, we were sure they'd always be feral, that is, *if* they even survived. Our contingency plan was to neuter and release them because the vet worried they'd never adjust to living with humans. But for the cost of a whole-house generator, two eye surgeries, and a couple of weeks in the kitty ICU, the vets made them healthy. Then we spent a few more weeks waking up in the middle of the night to administer medicines and months socializing them. And now? Not only was Odin able to keep his eye, but all the cats are so social they aren't happy unless they're touching one of us. Not long ago I was watching TV upstairs—Fletch came in and laughed when he spotted the three of them draped around my shoulders like a mink stole. I smiled and said, "Who's feral now, bitch?"

When we lost the last of our old cats earlier this year,[207] the Thundercats were a real comfort. They seemed to understand how affectionate Jordan and Tucker were, and they've since stepped up their games. Odin's big move is to sit on my lap while I'm using the bathroom and Chuck likes to press his face against the glass while I shower.

I appreciate the effort, but they need to work on their execution.

....

[207] RIP, you dirty old man and you cranky old lady. You are loved and missed.

The cats and I are resting amicably, waiting for the alarm to buzz. Drops tap against the window and there's some moderate thunder and lightning but in terms of storms, this is one of those relaxing ones that make me snuggle deeper into bed.

Then there's a huge pop and we lose power again. Using my skin for traction, the cats dig in and take off.

Argh! How are the lights off *again?* We just lost them three weeks ago! This is ridiculous!

ComEd was all over the news last time, gloating about having rebuilt the grid so efficiently. I kind of assumed said grid might last a little longer, but perhaps they rebuilt everything with balsa wood and tissue paper.

This is so frustrating. Just because I'm working on being better at living in the moment doesn't mean I *want* to experience the same damn moment so soon after last time.

Regardless, that's when our generator kicks in so it's all fine.

Ha! What I mean is, that's when our generator *would* have kicked in if Fletch and I weren't so deep in our analysis paralysis that we've yet to make a decision.

We talk about generators so much that the word "generator" is almost nonsensical now. Generator. Generator. Generator. Say it enough times in a row and it sounds exactly like the noise made from trying to start a recalcitrant . . . generator. Generator. Generator.

Our kitchen table's stacked with brochures and promotional DVDs and we've got a whole cost-benefit analysis charted out. By now we're probably both qualified to *sell* generators. Personally, I favor the Generac 1.6L Engine, naturally cooled, gas aspirated model . . . mostly because their Web site is interactive and you can click on different parts of the graphic to see stuff ignite.[208] Fletch is still undecided and I have to keep an eye on his research because he keeps meandering into survivalist message boards. I fear *Herd_Thinner666* and *Profit O' Doom* are not the best influences.

Point is I've gotten Fletch on board with the idea and our goal's to have one installed before the weather turns. Granted, we're buying a generator in lieu of taking a vacation, but when it's zero degrees and the snow's up to the garage roof and I'm not, you know, freezing to death à la *The Shining*, I'll be glad I didn't get to go to the Hamptons this year.[209]

Anyway, confident that a long-term solution's in the works, I go back to sleep.

When I wake up an hour later, the sun's already out and I'm covered in a blanket of cats. For a second I wonder if I dreamed the whole thing but then I see the blank display on the digital clock and confirm it really happened.

I have a number of boring tasks on my to-do list today, but since they all require electricity, I've given myself a get-out-of-jail-free pass. Hot-weather snow day at my house, yay! I have a leisurely breakfast while listening to the radio, where I learn that more than one hundred thousand Chicago residents are in the dark. Whoa! For a storm that lasted maybe fifteen minutes start to finish? Really? I can pee harder than it was raining. I don't understand what went wrong.

After the last outage, I'm super-meticulous about putting my electronics on the charger, so I've plenty of battery life and I'm not going to be disconnected from the real world. I send out a quick

....

[208] I very much enjoy clicking the electric stove button to see the oven get all fiery.

[209] At least that's what I'm telling myself.

status update to my friends and about half of them are in the dark, too. I invite everyone up for an impromptu pool party, but they're all busy with "meetings" and "day jobs" and "children." More sun for me then!

I kick back in a lawn chair, reading the books I've been meaning to get to forever and I spend this gorgeous day chilling out, maxing, relaxing all cool.[210] Fletch runs out to buy more ice for our coffin and when he returns, we transfer the contents of the freezer.

Every couple of hours, I wander back into the house for radio updates. The last time, the outage affected a quarter of a million people and as I checked the radio all day, those numbers rapidly diminished. But today, every time I tune in the numbers rise. Earlier this morning we hit three hundred thousand and at this point, it's six hundred thousand.

Today would be an excellent day to start my new career as a generator salesman.

A few weeks ago, the outages were really random. Like, one side of the street had electric and the other didn't, so the roads were crisscrossed with orange extension cords as neighbors helped one another not lose a fridge full of groceries. Joanna said the whole thing turned into a huge block party where people grilled up everything they could before it spoiled and kids got massive bowls of melt-y ice cream. I bet when her children look back at the blackout, they'll do so fondly. Up here, except for on one side of our fence, we're separated by woods and are easily a couple of tenths of a mile from all our neighbors, so even if we knew anyone, we couldn't find a cord long enough to tap into their generators.

While exchanging a couple of brief messages with my agent, I

....
[210] Ten points if you caught the Fresh Prince reference.

mention we're out again and she's all, "Did you move to the 1970s?"

However, the situation feels different this time, probably because I'm actively working to adjust my attitude. I'm coming up on a busy part of the year, so stealing a little break isn't the worst thing ever. I'm learning that once in a while it's nice to have a quick TV time-out and it feels like we're camping. But we're camping in a house with all our pets, my favorite antiques,[211] and flushable plumbing, so it's all good.

The power doesn't come back until midafternoon, thirty hours after it goes out. Honestly? Last night was fun! The sun set around eight forty-five p.m., so we had plenty of natural light. Then Fletch and I listened to talk radio and just hung out telling stories for a few hours before going to sleep. Because I'd soaked in the pool for so long, I lowered my core temperature and was actually chilly when I went to bed. We had such an adventure that I was a little disappointed when everything came back to life. I had at least two more days of good attitude left in me and I, dare I say it, found a way to enjoy the experience.

That is, except for the frogs.

When I let the dogs out this morning, I saw some stuff floating at the surface of the pool, so I grabbed the skimmer. Upon closer inspection, I realized they were frogs, a hundred mini-frogs, all clustered together! OMG! So adorable! Wee and grass-green with comically bulgy eyes! For a second, I considered running inside to grab my camera so I could document the find for CuteOverload. com. I mean, how often do you stumble upon a little froggy fraternity party?

....

[211] Zinc lion heads, I'm looking at you!

Last summer, we found a couple of small amphibians swimming in the pool but we haven't seen any since then. There's something about the noise of the pumping system that keeps wildlife away. I guess with the system silenced, the Itty Bitty Froggy Committee assumed they'd found themselves an ocean! Last one in the pool's a rotten toad!

I didn't notice the problem at first. I assumed when my tiny new friends spotted the net coming at them, they'd go all Calaveras County Frog Jumping Competition on me, with teeny fern-colored bodies making spectacular leaps and bounds. It wasn't until I got my first scoopful that I realized none of them were leaping.

Or bounding.

In fact, they weren't moving at all.

My pool wasn't full of dozens of happy mini-frogs, delighted at having found sweet new digs; rather, my pool was full of a hundred mini-frogs who met an untimely death.

Oh, the screaming that followed.

Fletch wandered outside then, asking, "Hey, what's with all the shouting?" When I showed him, he paled and made the excuse that there was something urgent requiring his attention inside the house. If the predicted zombie war has anything to do with small, dead amphibians, Fletch isn't going to be quite the warrior he envisions.

I tried to keep the hollering to a minimum as I scooped them out and chucked netful after netful towards the woods. In the middle of my gruesome task, I had to shuffle the dogs into the house.

"All finished?" he asked, looking relieved.

"Nope," I replied. "Libby was snarfing up frog carcass as though *cuisses de grenouilles* were her new favorite dish." That's when Fletch decided he needed to go out for more ice.

Fifteen increasingly screamy minutes later, I successfully strained the tiny bodies out of the Dead Sea . . . or so I thought. That's when I spotted the sole survivor, tucked away inside the hollow core of a fun-noodle like a small, web-footed Anne Frank hiding from the German Security Police, otherwise known as chlorinated water.

Gingerly, I liberated her orange foam life preserver from the water, placing it on the other side of the yard, and breathed a little sigh of relief as she hopped towards the wood line. Then I set up the hose to ripple the surface of the pool, hoping to signify danger to any other mini-frogs currently lurking in the grass.

So, yeah, other than the Frog-o-caust, the power outage was fine.

After the electric kicks on, I decide against running the air-conditioning, opting to air the stink out of the joint. One of the best parts of moving out of the city is being able to open a window without encouraging unwanted visitors, be they rats or homeless people or criminals.[212]

I leave the door open between the kitchen and the screened porch so the cats can enjoy the weather, too. They're happy to hang out on what we call their "catio" all day, lazing on the couch while glowering at chipmunks and letting the sun warm the downy fur on their bellies.

I keep the dogs inside because I don't want them eating any more frogs. I'm surprised not to see the cats on the porch, but the dogs are out there and sometimes Libby annoys them. Although she's gentle, she's yet to figure out the concept of personal space, so she's often on the receiving end of a few good swats.

....

[212] I've battled all three.

A couple of hours later I come inside to shower. As I pass the spare bedroom on the way to the master, I notice something's askew. Upon further inspection, I realize the problem. The screen's been removed and it's five feet away in the rosebushes.

What the . . . ?

How did . . . ?

Clearly no one broke in because we're home and the dogs would have lost their minds. And I know the screen was securely attached to the window because that's the kind of thing I'm fairly neurotic about, kind of like when I check three times to make sure the iron's unplugged.[213]

That's when I realize that our little family is missing three feline members.

Oh, no.

No, *no*.

My cats can't get out. My cats have *never* gotten out. Never. Not one of the six cats I had before the Thundercats ever made an unauthorized exit. I've now owned cats for twenty years and nobody's ever escaped, sort of like Stalag 13 on *Hogan's Heroes*.[214] I have a perfect record. If I were a factory, my sign out front would read: This Organization Has Gone 7300 Days Without an Incident. I employ Constant Vigilance™; this shit does not happen on *my* watch.

I immediately break into a sweat. I scream for Fletch, shut the window, and conduct a thorough whole-house search for the Thundercats. None of them are in any of their usual spots—between the tasseled curtains and the sliding glass door, inside the

....

[213] Solution? Never iron!
[214] Whether or not the old cats had an entire secret bunker set up under the house is still in question.

lining of the couch, on top of the Zombie War boxes in the basement. They're nowhere to be found.

I throw on a pair of shorts and shoes and we spend the whole afternoon calling them and combing the woods around the house. We're surrounded by trees on all sides except for the narrow path that winds from the road down to the house.

The road.

NO!

These guys haven't seen any road for two years. And even though we're tucked away behind all the trees, ours is a fairly busy street and we're not far from the highway. What's going to happen if they decide to cross? They don't know to look both ways. The idea of finding one of them by the side of the road makes me feel ill. We worked so hard to get the feral out of them that now I'm afraid they can't take care of themselves.

Also?

EVERYONE ON THIS ROAD IS DRIVING TOO FAST.

There are cats in these woods! Be careful, you assholes in your zippy cars! Give 'em a BRAKE. I stand at the end of my drive, hands on my hips, glowering at everyone going over fifteen miles an hour. It doesn't help me find the cats, but it makes me feel a little better.

A couple of hours into our search, we spot Odin in the woods to the west of us but he runs away because he thinks we're scary monsters. The fact that I'm sobbing hysterically probably doesn't help.

When we finally come in, we're covered in bug bites and we're all slashed up from the brush. Fletch calls our vet to see what our next move is and to confirm that their microchip information is up-to-date. The vet explains that the cats will likely just come home when they're bored or hungry and all we need to do is set out some tuna and they should turn up.

This? I paid the price of a used car on cat upkeep and *this* is the advice I get? For what we spent, I want the whole veterinary office up here in S.W.A.T. gear and for us to make a human chain and comb the woods inch by inch. Tuna? Come on!

We set out the tuna and then Fletch decides to retrace the cats' steps. "We have to think like a cat," Fletch tells me.

"Okay, would you rather bang open some cabinets or throw up in the cleaning ladies' shoes?" I ask.

"Shh, give me a minute. I'll figure this out," he replies.

I don't understand how one of them got the screen off because they're sturdy; I test-push them all the time and they won't budge. I'd have never opened the windows if I didn't trust them to hold.

Fletch pores over the point of exit. "Aha!" he exclaims.

"DO YOU SEE THEM?" I shriek.

"No, but I figured out what happened. Look here." He points at the body of a dead chipmunk and then another a few feet down, plus a stiff mouse ten feet past that.

"Oh, God." Tears spring to my eyes when I see the furry little victims. Can every woodland creature please not DIE up here today? Hey, Bambi and Thumper! Stay away from my yard or face certain doom! Tell your friends!

He continues. "They must have seen all the rodents and it was too much. My guess is they all worked together to bash out the screen, which is why it flew into the roses and then they went on their killing spree." Fletch points out where the hedges are trampled on the side of the house and the flattened daylilies. "My Boy Scout training tells me that's where they left the protection of the side of the house."

"And then where did they go?"

Fletch looks puzzled. "I don't know. I wasn't a very good Boy Scout."

"Do you want me to keep crying?" I demand.

After more searching and another bout of hysterics on my part, Fletch convinces me to go inside with him. "All we can do right now is wait. They'll come back. They've got it too good here not to come back."

"What if they don't? What if they're hurt or they decide they like the taste of freedom too much? I cannot lose five goddamned cats to death and attrition in one year. Do you understand me? *I can't do it*. This will be the straw that breaks and has thus far prevented me from being The Crazy Cat Lady. *This* is what's going to earn me a spot on *Animal Hoarders*."

Fletch grasps me by my shoulders. "Jen, it's going to be okay. I promise you we will get them back. Whatever it takes, we'll get them back."

Fletch tries to distract me with a late dinner and free rein of the remote control but I can't eat and I'm not interested in TV. I mean, I know that they're just cats and in the scheme of things, kittens are pretty much free . . . at least until you take them to the vet. Plus, they'd probably prefer to live in the wild anyway.

Despite the fact that I equate the cats with being my children, it's so not the same. As untethered as I feel right now, I have to wonder what happens to families who have to deal with a real missing child, and not just a furry surrogate. I feel awfully self-indulgent right now, wallowing in my own unhappiness. I can't even imagine what parents must go through; it's unthinkable. Part of why we never opted for children is that I couldn't handle it if anything ever went wrong. I'm already so neurotic and controlling that if I had to worry about a tiny person's life, I fear I'd go over the edge. My constant anxiety and worst-case-scenario-ing would consume me.

Angie, mother to four healthy, happy sons, says you eventually learn to balance the need to protect your kids with their need to explore boundaries, but I wouldn't be capable. I'd want them in a full set of pads and a helmet and I wouldn't ever want them out of my sight. I would be the poster child for helicopter parents everywhere.[215]

My children would likely resent me for my overprotection and we'd all be miserable. Plus, since I can't even keep a damn cat safe, apparently, I'm sure I'd be a huge failure. The whole secret to my success is avoiding anything I wouldn't immediately be good at; ergo I'm never going to be anyone's mother.

No, let me rephrase that.

I plan to be good at catching these damn cats, so after dumping additional tuna juice and handfuls of catnip all over the front step, I sit by the door and watch and wait.

Not more than ten minutes after I rebait the trap, Chuck Norris appears out of the bushes!!

Opening the front door startles him, but the lure of the tuna is too great and I'm able to scoop him up while he stuffs his maw with fish. I'm somewhere between euphoric and devastated—I'm thrilled to have him back, but Chuck's the ringleader, so I sort of thought he'd bring everyone with him.

Chuck appears no worse for wear. Actually, he seems a bit smug.

Hope you enjoyed your walkabout, you little asshole, because

---

[215] Yes, there would be leashes. Laugh at me all you want in the mall, but I'm not letting these guys wander away.

it is never, ever happening again. I lecture Chuck on how he's lost "catio" privileges before I resume my vigil by the door.

Every few minutes I leave my perch to go outside and call the others. Earlier I walked up and down the wood line with an armful of cat food cans, willing the sound of opening them to bring them running. Finding this unsuccessful, I left all the open cans out there for the coyotes so they'd be full and wouldn't need to eat the tender young Thundercats.

About an hour later, I notice a gray ball of fluff in the darkness. Odin! It's sweet little Odin! He's come home! Carefully I pry open the door and attempt to grab him, but Odie's way too skittish to stand still. He immediately streaks out into the darkness. But that's good news because it means his instincts are to come back. Now all I have to do is convince him I'm not a scary monster.

I get Fletch and we both strap on our headlamps and begin to sweep the bushes. "You see anything?" I ask.

"Something over here has one and a half lasers. Unless there's another creature who's had eye surgery, I'm looking at Odie. Here's what we're going to do—I'll flush him out and then you grab him," Fletch says, cutting back behind the lilac bushes.

But every time Fletch herds Odin in my direction, he gets spooked and dashes under the boxwood hedges. I'm afraid we're terrifying him, so I insist we speak in super-soothing tones. "Odie, sweetie, please come to your mama because she loves you," I beg.

Fletch adds, "Nice, nice, little Odie, please go to your mama because I'm being eaten alive by mosquitoes and I'm about to pass out from blood loss, okay, good boy?"

"Stop that! He understands sarcasm," I hiss.

"He's afraid of paper bags and the dishwasher and thinks

we're scary monsters," Fletch replies. "Sarcasm isn't even in his top ten of what bothers him."

After a solid hour of playing cat to Odin's mouse, we decide to take a break. "Maybe if we sit on the step and toss tuna to him, we can lure him over?" I suggest. I'm so frustrated sitting here, knowing Odin's so close to safety, yet being unable to bring him in.

Fletch tosses chunks of tuna down the bluestone path and Odin inches closer and closer. "Those pieces are too big! He's going to be stuffed before we get him over here," I say.

Then I get the genius idea to rub catnip all over myself and douse my hands with tuna juice so I'll smell irresistible. And I am irresistible. To every biting bug in Lake County. I'm going to need my own flea collar after this.

After woofing down big chunks of tuna, Odin seems satisfied and we can't lure him any closer.

"This isn't working," I cry.

"This cat is coming in this damn house right damn now," Fletch says.[216] "We'll funnel him into the hedges and I'm going to force him down by you. Grab him and throw him in the house. Let's do this!"

And then we do this.

Unsuccessfully.

Whole buncha times.

We're almost three hours into the hunt when Fletch gets an idea. "Odin keeps going to the window where he escaped. What if you went inside and popped the screen to see if he wants to come in that way?"

....

[216] I love when he goes all General Patton.

"Couldn't work less than what we're currently doing," I agree. I hurry to the bedroom and ease the window open. Gingerly I pop the screen, the whole time saying, "Odie, come! Come on, little guy, come see your mama."

And then that little son of a bitch walks right up to the window, arches his spine, and raises the back of his neck as though he wants me to pick him up.

As though I hadn't been *trying to do exactly that* for the past three hours.

I'm able to grab him and whisk the window shut and the whole time, Odin's purring contentedly in my arms, all, "You shoulda seen the scary monsters that was chasing me!"

Two down, one to go.

After we got Odin back and I washed all the fish juice off myself, Fletch insisted we call it a night. We left the screen off the window and lined the sill with tuna in the hopes that Gus would follow suit.

In the morning, the meat's gone but there's no sign of Gus. I'm sure any number of animals could have eaten it, but I choose to believe it was Gus. Because he's the most skittish of the group, we need to rethink our strategy. I feel he's too nervous to come out on his own, so I send Fletch out to buy a cruelty free trap while I spend the day in the woods. I catch nothing, save for the possible exception of malaria.

We set the Havahart trap and cover it with a towel and I dash out the door in the morning to find the tuna gone and nothing in the trap except an enormous toad and some mouse droppings.

I really thought Gus would be back within twenty-four hours, but he's not. What's he doing out there? Is he hurt? Is he scared? What's he eating, other than the possibility of windowsill tuna? It's so hot—is he able to find a water source? Does he even want to come home?

Maybe that's it. Maybe I've spent so much time anthropomorphizing him that I just assumed he loved me back and wanted to live here. I mean, he's not a person; he's an animal. Maybe he got out in the wild and the feral part of his brain took over. Maybe he's been miserable here and all he's ever wanted to do was roam free. Maybe he's still pissed off about the time I stuck him in a pumpkin costume and put his picture on the Internet.

Yet I'm not about to give up on him. I'm scouring the Web for information when Fletch comes up behind me.

"Any news on Gus?" he asks.

"Um, so far he hasn't checked in on Foursquare or updated his Facebook status, so, no. No news," I reply. (Except Stacey who sent me a note saying, *"He'll come slinking home smelling of clove cigarettes and wine coolers, having made out with someone inappropriate. Oh, wait, that was me in high school. But he'll be back, don't worry."*)

"That's not what I meant. Why don't you ask your readers for help? They know everything," he suggests.

The thing is, he's right. I swear I have the most plugged-in readers in the world and there's pretty much nothing they can't resolve. They figured out when my tree was infested with Emerald Ash Borers and informed me it was Tatiana Patitz in my favorite George Michael video, and not Elaine Irwin.[217] When I was hit with my second instance of those bastard ear crystals, alert fans

....

[217] *Freedom '90.*

pointed me to the Epley Maneuver and in ten minutes, I was able to fix what my primary care physician couldn't in three months. How did I not think to ask these guys two days ago?

As soon as I post a status update, advice pours in. Those who don't have a specific strategy offer support and I'm grateful for their kind thoughts. I'm overwhelmed with all the useful information, from setting the trap on the lightest possible setting to leaving the garage door cracked so Gus can come inside on his own. We also plan to set out baskets of dirty laundry and used cat litter, so Gus will be attracted to a familiar smell.[218]

Putting the suggestions into action requires a trip to Target for sardines and a baby monitor. Now it's no secret that I'm a Target aficionado. From Archer Farms and Merona and Mossimo to Up & Up, I have intimate knowledge of almost every product and aisle. I speak bull's eye. I can even tell you which Target carries my favorite brand of milk[219] and which stocks my favorite moisturizer[220] and I plan my shopping trips accordingly. But until today I've not had much reason to set foot in the baby aisles.

Let me just say this—I had no idea having a baby required so many accessories. From onesies to crib bumpers to lanolin-based n-i-p-p-l-e salve, how does anyone have a kid without going completely broke? Just getting a nursery ready for Day One of a baby's life has to cost thousands of dollars and that's way before they start crying for Air Jordans or flip phones or whatever it is the kids need these days to preserve their self-esteem. You have one kid and you're *never* going to be able to afford that generator. And didn't

....

[218] Fletch drew the line at the suggestion he pee in the bushes. But if the above doesn't work, I'm not opposed to trying myself.
[219] Grassland at the Target Highland Park.
[220] Johnson's Deep Hydrating Lotion at the Target Vernon Hills.

people used to have their babies sleep in drawers fifty years ago? Where did all these products come from?

There's even a million choices when it comes to baby monitors. I'll probably opt for the thirty-dollar model because all I want to do is hear if the cat comes into the garage. But how does any new parent see the option with the video feed and *not* buy it?

As I stand next to the monitors, a couple of people give me big, happy smiles while Fletch and I compare features. In every other part of this store, everyone's always rude and wedging in front of me. But in this aisle, the assumption is that we're first-time parents and the attitudes are adjusted accordingly. I haven't the heart to tell anyone I have a missing cat.[221]

After Target, I spend more time in the woods, but find nothing. Yet I feel hopeful that something good's going to happen because I've employed every possible suggestion I was given[222] including taping some of the cats' whiskers to an unseen part of the wall. I have no clue as to why this is supposed to work, but damn it, I'm trying anyway.

Before we get ready for bed, we slosh sardine juice all over the cage and place the bits of fish into a plastic bowl. I've been told the more highly scented the lure, the better. If I don't catch a freaking bear with this stuff, I'll be shocked. And even though I've happily eaten far more disgusting stuff, I have to put a scarf over my mouth when doling out the sardines.

We set the trap and once I'm in bed, I concentrate on Gus extra hard when I say my prayers. It's been three days—my feeling is he's coming back tonight or he's not coming back at all. For the

....

[221] And really? I'm just kind of fat.
[222] Except for the peeing and I'm not above doing that.

past two days, Odin and Chuck have been wandering past the doors and windows all confused, like something's out of place, but they're not sure what. It's a little heartbreaking.

So tonight is my line in the sand—if Gus doesn't come back, I'll have to accept he doesn't want to. Tonight determines if we actually have the bond that I imagined. I have such trouble believing that the little guy who curls up with me every night was just biding his time until he could make his escape. I think of last week when I was watching *So You Think You Can Dance* and he was sitting on my chest. Whenever Gus is really happy, he drools. And he must have been delighted because long strings were hanging out of either side of his mouth. Had I known then that might have been our last time, I wouldn't have been so quick to be annoyed when he slobbered all over my shirt.

I fall asleep cradling the baby monitor. Fletch and I laugh that this is likely the first and last time we'll ever do so, but there's a part of me that's intrigued to experience one small parenthood rite of passage.

I wake up at dawn and immediately dash out the front door. The trap has been sprung and there's something inside. I can't tell what because the towel's obscuring the contents. I'm hoping desperately that it's my boy, but whatever it is we've caught, I'm keeping it and I hope it likes to snuggle. I hold my breath and bend to retrieve the trap.

I hear him before I even see him. The yowl coming out of those bars is unmistakable. I heard those sounds the first time when we were trying to move three very small, sick, angry kittens from one cat carrier to another. Then I heard them again when administering ear mite drops and checking on stitches. Sometimes

I hear it when Libby gets a little pushy with where she places her snout.

The sound is unmistakable and it can come from only one source.

My little guy is home.

I rush him in the house and give him a quick inspection before I open the trapdoor. Other than a scratch under his eye, he looks the same, only a little skinnier. He dashes immediately to his litter box in the basement and I idly wonder exactly how long he held it. Then he saunters back up the stairs to his food dish and digs in. The other cats crowd around him, their itch from the past few days finally scratched.

But after he's done with his usual business, he begins to head-butt me like he does every time he wants to be picked up. I hug him and kiss him and inhale the scent of freshly cut grass. He purrs loudly before passing out.

I suspect that although he's been on a grand adventure, he's very happy to be home.

Ever since the cats' triumphant return, they've been extra-affectionate. They've taken to sleeping with us and now I can't sit at my computer without a cat curling up between me and the keyboard. Although they can't say they're grateful to us, they certainly show it.

The way Fletch sees it, the cats went on Rumspringa—they went out and lived their lives away from us to determine whether or not they wanted to commit to being a permanent part of our family. And now that they've seen what's out there, they decided that driving cars and smoking cigarettes and listening to Judas Priest[223] just doesn't have the same appeal of being here.

They chose us.

Okay, fine, we had to result to some trickery for them to choose us, but we couldn't have rounded them up if they didn't make the effort to come home.

As I survey my little kingdom, I'm happier than I've ever been.

Now that they're back, I can return to the important business of picking a generator.

Because I am never opening a window again.

> ### Reluctant Adult Lesson Learned:
>
> *No one knows everything. Never be afraid to ask for help, even if that entails a quick leak in the bushes.*

---

[223] They seem like they'd be Judas Priest fans.

When Bad Things Happen to Bad People

*I*t takes a strong person to admit she's weak.

Yeah.

That sounds like a load of crap to me, too.

But after everything that went down with the couple next door back in the city, it was never my intention to return to my usual habits. I learned my lesson about minding other people's business. I was strong enough to give up the spying game. Or so I thought.

Once we moved into our house, I was pleasantly surprised by the level of solitude up here. Even though I'm on a through street, and despite being walking distance to railroad tracks, there's a half acre of trees between me and the rest of the world.

It's bliss. Sweet, silent bliss.

(Full disclosure: the trees actually do piss me off but passively, not aggressively.)

(Also, who circles a goddamn pool with trees? Like three feet from the water? Like there's no such thing as "gravity" or "change of seasons" and I've already had to replace a motor and a pump because the leaves put such a strain on the filtration system.)

(Point is those sons of bitches are going DOWN very soon.)

Anyway, when we were house hunting, we toured a place on Everett, one of the town's busier roads. The listing agent told us, "You'll hear some noise from the street and I want to make sure you're aware of that."

"What kind of noise?" Fletch asked. "Gunshots? Ambulances?"

"Err, no . . ." the agent replied.

I jumped in. "Salsa music?"

"Thumping baseline?"

"Missing mufflers?"

"Gang fights?"

"Fireworks?"

"You should come to our place during the two weeks surrounding the Fourth of July—it's like Jalalabad out there!" Fletch added. "Last year I heard a scud missile."

The sweet suburban Realtor blanched. "I was referring to traffic noise."

We both looked at each other and laughed. "Oh, please. We used to live across the street from the Kennedy Expressway." I gestured out the window where two vehicles had passed in the last five minutes. "Traffic? *That's* a couple of cars. *Traffic* is eating and sleeping and watching TV and breathing in a steady diet of exhaust fumes thirty feet away from an entire convoy of truckers all hopped up on methamphetamines, using their engine brakes to make that deafening WOOOOOOOT sound in order to save five cents on gas while surrounded by eight hundred motorcycles on their way to Bike Week in Sturgis, who have thus trapped one thousand impatient Lincoln Parkers driving their base-model Beemers to work and who honestly believe that honking will get them to the Sears Tower[224] thirty seconds sooner. Traffic. Ha! You people up here are adorable."

Although we didn't buy that house, we did give the Realtor a whole new perspective on how to sell to city buyers.

I was amazed at how productive I could be when I didn't have to get up from my seat and glower at disturbances every five minutes. Plus, because we have a decent yard,[225] the dogs get a ton of exercise and they're no longer compelled to sit across from me and stare until I entertain them. Once in a while they bark, but only when they spot a deer and that's just a badass reason to take a break anyway.

Back in the city, my office overlooked a traffic light on a busy street and a bus stop. There was an illegal day care across from me, where children would be herded into a small cement-and-metal enclosure for the sole purpose of shouting eight to ten times a day. I was a few doors down from a public park, so between yard time, drop-offs and pickups, and park traffic, there was never a point in the day when the street wasn't filled with kids.

And they were shriekers. Every last one of them.

Coincidentally our gate doorbell was at the exact height reachable by your average preschooler, so people rang all day long.

....

[224] Not the Willis Tower. Not now, not ever.
[225] Annoying pool trees notwithstanding.

At first when the door chimed, I'd run to the intercom system and ninety-nine times out of a hundred, no one would be there. Eventually I smartened up and went directly to the window where I'd watch the kids and their families ding-and-dash.

Yet *I'd* be the jerk for chasing them down with my good whacking shovel.

So not right.

One time after hearing my bell go off a dozen times in a row, I stomped down the stairs in a swirl of righteous indignation and polar bear pajama pants. Before I could step outside to confront the stupid lady holding her toddler up next to the gate, I had to wrestle the two dogs completely losing their shit over the constant bing-bonging.

"What are you doing?" I shouted over the thirteenth chorus of "Hear the Bells Chime" and the resulting dog melee.

The woman merely shrugged at me while her child continued to stab at the doorbell with a sticky finger. "She push button." From behind the door, dogs were headed into full-on-Pavlovian-bitch-panic mode.

"Uh-huh, I noticed. But that's *my* doorbell you're ringing."

She shrugged again while the yelping reached a new crescendo.

"Tell your kid to stop pushing it."

Shrug. "She like."

"I *don't* like." I pointed at the window beside the door that had since become opaque with doggie nose smudges and slather. "*They* don't like. *No one* like."

Shrug. "She like."

While I stood shaking in impotent rage and the dogs clawed the door, the kid got bored and the mother moved on.

A few days later they came around again, pulling the same stunt. Only this time instead of arguing, I simply released the hounds. They tore down the steps and bolted right up to the fence. If you have a single clue about dogs, you'd immediately be able to tell that Maisy and Loki were barking with unadulterated joy and nothing could have made them happier than a quick ear scratchy-scratch. Their tails were wagging like crazy, making a clanging noise against the bars of the iron fence, and their ruffs were completely smooth.

But if you're a fucking dolt who believes it's your right to ring and re-ring my bell, an understanding of dog behavior may not be in your wheelhouse. While they beat a hasty retreat, I stood at my gate shouting, "What? You don't like?"

Up here, anyone who wants to ring my bell has to take one hundred and fourteen paces to get there from the mailbox.[226] Plus, we don't live walking distance to anything (save the railroad tracks) so there's almost no foot traffic, which means that in moving here, we've neatly eliminated external distractions. I can literally sit at my desk and not be disturbed for hours . . . except maybe by my tree-cutting bloodlust and the lure of Internet gossip.

So my return to neighborhood watch is completely inadvertent. I'm reading the local online community newsletter, which is a perpetual source of comedy, particularly the police beat. Whereas the crime blotter in the old 'hood routinely detailed grisly crimes best suited to an episode of a fine CBS drama, the new one comes straight out of Mayberry. Folks are always calling 911 on reports of found bicycles and raccoons trapped in garages. Last fall

....

[226] Related note: sometimes an entire week goes by before I pick up my mail.

there was a real crime wave when an elderly man dialed 911 after waiting an hour to see his primary care physician and *then* didn't receive an adequate checkup.[227]

As I scan the blotter, I notice an entry about a traffic stop close to my house. I remember that day because the police pulled up next to my mailbox to issue the ticket and . . . I may or may not have lain on the floor of my dining room watching the action unfold from behind the curtain sheers.

But come on, how can a traffic stop *in my driveway* not be intriguing? In a town where the greatest transgressions involve wearing white after Labor Day and improperly tasseled loafers, any police action is interesting.

So I do a little Googling. If there's someone in the community, say, not properly RSVPing, then *I'm* a part of this community and *I* should know.

Then I Google a little more. Pretty soon I've wasted an hour clicking around the Facebook page of the poor bastard who'd forgotten to renew his city sticker.

I'd like to say I stop here.

I don't.

Constant Vigilance™ returns with a vengeance.

Soon the police blotter becomes my *National Enquirer/Page Six* and my snoopy nature takes on a decidedly white-collar feel. Each week I find myself nosing around for more and more information.

For example, did you know that the guy who made an illegal turn on red at Waukegan Road gave money to the Green Party? That boy who was caught driving drunk on Gage Lane? Accord-

---

[227] Police advised him to find a new doctor.

ing to Zillow.com, he lives in a multimillion-dollar home with (what I believe to be) overly permissive parents. And don't even get me started on what I'm sure was an inside job in that big ol' mansion a couple of miles up the road from here—I mean, how else would thieves have known about the hidden safe?

While I step up neighborhood patrol, Fletch involves himself in an entirely different kind of hobby. One of the reasons we bought our house is because our basement has higher than usual ceilings. Someday we'll finish it off and make it into a rec room, but for now, it's the perfect size and shape for a woodworking shop. As he's been looking for a project, I suggest he refinish an old dresser that I've been dragging around from musty basement to dusty garage for fifteen years.

Originally, I planned to paint the dresser myself.

Until I saw the spider.

Correction, *spiders*, whereupon I immediately morphed from the strong, independent, primary breadwinner to a prototypical fifties sitcom wife, tottering around helplessly as though deeply encumbered by heels, a frilly apron, and the right to vote.

"This will take, what, two or three days?" I ask as we inspect the lines of the old dresser. I'm pleased that his new hobby is actually useful. A few years ago when he was into Airsoft, our house turned into a veritable Army Surplus store, with uniforms and BB guns all over the place. I always thought I was going to break an ankle slipping on one of the ten million white pellets on the basement floor left over from his target practice. But this? I could be very happy having a husband who builds stuff and doesn't accidentally hobble me while I do a load of laundry.

I imagine all the cool projects he'll undertake, like constructing a lighted hutch where I can display my Carnival and Depression glass pieces.[228] A few years ago he'd have insisted on storing his Airsoft rifles in our kitchen gun cabinet[229] but now he'll have the tools to turn it into a shelving unit where I can show off my teapot collection.

I assess the scope of the project and determine it should take no longer than a week. I tell him, "We've got leftover paint from the cabinets and a couple of brushes, so we should be all set."

Oh, if it were only that easy.

What I always forget is that Fletch doesn't share my compulsion for half-assery when it comes to home improvement projects. He's never once hemmed curtains with a steak knife, nor used a wad of gum to make a framed picture hang straight.

Before he can even begin to envision slapping a few coats on the dresser, he has to ready his workshop. Clearly the basement is too dusty for paint to properly adhere, which necessitates the purchase of an enormous, expensive shop vac.

After his work space is sterile enough to perform your garden-variety tracheotomy, he realizes he doesn't have enough places to set things down. I suggest perhaps he use the now-immaculate floor. He laughs, but I'm not sure why that's funny.

Instead, he invests in a hammer drill to hang studs on the cement basement walls. Then he mounts Peg-Boards on the studs and loads them up with tools artfully displayed by make, size, and shape. Dissatisfied with his handiwork, he takes all the tools down to paint the Peg-Boards. My suggestion of, "Why not hit the dresser while you've got the brushes out?" falls on deaf ears.

....

[228] If you're doing any birthday shopping, I'm all about orange Carnival bowls/vases and the pink Jeanette Floral Poinsettia pattern in Depression glass. But, really, only if it's my birthday.

[229] No, I'm not kidding about the cabinet or his proclivities.

Workshop complete, Fletch disassembles the dresser and begins to sand. He doesn't care for the job the finish sander is doing, so he declares the need for a random orbit sander.

"How much does that cost?" I ask, growing more and more annoyed.

"You can't put a price on a job well done," he replies.[230]

But the random orbit sander works well. In fact, it works so well that Fletch accidentally smoothes out some parts meant to stay pointy, which requires the purchase of a table saw.

"You need a saw? To *paint*?" I demand.

"All part of the process," he assures me, while lovingly assembling a machine costing roughly the same amount as my first year of college tuition.

"Wait a minute," I say, recalling the dismemberment stories he'd shared about his father, uncles, and maternal *and* paternal grandfathers. "Don't you come from a long line of nine-fingered Fletchers?"

"Everyone gets ten—that way you have some extras."

To date, he's forked out hundreds of dollars on this project and that's without factoring in the cost of three weeks' labor. For a dresser that's still in a dozen pieces and has yet to see a single drop of primer.

Next time? I'm just going to paint over the spiders myself.

As weeks pass, the dresser becomes my Godot. Every time I think there's progress, something else happens—e.g., the primer isn't setting properly—and he has to take one step back.

Mind you, I have plenty to occupy myself, especially now that I've found the official online version of the police blotter, but I am

....

[230] Um . . . when it's a fifty-dollar dresser you can.

not a patient woman and the process is slowly driving me to distraction.

Six weeks into the project—SIX WEEKS—Fletch bounds up the stairs to my office. "Small problem."

"No shit." He's been "small problem"-ing me for weeks now, from rebuilding missing drawers, to reimagining an entirely new base. This dresser has taken me through all the stages of grief, although getting past the anger and bargaining point was touch and go there for a while, and I'm finally at the point of acceptance. I didn't need the damn thing in the first place and the only reason I wanted it was so we could use up the extra Tiffany-box-blue paint. But it's fine. I don't care. I'm okay with living in world without an Easter egg–colored dresser.

"There's a missing hinge and because it's so old, Home Depot doesn't carry anything that size, nor does Lowe's or the woodworking shop. It's on the outside, so it really needs to coordinate with the other hinges."

I simply shrug and say, "Who is John Galt?"

"Of course, I could order one on the Internet. It won't be an exact match, but it'd be close. They're kind of pricey, though."

"How pricey?" If it's less than the scrillion dollars we've already put towards this, I'm willing to negotiate.

"Fourteen dollars."

Fourteen dollars. The man who happily invested in six different types of handheld drills really believes I care about fourteen dollars at this point?

"What's fourteen dollars compared to what you've already spent?" With every purchase, he's justified the expense saying that he'd use all the tools over and over again. Yeah, pal, I've got a closetful of bridesmaid dresses telling me the same story.

I continue. "My concern is not the price. My concern is that in receiving the hinge and finishing the project, you'll have accidentally opened the portal to Hell. This dresser was never meant to be finished and if somehow you manage to do it anyway, you're going to unleash some Pandora's box–level of plagues on this world. Buy the hinge and finish the project or leave it off and save the world. Either way, I'm not picky."

A week later I'm in my office reveling in a particularly dishy story. There's some batty old socialite on the lakefront who hates when people walk on her part of the beach, so she's always turning her enormous dogs on trespassers. While everyone else is up in arms about the situation, I'm trying to figure out how to make friends with her.

Fletch wears an odd expression as he walks into my office carrying a couple of packages. "You'll be pleased to hear that you were right."

"How so?"

He shakes one of the big mailer envelopes at me. "I got the hinge today so I should have your dresser done in a few minutes."

"YAY! That's fantastic!" The piece has been hanging out in the guest room for a couple of weeks, finished save for the missing door. To Fletch's credit, he did such a professional job with the reconstruction and the paint that it almost doesn't need the door. Almost. "Wait, how was I right?" Not that it matters, but it's nice to force him to say it.[231]

....

[231] That's what keeps our love alive.

He hands me the other package. "The portal to Hell has been unlocked."

"Beg pardon?" Then I take a good look at the package's return address. "Motherfucker."

I realize that I write tell-all memoirs, but that doesn't always mean I share the whole story.[232] Sometimes things happen in my life that are so stupid and frustrating and unnecessary[233] that it's not appropriate to share those stories, satisfying though it may be.

Particularly when I'm in the right.

In this case, I've moved twice without giving the person who sent the package—now referred to as My Mailer—a forwarding address, so you'd think that would be a heavy clue that we've reached an impasse in our relationship.

You'd think, anyway.

I'm a big fan of Dr. Laura[234] and recently she discussed the best description of my situation. She explained how when a one-celled organism senses trouble, even though it doesn't have a brain, it instinctively swims away. That's what I finally had to do—I swam away. I'm not an unreasonable person and I have an unmitigating sense of loyalty. But there's only so much I'm willing to take before I call it quits. My Mailer and I reached that point long ago.

"How'd she get my address?"

He shrugs and then sits down across from me. "You need me here while you open it?"

"No, because I'm not going to open it."

"I appreciate your liberal use of denial."

....

[232] For example, I have seen Fletch naked. More than once, even.
[233] Not referring to the naked part.
[234] She calls people "whores" on the air. I can't not get behind that.

I shove the envelope into a file drawer and make shooing motions. "Thanks. Now please go finish my dresser."

Turns out I'm not so skilled in denial and I end up opening the package.

The more I cogitate, the angrier I am, because her tracking down my mailing address feels like an invasion of my privacy. I never shared my address not because I was trying to hide; rather, I kept it to myself because I didn't want to be bothered.

Yet here I sit with a big old envelope of Bothered.

It would be one thing if being Bothered just impacted me, but it actually affects my readers, and that's unacceptable. The fact is, in order to avoid confrontation, there are entire cities I won't visit after having previously been ambushed by My Mailer.[235] I'm angry that My Mailer's inability to behave has kept me from connecting with those who love my books.

You know what? I'm going to take action because this isn't right. We're in the process of booking my tour and I want it to go down without incident.

We used a real estate attorney for our closing and to handle a couple of business matters related to corporate filings for our LLC. At our last meeting, I mentioned the issues with My Mailer and asked if there was a legal way to keep her away from me and my events. He told me all I had to do was file an Order of No Contact. That way, My Mailer couldn't come to my events, couldn't call or

---

[235] I swear it's not just me. I've heard horror stories from other authors about the exact same thing.

e-mail, and wouldn't be allowed to have others act as an agent for her. I simply needed to fill out a form on the Internet and drop it off at the county courthouse. Easy-peasy!

I find the forms, complete them, and tell Fletch we need to swing by the courthouse in the morning. Plus, I want to check out the antiques stores north of here, so this little road trip will dovetail nicely into my quest for a full set of Depression glass.

I've never been to Waukegan, but it's not too far from here and it borders the lake, so I picture it filled with darling antiques shops and cute lunch places overlooking the water.

What I find is a smaller version of Gary, Indiana, minus the charm. The town is basically nothing but criminal law offices, a massive courthouse next to an even larger jail, and the only people here are either visiting relatives in lockup or having their day in court.

I clutch my purse and my husband as we make our way to the main building and I'm pretty sure I hear the woo-hoo-hoo, chh-chh-chh, hah-hah-hah that plays right before Michael Myers pops out in a hockey mask wielding a machete.

As it turns out, the only asshole with a knife is *me*.

Whenever I'm not traveling, I like to carry my good stabbin' blade and I often forget I have it on me. As I stand in line with all the criminals—whom I'm totally judging, by the way—*I'm* the only dirtbag attempting to[236] smuggle in a weapon.

Perhaps hardened criminals don't wear loafers and slouchy socks with their boyfriend jeans cuffed to Capri length, so the lady

....

[236] Again, inadvertently.

running the metal detector allows me to keep my knife. She doesn't confiscate it, but we have to go all the way back to the car to check my weapon.

In my novel *If You Were Here* the character Mia is obsessed with omens, both good and bad. She believes that our paths are predetermined by the universe and that all we need to do to live our best life is to follow the signs. Mia would say that the knife thing was the universe's way of telling me to GET OUT, GET OUT, GET OUT, WE'VE TRACED THE CALL AND IT'S COMING FROM INSIDE THE HOUSE, but I'm not a huge proponent of that kind of hooey so I proceed blithely on.

Fletch and I take my stack of paperwork to the clerk and I tell her I want to file an Order of No Contact.

"You don't do that here," the clerk tells me. "You've got to go upstairs."

We head upstairs and file in line behind a bunch of haggard ladies. The line moves interminably slow and we find out that's because only one woman's doing the intakes. After an hour, I say to Fletch, "Do you want to go? Maybe I'm overreacting and this is probably just silly, so we should go."

"Up to you," he replies. "You've waited this long and you want a resolution, so maybe we should stay. Besides, I don't have anything else on the docket[237] for the afternoon."

"Reason enough," I agree.

Not long after this, another woman comes out, takes one look at the line, and immediately jumps in to help. "Hi, please come in. I'm Lana, and I'm a volunteer victim's advocate."

....

[237] Sign. SIGN. BIG FAT LANGUAGE USE SIGN.

At no point yet does it occur to me that the court might consider me a "victim" and not just Bothered.

I brief Lana on the situation while Fletch wanders over to help himself to coffee. When I show her my paperwork, she says, "You don't want an Order of No Contact—you need an Order of Protection."

"I disagree. I'm in no danger; I need to be *very* clear on that. I'm just annoyed and I need to protect myself against having my events disrupted," I explain.

From the other desk, the woman who's employed by the courthouse barks, "Order of Protection!"

Fletch meanders back over, blowing on his hot Styrofoam cup. "That doesn't sound right."

"Order of Protection!" she calls again.

The whole staff seems to agree that this could affect my business, so I begin detailing various annoyances for my Protection Order and I have to fill in all kinds of paperwork. I don't understand why they can't use the forms I already filled in, but whatever.

SIGN.

I'm trying to pay attention to what Lana's saying, but there's a woman next to me who keeps talking about safe houses and being thrown down the stairs and, frankly, it's hard to concentrate. All my instincts say to grab this woman and bring her home to live in my guest room.

After we finish, Lana tells me, "We'll get you your court date now, so follow me."

Um . . . what?

Fletch and I flash each other confused looks while we pass

down a long hallway. We enter a room that looks a lot like a courtroom.

That's because it IS a courtroom.

I'm placed in a row with a number of women, many of whom
seem to be bruised or missing teeth. Fletch is ferried off to the seats
in the back and I notice that he's the only man in the room who isn't
the judge, the bailiff, or the defendant.

Woo-hoo-hoo, chh-chh-chh, hah-hah-hah.

I don't understand what's happening with the pregnant lady
with the black eye currently standing in front of the judge because
everything she's saying is going through an interpreter. However, I
get the gist of it when her *esposo* comes shuffling out in an orange
jumpsuit, shackled at the hands and feet.

Oh, dear.

I'm now fully convinced that my victim's advocate had absolutely no idea what she was doing and that I *should not be here*. Yet
I have no idea how to extricate myself.

The judge confers with the translator and then bangs his gavel,
saying that a two-year order of protection has been granted. The
translator tells the woman this, but instead of being happy, she starts
to cry slow, fat tears down her face and all I want to do is hug her. I
feel sick about this poor woman being stuck in a country where she
can't speak the language, watching her only form of support being
hauled back off in chains because he's a fisty douche bag.

Kind of puts that whole Bothered thing into perspective. The
minute I get out of here, I'm finding a battered women's shelter and
writing them a check.

While this is happening, the woman who'd been in the other
room with me sits down next to me. In her lap she holds five sheets

of paper, each line filled with details on how her husband beat her and threatened her life.

Suddenly Fletch's expensive woodworking habit seems charming and endearing, not annoying.

Okay, universe, message received.

I've gotten plenty of perspective. Now *please get me out of here*.

The next case is called and a woman approaches the judge and says she's mad at her husband because, "He be drinking all the time."

"Has he physically harmed you in any way? Does he threaten you? Has he threatened to harm your children?" the judge prompts.

She considers this for a moment. "No. But he be drinking all the time and I don't like."

Her husband interjects, "I don't be drinking all the time. I go to work all day, six days a week. When I get off work, I like to drink because I be working all the time."

The expression on the judge's face hovers somewhere between aggravation and resignation. If the past five minutes is any indication of what he has to listen to on a daily basis, then I'm totally voting for judges to get a pay raise during the next election. "So what you're telling me is you're not in any physical danger and there have been no threats. Ma'am, I have to ask—what is it you'd like for me to do?"

The wife replies, "Make him stop drinking all the time."

And that's when Fletch lets out a bark of laughter that's so loud that every single person in the courtroom turns around to look at him. He tries to cover it up with a coughing fit, but no one's fooled.[238]

....

[238] Hey, Bravo? Bet you wished you'd approached me for a reality show right about now, eh?

The judge decrees a two-week Order of Protection, yet when they're done, the couple walks out holding hands.

I weep for their children.

Then, it's my turn. Lana accompanies me to the bench and gives me a couple of reassuring pats on the arm, sensing that I'd like to die right now, but probably not for the reasons she thinks.

The first words out of my mouth are, "I'm in the wrong place." I explain how I'm here only upon the advice of counsel and that maybe I should have consulted someone other than a real estate attorney.

The judge assures me I'm in the right place, but it seems more like a technicality he's obligated to honor, rather than any sort of tacit approval. I briefly touch on My Mailer and why I'm exasperated, stressing again and again that I'm not in any danger, except possibly from having a stress-induced stroke, and, really, it's not like my butter and heavy cream intake are helping my whole artery situation.

The judge removes his glasses and rubs his eyes. I can't say for sure, but I'd guess if it were allowed that he'd like to punch me in the face even more than Mr. and Mrs. Be Drinking All the Time.

"Ms. Lancaster, I'm not going to grant your order and I'm not going to deny it. What I will do is give you a court date so that you and Your Mailer can give your sides of the story."

Um, wait, no.

I want to AVOID her. I want to be NOT NEAR HER. I want to SWIM THE FUCK AWAY FROM HER. I do not want to have a day in court with her.

Crap, crap, crap. How do I get out of this?

The judge pages through his calendar. "I'm going to have you back here on April eighth."

I shift in my loafers and twist my pearls and I start making statements in the form of questions. "Ooh, that's kind of a problem? You see, Your Honor, there's a banquet for me that day? My alma mater has named me one of their Distinguished Alumni for 2011, so I've got to be there? I'm the keynote speaker?"

That's when the judge basically kicks me in the 'nads with his eyes. He says, "Well. *Congratulations on your award.* Might there be another date that would work when you're not being honored?"

And then I die.

We figure out a time and I pretty much run out of the courtroom once I receive my paperwork.

"What THE HELL was THAT?" Fletch shout-whispers as soon as we're out the door.

I turn to Lana, who's still next to me, rubbing my arm.

REALLY NOT USEFUL RIGHT NOW, LANA.

I blurt, "This needs to *not happen*. How do we make this *not happen*? Can we withdraw the complaint?"

Cheerily, Lana replies, "Gosh, no. Now that you've seen the judge, it's an official action of the court and a public record." When she realizes *I'm* kicking her in the 'nads with my eyes, she adds, "If you choose not to pursue the matter, just don't show up for your court date. Your case won't be heard and the case will be dropped."

So then it's settled.

Denial it is.

I wish I had some snappy resolution to share about My Mailer, but I don't. The situation is impossible with no chance of improvement and she did nothing to endear herself after her (solo) day in court where she later gloated how she "won my case against you." It wasn't worth the effort to respond that as the defendant, she didn't *have* a fucking case. Also, I guarantee the judge didn't say, "I was going to rule for you even if she did show up," because admitting a preconceived bias towards one of the litigants is the kind of statement that gets you removed from the bench.

Regardless, because my professional events are on private property, we're able to prevent her from causing another scene and that's resolution enough, so basically, the show's over.[239]

My big takeaway has been a newfound respect for other people's privacy. The idea of strangers sorting through my dirty laundry (metaphorical or otherwise) makes me super-squirmy. With Karma being the bitch that she is, I've learned that if I have the expectation of privacy, I can't keep invading that of others.

No longer being Gladys Kravitz isn't easy because temptation (and information) exists everywhere. Some days all I want to do is Google stalk the new family on the corner with the expensive house and the cheap, cheap, seriously-what-were-they-thinking plywood fence they just built, but their business is none of mine.

I keep telling myself to snoop not, lest I be snooped and so far, I've kept those compulsions under control. And that makes me feel like I've taken another positive step towards full-blown adulthood.

....

[239] Apparently she's been trying to contact Oprah to settle our dispute. As this is Oprah's final month of filming, perhaps she'll bump her interview with President Obama and Tom Cruise to accommodate us.

But if I ever do meet those people with the amateur fence, I might mention that Fletch does woodworking.

Just because I'm a nice neighbor.

Reluctant Adult Lesson Learned:

Don't bring a knife to a gunfight or a real estate attorney to family court.

If you're going to lawyer-up, do it right.

C·H·A·P·T·E·R
T·W·E·N·T·Y-S·I·X

Death and Taxes?
Can I Select Neither?

When I told Fletch nothing could be more simultaneously boring and terrifying than meeting with the tax attorney, I was wrong.

That's because we hadn't yet met with the estate-planning law firm.

At least with the tax guy there was some raucous laughter, although it primarily emanated from him once he saw the mess our discount ex-accounting firm created.

I've said it before and I'll say it one final time:

Never economize on handbags, parachutes, or CPAs.

Fortunately, there's little a healthy retainer fee can't fix, so all's well in that department.

Anyway, today we're in this white-shoe law firm discussing

what's going to happen when we die. I hate that we're here, I hate what we're talking about, I hate how much it's going to cost, but it's got to be done. At this juncture in our lives, we need an estate plan more elaborate than the cocktail napkin where I drunkenly scribbled "I leave everything to Maisy!!" before doodling a bunch of bananas and a sheep. After canceling and postponing this appointment more times than I care to mention, here we are.

The tenor of the conversation has my palms sweating, but they're not visible because I'm currently sitting on my hands. See, last week I discovered that OPI makes nail polish called Jade Is the New Black. I normally have an aversion to any color polish that couldn't double as lipstick, but come on, with a name like that I couldn't not buy it! I brought the bottle to my manicure yesterday and now my nails are an exceptionally festive shade of green.

Considering I spend ninety-nine percent of my time either in the pool, at my desk, or going to the grocery store, I figured I could get away with a goofy color for once. That is, until I shake the estate planning attorney's hand and feel exactly like the kind of asshole who thinks green nails are a fine idea.

Perhaps when we're done here, I'll have my name tattooed on my neck and paint a rebel flag on the hood of my car before allowing my children of dubious, multiple parentage to wrestle freerange in the back of my pickup truck while we head to the minimart to procure the ingredients for tonight's dinner—Wonder Bread sopped in meat grease.

Fortunately, I'm not sure the lawyer notices the polish color because of my outfit. I wanted to be dressier than my usual khaki shorts and alligator shirt, so I went to put on one of the sweater-set/sundress items I normally wear on book tour. That's when I realized that every piece of appropriate clothing I owned had not only been sitting at the bottom of the dry-cleaning basket since I finished touring three months ago, but at some point had been used as a litter box, likely when I accidentally shut Chuck Norris inside the closet.

I panicked and began to paw through the rest of my wardrobe, quoting Cher Horowitz as I made a vain attempt to find my "most responsible outfit." I settled on a white pair of Capri pants, a flowered pastel tunic sweater, and a pair of silver sandals topped with a big silver cabbage rose, all of which I've previously worn separately without issue.

I thought I looked adorable until I saw my reflection in the shiny law firm windows. Instead of taking in my freshly touched-up roots or deep tan, I thought, "I should hold the door for the lady who came straight from Nana's mah-jongg game down in Boca."

Seriously, I'm one pair of Easy Spirits away from booking an Alaskan cruise in this stupid getup. I look exactly like Michael Westen's mother on *Burn Notice*. I could go dressed like this to the movie theater and demand discounted seats. All I'm missing is a jeweled cigarette case and a crooked wig. I'd say that I'm ready to drive ten miles under the speed limit on the expressway, bitch about Congress, and yell at kids to get off my lawn, but I've already been doing that for years.

Anyway, I'm glad my SeniorWear[240] distracts everyone from my junior high school manicure, but I'm sitting on my hands nevertheless.

We're being schooled on the four facets of estate planning and Ben, our lawyer, is asking us hard questions, like who we want to give health care power of attorney should we become incapaci-

....

[240] Trademark pending.

tated. Ben explains if something happens to one of us but not the other, certainly we'll make that decision for the injured spouse, but what happens if we're both incapacitated? Normally this task falls to family.

That gives us pause and Fletch and I both gawp at each other. Finally, I tell Ben, "We'll need some time to discuss this. All I know is I don't want my brother in charge. He'd be all, *'Broken leg? One hundred percent chance of recovery? Pull the plug anyway; I'll do it for you!'"*

Since we're not opting for family, who will we choose to make medical decisions for us? How do we put that burden on anyone who didn't share a backseat with us on the kind of interminable family vacations where we tried to catch and eat flies because my dad believed stopping for lunch was for amateurs?

I have great friends—the best, really—but have I been a good enough friend to request such a favor? What am I going to say: *"Hey, remember when I didn't come to your birthday party because it was rainy and my hair was frizzy? Yeah, sorry about that. Listen, do you mind being the one who decides if I live or die? Thanks!"*

We awkwardly stumble through more assignments under the other facets until we get to the actual will.

Ben explains that what we want to do is draft a will where everything's assigned to a trust. The trust (a private document) is where stuff gets specific, like who gets my porcelain Royal Doulton Union Jack bulldog. Because wills are public, anyone can go to the courthouse and request a copy. The trust portion will protect our privacy while we're still alive.[241]

"Someday if you're bored, Google 'celebrity wills,'" he tells

---

[241] After that, I don't care.

us. "You'd be shocked at how much information some of them contain. Probably because instead of using estate planning attorneys, they used attorneys who also planned estates.[242] For example, did you know that Michael Jackson assigned Diana Ross as his secondary decision maker on some of the facets?"

"Huh," I reply. "Hey, Fletch, we ought to ask Diana Ross if she wants to be our second, too. Clearly she's not afraid of the job."

After we work through the draft of the will itself, we get to the trust and that's where it gets interesting. By "interesting" what I mean is where I realize I'm an asshole yet again because in divvying everything up, my first thought is, *"Dance, monkeys, dance!"*

I'm all cavalier, determining who I'd like to gift upon my demise and I'm particularly delighted when Ben explains how I can write in terms and conditions. Funny, I thought that kind of stuff only happened in the movies. Clarification: bad movies.

I kind of love the idea of being able to run shit from the grave! Like if I want my alma mater to get money, I can make it so they're getting paid only if they endow a chair in my name. (Of course, whether it's a university honor or something with four legs, a back, a couple of arms, and my name on a plaque will depend on my industriousness going forward.) This is like a legal form of extortion!

As I cackle and rub my green-tipped hands together in delight under the table, it occurs to me that I shouldn't be quite so gleeful.

I mean, this isn't a hypothetical arrangement and for all my bravado, I actually am planning for my eventual demise. No matter how I spin it, I am going to die. I might not die soon (at least I

---

[242] He said this enough times for me to gather that the distinction is important. But what do I know? I have green nails.

hope) but I am going to die. No matter how many books I sell, no matter who loves me, no matter what color my nails are painted, it's all going to end for me exactly like it has for every other person who walked this earth.

Suddenly everything feels very real.

Although I've considered my own mortality many times before, I've never contemplated it on this level, except for that hour last year when we talked about life insurance.

Rather, my fear of death has always favored the how-to-prevent-it-from-happenings, and never the what-happens-when-it-happens-because-make-no-mistake-it-will-happens.

But in putting together these documents, I'm forced to come to terms with the fact that I'm no different from a carton of milk. I have an expiration date and there's no getting around it.

That's when Fletch and I really begin to talk. Do we want our legacy to be making everyone we know arm wrestle for the spoils? Or do we want to take what we've earned to do the kind of good that we—to this point—have not quite accomplished on earth?

We're opting for the latter.

Ever since I stopped volunteering, I've felt this sense of guilt that I wasn't doing enough. In terms of doing charity work, I learned that I'm better at giving money than myself so I've been as generous as I can whenever I can. Yet the guilt remained.

After earmarking the bulk of our net worth to deserving non-profit organizations, I feel an enormous sense of relief as we leave the law office. There's an almost indescribable satisfaction that comes from knowing my life will not have been lived in vain.

No matter how silly or vapid or mean I've been at times, I'll go out confident that my life will have made a difference and that fills me with a sense of peace and calm.

Despite my reticence, I'm glad we made these decisions. Although we still need to talk with those we've chosen as our second[243] I feel like we've leapt an enormous hurdle today and we're coming to the end of our Reluctant Adult Decathlon.

We shake hands on our way out the door and we head to the car having made the decision to begin concentrating on what's really important in our lives.

But before that happens, I'm probably going to get a fresh manicure.

Reluctant Adult Lesson Learned:

Estate planning sucks. Do it anyway.

---

[243] Not Diana Ross, FYI.

C·H·A·P·T·E·R
T·W·E·N·T·Y-S·E·V·E·N

Distinguish Myself

"What does this mean?"

I read and reread the letter and I still can't make sense of it, so I have to ask Fletch.

"Is this . . . something?" I wonder, handing the heavy sheet of paper across the counter to him.

According to what the letter says, I'm receiving a distinguished alumni award from the Liberal Arts department at my alma mater, but I'm not sure it's legitimate because I . . . didn't exactly have a distinguished college career. I mean, why would *I* receive this? What are they going to recognize me for, specifically?

Flunking out after my sophomore year?

Swimming in the fountain after every home football game?

Climbing up the fire escape of the old Education building to throw rooftop parties with my fraternity friends where the Dutchie may or may not have been passed to the left-hand side?[244]

Spending more nights in a row warming a barstool at Harry's than any other female student in university history?

Accumulating a record number of campus parking tickets because I refused to walk to class since getting sweaty would mess up my hair?

Taking eleven years to earn a bachelor's degree and then graduating, *finally*, with a solid C average?

Seriously, if my college career was distinguished, I'd hate to see whose wasn't distinguished.[245]

I tell Fletch, "I remember getting one of these letters in high school, too—you know, those *Who's Who Among American High School Students* awards they gave out for 'outstanding students'?"

"Not familiar," he replies, eyes scanning my letter.

I pause, remembering the volume I'd been so proud to receive until I realized that my information filled approximately one square inch in a five-hundred-page tome. I wave my hand dismissively. "Oh, everyone got them. The whole thing was kind of a scam. Some private company recognized students for their 'outstanding achievements' but if you ask me, the only thing really 'outstanding' about them is that their parents were willing to shell out forty-five dollars for a genuine leatherette-bound yearbook."

"Yeah, never saw one. But, Jen, this? This is real." He hands the paper back to me.

....

[244] If I ever have to testify before Congress about this, I'll claim the Bill Clinton defense.
[245] To be fair, I probably dated him.

I flip the paper over to see if there's any fine print on the back. "How are you so sure? Seems to be the kind of thing a college would send out to troll for a donation check. Ooh, or like when police departments send people notices saying, *'Hey, you won a boat! C'mon down and claim it!'* but really, it's just a way to bring in those with outstanding warrants? And even as those poor saps are slapped into cuffs and loaded into the police bus behind the decorated storefront, they're all, *'Do I still get my boat?'* Am I going to be hauled off to campus jail for not listening to Nancy Reagan and Just Saying No a couple of times in 1985? How do we know that this isn't an elaborate sting operation wherein—"

Fletch sighs deeply. "Joanna nominated you, dumbass. She met some ladies from the Liberal Arts department at your last book event and they suggested she do so. She spent months putting together an essay and going through the application process. I assure you, and I tell you again, *this is legitimate.*"

Joanna and I have been friends ever since the vagaries of the University housing department saw fit to put us together freshman year. I cherish her for a variety of reasons but a big part of that is because we knew each other back before we had any idea of who we might be when we grew up. Author Laura Dave has the most spot-on quote in her book *The First Husband*, where she explains how her old friends *". . . knew each other in that honest, unmitigated way that people get to know you who meet you when you're still young. Before all the rest of it. Before it becomes both easier and harder to know yourself."*

So, yes, we're Laura Dave–kind of friends.

Joanna's one of the most honest, straightforward people I've ever met, so the idea that she'd pull one over on me is difficult to comprehend. "She never once mentioned this to me!" I exclaim. I mean, secret things almost never happen around me because I'm so suspicious. I take great pride in that it's almost impossible to catch me unawares.

Okay, a lot of times I see conspiracy theories in coincidences, and sometimes Fletch isn't the only one around here requiring a tinfoil hat, but still. I even hate good surprises, and woe to anyone who tries. Like if Fletch actually *had* been able to pull off bringing my New York girlfriends Karyn and Caprice here for my birthday without my first cleaning and shopping and coloring my hair? You'd have seen me on the news.

Fletch nods. "Yeah. She knew you'd be mad but did it anyway because she thought it was important you were recognized. She's very proud of you, so we kept the nomination under wraps until everything was official." He points to my letter. "Now it's official. Congratulations."

Huh.

"What I fail to understand is why me? I had the least distinguished college career out of anyone I know." I reflect for a moment, scanning the internal databases for someone who screwed up as much as me. "Oh, wait—I was friends with a guy named Hoff who was in chemical engineering so he could make his own drugs. So my college career was more distinguished than Hoff's but that's it."

Fletch gives me the kind of indulgent smile one usually reserves for LOL Cats or toddlers with upturned bowls of oatmeal on their heads. "Jen, the award's for what you've achieved as *an alumna*. Trust me, no one's giving you anything for your undergrad career." And then he snorts, which is kind of unfair. I mean, I didn't even meet Fletch until well into my ninth year of college, so he never knew me when I was in my late-eighties *Girls Gone Wild* phase. Without the Kissing of the Other Girls or the Photographing of the Ladyparts, I mean.[246]

Even so, although Fletch and I generally hit the bars together once we met, there were instances when I'd head out with my girlfriends and I'd turn into what Fletch described as "a handful."

Fletch still gives me the business about the time his bar manager friend called him to come fetch my friend Sloane and me from the parking lot. Apparently after Sloane and I stole a bunch of steak knives, we attempted to use them like crampons to scale the building. Due to a flaw in the steak knives' design and an unyielding brick wall (or possibly the three pitchers of Molson we imbibed), we abandoned our task.

Plan B involved going into hyperstealth mode, digging foxholes in the snowbanks outside the bar, obscuring ourselves by draping white cloth napkins over our heads in order to be completely camouflaged while we shouted obscenities at the snotty patrons who'd been shooting us dirty looks inside when they walked to their cars.[247]

Once Fletch arrived and patiently explained that this was, in fact, *not* how Superman combated forces of evil, we grudgingly abandoned our Fortress of Solitude. Sloane caught a ride[248] with other friends, but I refused to go home until I had a burrito. In an

---

[246] That kind of stuff didn't go down on campus until I was toiling away in corporate America wearing an ill-fitting business suit. Frankly, I'm relieved.

[247] Listen, we can't not sing along to "Love Is a Battlefield." It's, like, against the law or something.

[248] Read: was wrestled into a car.

attempt to placate me—or out of concern that I might still be packing steak knife heat—we went to La Bamba, home of the Burrito as Big as Your Head.[249]

Anyone who attended a Midwestern Big Ten school knows the magic of a La Bamba burrito. This is the only restaurant I've ever seen with a dinner rush that hits between two and four a.m. I fondly recall standing with all the other drunken students in lines that looped out the door and down the street, all of us waiting for the enchanted elixir.

There's nothing particularly special about any of the burrito's ingredients, outside of them being fresh, crispy, or nicely seasoned. Yet somehow the act of stuffing them all into a clammy white flour tortilla (that is literally larger than the circumference of my head) turns this innocuous concoction of lettuce, rice, and meat into a silver bullet of sorts, capable of stopping a speeding hangover, no matter how many Harry's World Famous Long Island Iced Teas I tossed down my gullet.

The La Bamba burrito was and is a genuine booze sponge and is thus the Golden Ticket to not barfing/getting the spins. Everyone I knew used to order the Super as an insurance policy. We'd eat half the night before and we'd have the second half in the morning.[250]

Anyway, that particular night, after securing my precious, delicious cargo, I slipped on the ice next to Fletch's truck. I slid directly beneath the passenger side, where I laughed myself into an asthma attack because I was so pleased at having the foresight to

---

[249] And still one of my most favorite foods ever.
[250] Sort of like a refried bean–based Day After pill.

save my Super-steak with extra *queso* and sour cream, despite ripping my pants and banging my head.

I stayed under the truck eating my burrito, while Fletch craned his neck all over the place trying to figure out where I might have gone. When he finally found me under the truck, he assumed I was dead, not happily cramming my cheeks with carne asada.

Handful.

I ended the evening by blowing my nose on his tie because "it looked all soft and flannel-y."

FYI, this is why it took me eleven years to graduate.[251]

I digest Fletch's news for a moment. "I . . . guess that makes sense. But it seems like they should be giving this award to an astronaut or something, not me."

Fletch rolls his eyes. "Purdue has surprisingly few astronauts in the Liberal Arts department."

I reply, "This lack of critical thinking skills is exactly what leads me to believe I don't deserve any kind of award." Fletch leaves the kitchen and begins to head back towards his office while I'm left to review supporting documentation for my major award. "Hey, honey—wait. The information packet says something about a ceremony and a dinner and stuff. I don't have to go, do I?"

Fletch shakes his head. "Of course not. If you don't mind disappointing Joanna, you're welcome to stay home."

Oh! Hoisted on my own petard!

"*Wow.* You rarely do guilt, but when you do, it's a doozy." Seriously, *ouch.* I'm very protective of Joanna and the idea of upset-

....

[251] And, likely, eight years before he agreed to get married.

ting her intentionally is far too much to bear. "Looks like we're going to the award ceremony."

"Cheer up!" he replies. "It'll be fun. You eat some rubber chicken, you get your picture taken, and you give a little speech. How hard can it be?"

I guess we'll find out.

Four months before the ceremony, I think: I should get a head start on that speech.

Three months before the ceremony: Maybe I should jot a few thoughts down before it's April and I'm slammed with pre-book-launch publicity in May.

Two months before the ceremony: Ooh! Snow! I'm not going to write a speech today. Imma build a fortress!

One month before the ceremony: I should think about that speech.

One week before the ceremony: I should work on that speech, but my desk is so messy and I have all these dog pictures to post . . .

One day before the ceremony: *Well, shit.*

Okay, I'm writing this.

I can do this.

I mean, I write for a living, yes?

I click open a Word document and I adjust all my settings. I'm unable to think about writing until I have the font set to Bookman Old Style, 12 point, double-spaced. I'm actually a bit of a lunatic about this and I won't even read any document online until I convert it to this format.

Ready, okay.

I have to write the keynote address right now. There's no more *I'll do it tomorrow.* Tomorrow is too late.

As there are three other recipients, this speech can't be all about me. Although the truth is I'm secretly disappointed at being one of the Outstanding Alumni and not THE Outstanding alumnus,[252] yet this takes some of the pressure off me.

Let me just Google these other recipients' names and . . .

Shit.

Shit, shit, shit.

The more I dig into my peers' backgrounds, the sicker I feel. If my Google-fu is strong (and it is), it would appear that the first

----

[252] If I'm getting an award I don't deserve, then I should be the only one who gets it.

gentleman also getting recognized has devoted his life to the social justice surrounding capital punishment. He's a Sociology Professor and Department Chair at a huge university.

Yes, sure, I know all about that. I can talk at length about the Grisham novel I just read on that very subject.

Argh.

The second guy I research is . . . oh, goddamn it, he's an *Ambassador*. So, unlike me, he was actually able to find a job in our shared major of Political Science. That's just awesome and I don't feel like a dick *at all*. And certainly I'm not intimidated or anything. I'm just going to be all, "Hey, Ambassador, my claim to fame is swearing at Alec Baldwin at a charity event. Bet THAT never happened to you while you were out there ambassador-ing."

Jesus Christ, this night is going to be a disaster. I don't belong with these people. I'm not worthy. Yeah, I've written some books that people enjoy but they're not, like, literature or anything.

I freak out for a little while longer until my pragmatic side takes over.

You know what?

I'm psyching myself out and if I don't finish this speech, I won't have time to go tanning or get my nails done. Then I'll be at the ceremony feeling inadequate AND unkempt.

At least I can be kempt. I may be a dumbass, but I'm a well-groomed dumbass and that's half the battle.

Fine, moving on. I search for the last recipient and I see she's a writer, too. Okay, cool. I can get down with that. I certainly identify with another writer, yes?

Oh, wait. Says here she's a Pulitzer Prize winner and the Washington Bureau Chief for *The New York Times*.

Terrific. I'll be sure to inquire if she's read my recent think piece on Card Sharks.

I am so screwed.

"That you?" Fletch calls from the bedroom.

"I'm home," I say, as I walk down the hallway to the master. I have a seat while he packs. When it comes to travel, I'm kind of a Viking and I had my stuff together for this event days ago. Wonder if the Ambassador can head out for a three-week book tour with only carry-on luggage?[253]

"How was your afternoon?" he asks as he shoves six pair of socks and no underwear into his overnight bag. Fletch is not a Packing Viking, bless his heart.

"Not bad," I reply. "I had a manicure[254] and went to Palm Beach Tan. By the way, when I was doing my speech research, I saw that a bunch of NASA guys are receiving the same award tomorrow from the Engineering school. Wonder if any of the astronauts are getting ready for their big day with a spray tan?"

"Doubtful," he says, tossing in sneakers and some workout shorts.

"Um, are you going to the Co-Rec for a pickup game of squash or are you coming to a banquet with me? If it's the latter, why don't I help you pack?" I suggest.

....

[253] I feel it's best to find opportunities over which I can gloat, few and far between as they are.
[254] OPI's Conquistadorable seemed to be the most responsible-looking color.

Not long after this, we've got everything Fletch could need for the twenty-four hours we'll be gone. From pajamas to going-out shoes, I've helped Fletch neatly prepare for any eventuality on the road. However, he argues when I try to get him to put his shirt and suit in the suitcase.

"They'll get wrinkled," he complains. "I'll grab them tomorrow."

"No," I reply. "You'll put them in the car right now; otherwise you'll forget, if the last three weddings you attended in gym shoes are any indication. I am not about to receive my major award with you in a Donkey Punch T-shirt."

And with that, we're ready to go.

Joanna and her husband, Michael, were planning on driving down with us, but they have a schedule conflict tomorrow morning and need to leave at the crack of dawn, so it's just us in the car. Fletch breaks his cardinal rule of no eating because I was so busy not writing my speech that I also didn't go to the grocery store and there's no food in the house. We stop at Arby's and I do my best not to drip Horsey Sauce on upholstery.[255]

When we arrive at Purdue, I'm shocked at how much it's changed. I guess I didn't expect it to be exactly the same as when I left, but . . . that's a lie.

I totally did.

I wanted to see the Purdue of 1985 when Joanna and I used to

---

[255] Oh, forbidden potato cakes, you're the sweetest potato cakes of them all!

stumble home to our teeny room in Earhart Hall after way too much trash can punch, sweaty and happily exhausted from dancing to Modern English in Keds.

I hoped that somehow, even though it was April, I'd see kids in barn jackets using ironing boards and cafeteria trays to slide down a snowy Slayter Hill.

I was secretly expecting to drive by the fraternity houses and spot familiar faces out there, clad in khaki shorts and white oxfords, feeding sips of Little Kings Cream Ale to a bandanna-wearing black lab/house mascot named Murph.

Instead, I see an army of Justin Bieber clones, texting away as they hurry from one spanking new university building to the next. It's all I can do to not scream, "Get a haircut!" at each of them as we cruise by. Oh my God, I feel so old.

As we pull up to the Union, I'm melancholy when I realize that all my favorite spots are gone, paved over into parking garages or turned into Starbucks. I haven't been back at school since the late nineties specifically because I was afraid this would happen.

I never wanted to be that pathetic alum accosting a bunch of undergrads about all the places that ceased to exist decades ago, all *"Hey, kids, you could get a steak for a nickel over there and see a moving-picture show, too!"*

I never wanted to be the weird older lady pointing out the front corner of the Yacht Club, where the manager Ferris kept the topless bronze statue that I'd always cover in a paper-napkin bikini whenever I sat in front of it. No one cares that was the exact spot where we raised a glass to Kurt Cobain after his suicide, playing an endless round of Nirvana songs on the jukebox. I remember how we hugged each other, saying over and over with the kind of sincerity exclusive to kids in their twenties, *"This changes everything."*

No one wants to know how good the pizza at Garcia's was, or how bad the drinks were at Pete's. Or how I'd meet my best friend, Andy, at the little Chinese place every Friday for the three-dollar lunch special and how every week we'd laugh at how they refused to give us butter knives.[256]

Don't get me wrong—I prefer to live in the now. I love my life and the people in it and nostalgia generally makes me happy. I wouldn't relive my college days on a bet. No one tells you in your twenties how much better your forties are.[257] But being back on campus, in the one spot where so many of my best memories were created, and finding a setting that's completely changed is disconcerting.

Fletch and I check into the Union. We get ready for the reception before the awards banquet and I dress carefully in a black wrap dress, accented with a snappy plaid scarf/shawl. Truth? I'm not wearing this piece for fashion as much as for function. I call this my "good eatin' scarf" as it protects whatever I'm wearing underneath from errant mayo and salad dressing dribbles. As pleased with myself as I am at having created this solution, I remind Fletch to give me a kick if I try to tell anyone about it. Somehow I bet the Ambassador wouldn't be impressed.

The reception is in the room across from where the Student Check Cashing window used to be. Fletch, Joanna, Michael, and I all laugh, remembering how every Friday afternoon, the entire campus would line up at that window to cash a minuscule check for the weekend. The window's gone now, replaced with a large bank of ATMs. I make a mental note to return there later to get

---

[256] So, yeah, pretty much my equivalent of steak for a nickel.
[257] Primarily because if you knew how much your thirties would suck, you'd drink bleach.

money out of the machine, not because I need cash, but because it will be the first time at Purdue that I'll have stood in that spot and had more than $10 in my bank account.[258]

While we're in the reception, we notice all the large oil paintings of dour old men sitting in leather armchairs. Fletch insists we take a picture of him posed that way, too. He looks eerily similar to the University's founder and it makes me laugh, wondering if John Purdue was just goofing around with his old drinking buddies when he had his portrait done, too.

I meet the other award recipients and they're all lovely and in no way act like I don't belong with them. I may or may not suggest we pose in a human pyramid when we get our photos taken, but I'm pretty sure they know I'm joking.[259]

The most surreal moment of the night happens when I enter the ballroom because I've been here before. The last time was twenty-four years ago when I was working for the University's catering department. There I was, a few weeks from flunking out after my sophomore year and I found myself filling iced tea glasses at a banquet for the outstanding graduating seniors. As the speakers droned on about all the amazing accomplishments my peers had achieved, I felt very small and insignificant.

But here? Today? I get a sense of where I've been and how far I've come, and I feel a sense of belonging. So when it's time for me to step onstage and give my speech, I do it with confidence and panache and when I'm finished, I swear the audience claps louder for me than any of those graduating seniors so many years ago.

....

[258] Related note? I still seek out ATMs that dispense bills smaller than a twenty. Finding one that spits out five dollars is like spotting a unicorn!

[259] If I weren't, I'd be a base. Am very sturdy.

There's a point later in the ceremony when we accept our awards and everyone acknowledges those who helped them get there. During my acceptance, I thank all of the usual suspects, including Brian Lamb, founder of C-SPAN, who happens to be a special guest at the dinner. You see, he didn't hire me for a C-SPAN internship back in the day, primarily because the time I met him I'd been marinating in gin for a few hours and I may or may not have mentioned how much "I likesh Congresssshhhh."

I give a quick summary of the story, adding that he shouldn't worry and that everything worked out for me without the internship.

And in that moment, I bring the house down.

After the ceremony, hugs are exchanged and photos taken, and I finally feel like I've officially graduated from college and into adulthood. All in all, this has been a great end to a spectacular evening and the next time Purdue asks, they're getting the first check I'll have voluntarily written them and trust me, it will be for more than ten dollars.

This is where I wish the story ended.

It doesn't.

After hitting the ATM—two hundred dollars, because I can!—we change into our bar clothes and meet Joanna and Michael in the lobby. The plan is to hit Harry's for a couple of drinks and then head to more grown-up venues with our local friends. In the years since I've been gone, the town's become a bit of a destination, full of gastropubs and wine bars, which sounds really nice. Besides, Harry's is bound to make me sad because when I walk in there, it won't be like it was back in the day. Rather, I'm going to run into nothing but college girls in skimpy tank tops[260] as Ke$ha and Katy Perry tunes play on the jukebox in the background.

No, thanks.

Then the damndest thing happens—we enter Harry's and it IS 1993. The place looks—and smells—exactly like it used to and the old friends we'd hope to meet are right there at the door while Steve Perry wails in the background about holdin' on to that feelin'.

It's like Brigadoon.

Only with beer.

Shocked and awed, Joanna and I make our way to the back of the bar to see if our names are still carved into the wall . . . and they are! The jukebox begins to play Van Morrison and the college girls—who aren't all tarted up, by the way—shriek and begin dancing to "Brown Eyed Girl," exactly the way we used to do.

Um, what is going on here?

Did the Liberal Arts department re-create my favorite parts of college here in this bar? If so, color me impressed.

In honor of the occasion, I switch from the wine I'd politely sipped at the dinner to Long Islands because it feels so appropriate.

As for the rest of the evening, I've pieced together what I can via tweets, photographs, Facebook posts, and video.

9:00 P.M.—More Long Islands for everyone!

9:30 P.M.—What time is it? Why, it's Long Island time!

---

[260] That's what the kids today wear, yes?

9:44 P.M.—Pace myself? You want me to pace myself because I rarely drink and when I do it's a couple of glasses of wine? Pfft! I'm fine! No, I'm more than fine! I'm DISTIN-GUISHED!

10:00 P.M.—It's Moms' Weekend at Purdue and I'm a tad dismayed to realize that all those la-dies who look like me are here with their college-aged kids.

10:30 P.M.—Hey! I don't look like one of those moms. I look young! I bet those kids think I go here! Yes! Drinks for me and my under-grad friends! I HAVE TWO HUN-DRED DOLLARS, WOO!

11:30 P.M.—JUST A SMALL-TOWN GIRL, BORN AND RAISED IN SOUTH DE-TROOOOOOOIT!

11:45 P.M.—Why'd I punch you? Becaushe itsch a game! STEEEEEEVE PERRRRY! Now get me anodder drink! Itsch my birsch-day! Oh. Well then it *feels* like my birschday!

12:00 A.M.—Mike Alstott walks by. He's in town with a bunch of NFL dudes who've been standing next to us all night. I introduce myself, figuring he'd like to know that I'm the ~~dischtin desting jus destiningush~~

I won a major award! Then I tell him he made out with my friend Sloane back in the day. He can't recall. "Oh, itsch all right," I assure him. "She made out with a lot of people."

12:30 A.M.—HOLD ON TO THAT FEEEEEEE-EEELIIIIIN!

1:00 A.M.—Letsch throw gang symbols so every-buddy thinksch we're tough! Lake Forest represent! Our colors are pink and spray tan!

1:30 A.M.—STREETLIGHTS, PEOPLE! OOO-OOOOOOOH!

2:00 A.M.—And thus begins the random Hugging of the Strangers.

2:30 A.M.—Form a human toll bridge and stop all the undergrads trying to leave to explain what makes me a distinguished alumna. And that I have two hundred dollars. They are less "impressed" and more "fucking terrified."

2:40 A.M.—Fletch notices I'm eating stray pieces of popcorn off the table and decides it's time to drag me back to the Union. But before I go, Joanna insists I smuggle a beer pitcher out to commemorate this momentous night. Because I carry a mom-purse, this is exceptionally easy. I make elaborate plans to house this pitcher right next to my engraved Distinguished Alumni award.

2:45 A.M.—I leave, but not before announcing to the population at large that I'm returning to the Pi Phi house where I live because I'm totally twenty-one and who is this old perv dragging me out of the bar? WOOOOO! TWO HUNDRED DOLLARS!! STEEEEEEEEVE PERRY!

2:46 A.M.—Fletch refuses to take me to La Bamba, while muttering something about my being a handful.

2:51 A.M.—Face-plant across the bed, in full jewelry, shoes, and makeup.

8:00 A.M.—I wake up to discover that I am not, in fact twenty-one, and neither is my liver.

As we have to get back home to attend to other business, there's no time to hit the Triple X, home of the best biscuits and gravy in the world and, outside of the La Bamba burrito, the only known hangover remedy.

As the room spins and dips, I realize I'm not going to make it without some Starbucks. I'm suddenly very glad the powers that be paved paradise and put up a coffee shop. Oh, Starbucks, I will never doubt you again.

On the way to pick up the car, I pass the Pulitzer Prize winner and note that she does not smell like a fraternity party.

I do not distinguish myself in the parking garage trash can, but it's touch and go there for a minute. Now *that* is the true and fitting end to my illustrious college career.

And despite the shame (and nausea), I wouldn't have wanted it any other way.

Plus I still have two hundred dollars.

I'm claiming this in the win column.

Reluctant Adult Lesson Learned:

The biggest benefit of not being twenty-one anymore means you're not twenty-one anymore. Embrace this fact . . . or face the worst drive home ever.

E·P·I·L·O·G·U·E

OCTOBER 21, 2011

DEAR READER,

As I MAKE THE FINAL EDITS ON MY MASTER MANUSCRIPT FOR THIS BOOK, OUR WORLD IS IN CHAOS.

BOOMERS AND MILLENNIALS ALIKE ARE IN THE MIDST OF OCCUPYING WALL STREET, THROWING THE LARGEST TEMPER TANTRUM OUR NATION HAS SEEN TO DATE, PEEING IN THE STREETS, AND INHIBITING COMMERCE IN THE SMALL BUSINESSES DOTTING ZUCCOTTI PARK. MEANWHILE, THOSE OF US IN GENERATION X ARE JUST TRYING TO MEET OUR DEADLINES. (WHETHER OR NOT I SUPPORT THEIR MESSAGE IS IRRELEVANT. THE MINUTE THEIR DRUM CIRCLE WOKE UP PEOPLE WHO PAY RENT AND HAVE TO GET UP EARLY FOR WORK, I DECLARED SHENANIGANS.)

IF AND WHEN WE PULL OUT OF THIS COUNTRY'S FINANCIAL MESS—AND I BELIEVE WE WILL—I GUARANTEE YOU IT'S MY GENERATION WHO'LL BE LEADING THE CHARGE TOWARDS SANITY AND COMPROMISE.

ALSO, WE LOST ELECTRICITY AGAIN TWO DAYS AGO, BUT FEAR NOT, FOR WE HAD A GENERATOR. WE HAVEN'T HAD THE WHOLE-HOUSE ONE INSTALLED YET, BUT WE HAD THE FORESIGHT TO PURCHASE A SMALLER, GAS-POWERED MODEL. IT'S NOT EVERYTHING WE WANTED, BUT IT WAS EXACTLY WHAT WE NEEDED.[261]

IN ADDITION, THE CAPS LOCK ON MY KEYBOARD BROKE A MINUTE AGO AND THIS MANUSCRIPT IS DUE TODAY.

SO I FOLLOW THE LESSON THAT NO ONE UNDERSTANDS BETTER THAN MEMBERS OF GENERATION X...

I LEARN TO ADAPT.

XO,
JEN

---

[261] Of course the power came on ten minutes after we finally assembled the damn thing, but that's neither here nor there.

A·C·K·N·O·W·L·E·D·G·M·E·N·T·S

*L*earning how and when to say thank you is a key element to becoming a full-fledged adult, so here goes:

Maybe it's a little out of traditional order, but first I have to thank Anthony Ramondo and the rest of the art department for creating my favorite cover since *Bitter*. Home run, people. Total home run.

A million thanks go to my editor, Tracy Bernstein, for raising the bar. Knowing you'd be reading the manuscript made me push myself and I'm so pleased with what we've done together. Additional, heartfelt thanks go to Kara Welsh and Claire Zion for embracing my vision in seven books and counting. And Craig Burke and Melissa Broder? You're the hardest-working publicists in the business. All of you (plus sales and marketing and production) are my Dream Team.

I'd be nowhere without my family of choice—Stacey, Gina, Tracey, Caprice, Joanna, Angie, Wendy, Blackbird, and Poppy. You guys are my inspiration and you make everything more fun! (Except possibly driving.) (Listen, I'm sorry, but the GPS lady is very stern so I'm obligated to defer to her if there's a question.)

(Also, I have shitty night vision, and if the speed limit says fifty-five, then I'm going forty-five just to be sure.) (This has no bearing on my thanks, yet I want to have this on record so you don't mutiny again like that time we went to Wendy's house.) (Luff you!)

Karyn Bosnak, you get your own paragraph because that's how hard you rock. You're the best nemesis I ever had (even though it was unbeknownst to you), and I feel so lucky to be in your life. And your title? I'm not worthy! I'm not worthy!

For Fletch—thank you for putting up with what you call "writing season," which is defined by a dirty house, bored dogs, and nothing to eat. What you lack in administrative-assistant skills, you more than make up for in the husband department. You're the best partner I could have in business and especially in life, and I'm so proud of what we've built together!

For Douglas Coupland—thank you for writing one of the greatest novels of all time. You are truly a genius, and I hope you understand that *Jeneration X* is my homage to the generation you defined.

For all my readers—thank you from the bottom of my heart. I love seeing you at events, receiving your e-mails, and interacting with you on social-networking sites. Please know we would *totally* be friends in real life. (Unless you were my neighbors. As it turns out, I'm kind of weird about them.) I wish you all joy, laughter, and a lifetime supply of good whackin' shovels.

Jen Lancaster, the *New York Times* bestselling author of six books, has appeared on *Today, The Joy Behar Show*, and NPR's *All Things Considered*. She resides in the suburbs of Chicago with her husband and their ever-expanding menagerie of ill-behaved pets.

Please read on for a sneak preview of
Jen Lancaster's hilarious new memoir,

The Tao of Martha

Coming in June from New American Library.

*Y*ou think Martha Stewart shoves her clutter in a gun cabinet?"

Despite the fact that Fletch finished his Army tour of duty seventeen years ago, his bearing is still distinctly military. He's practically standing at attention, sporting his fresh short haircut, shiny shoes, heavily starched oxford, and flat-front khakis. I squirm under my meatball-stained workout shirt and yoga pants, with bonus unwashed ponytail.

I'm loath to admit that he's right—I'm sure Martha would have never stuffed her countertop untidiness in the bottom cabinet of the kitchen gun cabinet.

Martha probably doesn't even *have* a kitchen gun cabinet.

The only reason we currently possess the handy, fridge-adjacent firearm storage is that it came with the place. The previous owner was a retired naval officer and huge military history buff, so this house once showcased many of his treasures. Why he felt the breakfast nook was the best place to display his Enfield Muske-toons, I can't say.

Maybe he was a Civil War reenactor?

Maybe he was paranoid?

Or maybe he simply enjoyed gazing at his artfully lighted and secured vintage weapons stockade over eggs Benedict?

Personally, we moved from our sketchy Chicago neighbor-hood to the northern burbs specifically so we *didn't* have to eat breakfast fully armed, but who am I to judge?

At some point, I'm going to convert it to a china cabinet, so it's totally fine.

Of course, I've been saying that for over a year now.

I tell Fletch, "The good news is that I found my recipe."

Seriously? I've been tearing the house apart for three days looking for this one cookbook that contains the best Bolognese sauce recipe on the planet.

Fletch gingerly picks through the other items I've unearthed in the cabinet. He waves a handbag at me. "You felt the gun cabinet was the best place to stash this purse?"

I can't help but admire the gorgeous pea green leather with contrasting chocolate trim. "Show a little respect. That's a Chloe bag. Got it for seventy-five percent off at Nordstrom. You know how hard it is to snag a deal like that? Please. You'd have an easier time finding a unicorn or a professional athlete who hasn't banged a Kardashian. Point is, I've been meaning to have it reconditioned, so I brought it downstairs."

"When? Six months ago?"

I nod and he sighs, moving on to the next item in the pile. He reads a slip of paper. "And your prescription for blood pressure medication?"

I press my hand to my heart. "Huh. That would explain my racing pulse."

He peers down at a couple of orange packets. "What do we have here? Let's see, not one but *two* overdue parking tickets. How old are these? We haven't lived on Altgeld for three years!"

I shrug. "I was busy."

He frowns as he examines the rather important-looking letter from our accountants. "Help me understand why you wouldn't want to, say, store these items in the proper place. Walk me through the process where you said, '*Yes, the gun cabinet is the perfect repository for every random bit of crap to ever pass through our kitchen.*'"

Please note that over the years, I've upped my household game considerably. Seriously, if Martha Stewart herself were to step inside my home right now, she'd give my empty counters and the pristine baseboards two thumbs-up. Maybe I haven't quite managed to shower yet today, but it's because I've been busy cleaning. Martha would never find a mess in my sink because I can't sleep in a house where the dishes are dirty, even if it means scrubbing lipstick off of champagne glasses at three thirty a.m. while half in the bag.

Because I share my home with a number of pets that have no problem besmirching a Persian rug, I own three vacuum cleaners (not counting shop vacs, which brings the total to five), half a dozen types of mops, and a professional-grade Rug Doctor.

Yet my dirty little secret is that the place seems immaculate because I shove everything into cabinets, drawers, and closets to keep it looking that way. Today's foray into gun cabinet storage? So *not* my first rodeo.

The worst of it all is located in my nightstand, which Fletch has dubbed the Drawer of Shame. The Drawer of Shame is a big, knotty mess of dental floss, old hair bands, free-range antacids, uncapped half-chewed lip balms, pretzel wrappers, and eight thousand tubes of whatever was the big new antioxidant eye cream six months ago. Whenever I reach for one item, the whole lot comes out, too.

The thing is, all my drawers and closets are disgraceful, much to the hyperorganized Sergeant Fletcher's chagrin. Open the spice cabinet, and it rains bottles of oregano, garlic powder, and artisanal salts. Crack the drawer next to the kitchen desk, and scores of empty plastic grocery bags will explode as though being shot from a cannon. And my closet? Let's just say it's a testament to single right sneakers, solo socks, and a disproportionately high number of meatball-stained workout tops.

Yet, honestly, I'm fine with the behind-the-scenes chaos because I've been busy with personal growth.

Okay, that's a lie.

I might be a *tiny* bit lazy when it comes to organizing. But when I consider the process of getting organized, I feel overwhelmed. And there's so much else I'd prefer to do with my time—like drive to the city to have lunch with my girlfriends, or shop for antiques, or hang out in the TV room with Fletch and the dogs, which are perpetually draped across our laps. And are you aware of how many good books were published *this year alone*? Plus, if I stopped paying attention to the Real Housewives, they might cease to exist. I can't have that on my conscience; hasn't poor Taylor Armstrong been through enough?

My point is that everything looks super-neat and clean largely because I'm always stashing whatever crap accumulates. Maybe what's beneath the surface is a wreck, but SFW?

So, to answer Fletch's initial question, no, I'm sure Martha

Stewart would *not* shove her clutter in the gun safe. But that's not because I'm Martha-bashing.

Far from it, in fact.

I worship Martha Stewart.

I see her as our nation's overachieving older sister. Like, I might resent her a tiny bit, but mostly I'm in awe of how she makes everything look so damn easy. It's just that whenever something goes awry in my house, we seem to invoke her name, e.g.:

"I wonder if Martha Stewart has to chase her asshole cats off the appetizer buffet."

"I wonder if Martha Stewart spends four hundred dollars and an entire summer fertilizing a garden only to end up with two anemic tomatoes and an unholy army of slugs."

"I wonder if Martha Stewart rights the crooked mirror in her dining room with a wad of chewed Dentyne."

"I wonder if Martha Stewart's bourbon chocolate pecan pie is both so liquid and boozy that it's technically considered a cocktail in and of itself."

"I wonder if Martha Stewart's guests are greeted at the door with her sweating, crying, and shouting, 'Here's a recipe. Get to work or we're never eating Thanksgiving dinner!'"

I live for Martha and her perfect little universe, but I've yet to find a way to incorporate her processes into mine. I mean to, of course, but . . .

We're currently on our fourth visit to the Restoration Hardware outlet store in Wisconsin in pursuit of replacing the funereal drapes that used to hang in our bedroom. Before Thanksgiving, I found a great deal on some discontinued curtains and figured it was high time for a more modern update.

Not only were the old drapes fussy, but they weren't functional; they were made only to frame the window. We had decent pull-down blinds for privacy and light blocking, but Nibble-y Libby and the Boredom Chews ended what should have been a long life span. Keeping the blinds open had come to require tying a system of Gordian knots, so most often, the bedroom was as dark as a tomb.

So Fletch tore down the blinds only to discover that the sun lights up the bedroom like the map room in the Temple of Doom every day at five forty-five a.m.

I fixed the problem by thumb-tacking sheets to the window frame.

Yes, I realize that Martha would shudder at my half-assery. But it was that or rising with the roosters until we found a solution that we liked and that didn't cost as much as a used Honda.

Once we removed the old curtain hardware, I estimated that installing the new rods would take an hour, max. Which it did.

The window-covering situation only became complicated once we determined that we'd hung the rods too low and that the curtains I insisted would match the rug . . . didn't. This development precipitated the second trip to Wisconsin and a fair amount of cursing on both our parts. Then, because we'd punched so many holes in the wall, we had to patch the paint.

The old owners were ridiculously organized, and when we moved in, they essentially gave us a guide to living here. We received binders full of appliance manuals and warranties. (What, you thought I was going to say "Women"?)

Therefore, what happened next is not their fault.

They left us every scrap of extra material, like carpet and wall-paper, all meticulously labeled and neatly stored. After the rods were finally hung and the walls patched and sanded, Fletch went downstairs to find the appropriate paint. When he came back up, he was flummoxed.

"I can only find beige paint labeled 'sitting room.' This doesn't mean bedroom, does it? Maybe this is for the TV room upstairs," he said.

We opened the paint and compared. As far as I could tell, it was an exact match.

"Seems a little darker," Fletch said.

I rolled my eyes. "Come on, Fletch—who would use two al-most but not quite identical shades of beige in the same house? I promise it's the same. The color will absolutely dry lighter."

Three days later, Fletch and I had to have a little discussion about promises I couldn't keep. The project continued to slide off the rails, but once we hang the last set of curtains we're buying today (because I can't count, apparently), we should be finally, mercifully done.

"I bet it wouldn't take Martha Stewart two months to hang cur-tains in the bedroom."

Something about Fletch invoking Martha's name lights a spark.

"Say that again," I demand.

"That it wouldn't take Martha two months to hang curtains?"

"Exactly!!"

Fletch shrugs and goes back to sorting through the bin of re-ject drapes while my idea takes shape.

Right now, Martha Stewart definitely wouldn't consider the way I live my life as a Good Thing. Yet that doesn't stop me from adoring her, you know?

I've been obsessed with Martha since I tried her butter cream cupcake frosting recipe. "Transcendent" doesn't properly describe this concoction and "delicious" is an insult. Her recipe creates something that feels like cashmere and tastes like it was whipped by angels and flavored by God's own vanilla beans. Seriously, it's strip-and-go-naked kind of good.

Although I wasn't a fan of the Martha back when she went to prison, she conducted herself with such grace and dignity that she eventually won me over, and that's when I started buying her magazine and watching her show in earnest.

See, instead of curling up and dying in that situation, she made the best out of it.

She made gourmet microwaved dinners.

She made friends.

She made *ponchos*, for Christ's sake.

She rose to the occasion, and I can't not get behind that.

Millions of women adore M. Diddy (what the gals in the joint called her) because she can break down even the most difficult tasks into something simple and lovely and doable. I read that she doesn't own a bathrobe, which means that when she rolls out of bed, she hops straight into the shower. That boggles my mind. I live in a world where pajamas have been worn to the dinner table . . . on days I wasn't sick.

I realize Martha Stewart isn't everyone's icon, but she *is* mine. I love her because instead of lording her superior skills over everyone and making them feel bad about themselves, she's out there breaking it all down for even the least talented amongst us. Had I thought to consult her guides, the curtains project truly would have taken two hours and not two months.

This is not to discount the Magic That Is the Oprah. Millions of women are Team Oprah over Team Martha. Actually, I believe there are only two kinds of women in this world—Martha people and Oprah people. That doesn't mean one can't have an affinity for both of them, but my theory is that every chick is more firmly in one camp than the other. The typical Oprah woman is all self-actualized and best-life-y and *Eat, Pray, Love.* The Big O seems like the kind of gal who'd insist we all spend the afternoon wearing jammie pants. And how fun would that be?!

But Martha?

She's not putting up with that nonsense, and that makes me adore her all the more. She'll tell you *what* to eat, *where* to pray, and *who* to love, and I appreciate the guidance.

I mean, I *have* a best friend; I *need* a drill sergeant.

(Related note? Were Martha and Oprah to cage-fight, smart money is on M. Diddy because you KNOW she's a scrapper.)

On paper, Oprah trumps Martha in terms of fortune and fame and felony convictions. But if the apocalypse my tinfoil-hat-wearing husband (bless his heart) predicts is indeed coming, I have to ask myself: Do I want to follow the lady who encourages me to make dream boards for a better tomorrow, or do I want to listen to the gal who can show me how to butcher my own game hen *right now?*

I'm Team Martha, no questions asked.

I wonder what would happen if I were to follow her advice from A(pple brown betty) to Z(ip-line-attached Christmas ornaments). Would my life be easier—and Fletch less twitchy—if I use her tricks to get organized?

Could my dogs be more satisfied if I feed them what she gives to her French bullies, Sharkey and Francesca, and her chow chow, Genghis II?

Might I grow closer to my girlfriends who knit and sew when I finally show some interest in their boring-ass hobbies?

Would I morph from the person who gives guests a recipe and instructs them to start cooking to the hostess who goes ballistic if someone dares wear cream to my White Party?

And would that be the worst thing in the world?

Most important, could I be happier if I were to pattern my life from her recipe?

I plan to find out.

As soon as I finish with these damn curtains.